M000098300

March 1996

For Max, with admiration
and gratitude, from Mort

Beyond the Classroom

Beyond the Classroom

Essays on American Authors

Merton M. Sealts, Jr.

University of Missouri Press

Columbia and London

Copyright © 1996 by
The Curators of the University of Missouri
University of Missouri Press, Columbia, Missouri 65201
Printed and bound in the United States of America
All rights reserved
5   4   3   2   1   00   99   98   97   96

Library of Congress Cataloging-in-Publication Data

Sealts, Merton M.
        Beyond the classroom : essays on American authors / Merton M. Sealts.
            p.   cm.
        Includes bibliographical references (p.   ) and index.
        ISBN 0-8262-1046-5 (alk. paper)
            1. American literature—History and criticism.
        PS121.S43   1996
        810.9'003—dc20   95-26149
                                                                              CIP

⊗ This paper meets the requirements of the
American National Standard for Permanence of Paper
for Printed Library Materials, Z39.48, 1984.

Designer: Stephanie Foley
Typesetter: BOOKCOMP
Printer and binder: Thomson-Shore, Inc.
Typefaces: Adobe Garamond and Berkeley

For Ruth Mackenzie Sealts

(1918–1995)

Ζώη μοῦ, σᾶς ἀγαπῶ.

It is time to be old,
To take in sail. . . .
                    —Emerson, "Terminus"

Contents

Preface   xi

Abbreviations   xv

Part One: 1982–1986

  1. Emerson as Teacher   3

  2. Melville and Whitman   15

  3. Herman Melville's "Bartleby"   21

  4. Melville's "Benito Cereno"   32

  5. Innocence and Infamy
      Melville's *Billy Budd, Sailor*   39

Part Two: 1988–1992

  6. An Author's Self-Education
      Herman Melville's Reading   65

  7. Melville's Reading, 1853–1856   74

  8. "Pulse of the Continent"
      The Railroad in American Literature   86

  9. Emerson Then and Now   96

 10. The Scholar Idealized   102

 11. "The Flower of Fame"
      A Centennial Tribute to Herman Melville   110

Part Three: 1993–1995

12. The Presence of Walt Whitman   129

13. The "I" of *Walden*   146

14. Hawthorne's "Autobiographical Impulse"   159

15. Whose Book Is *Moby-Dick*?   175

Postscript   189

Appendices

1. Questions concerning Herman Melville's "Bartleby"   191

2. Questions concerning Herman Melville's "Benito Cereno"   195

3. Questions concerning Herman Melville's *Billy Budd, Sailor*   199

4. The Melvilles, the Gansevoorts, and the Cincinnati Badge   209

Notes   211

Books, Articles, and Reviews by Merton M. Sealts, Jr.   248

Index   257

Preface

I man the rudder, reef the sail,
Obey the voice at eve obeyed at prime. . . .

—Emerson, "Terminus"

To the preface of my *Emerson on the Scholar* (1992) I prefixed another quotation from Emerson: "That statement only is fit to be made public which you have come at in attempting to satisfy your own curiosity." Emerson's words might well serve as a motto for everything I have "made public"—from 1940 through my career as a teacher and scholar and continuing in my retirement years since 1982. This affirmation needs no further comment here, in view of the convictions I expressed to my late friend Harry Murray in the "Letter" that concludes *Pursuing Melville* (1982) and in the Postscript that appears below.

"Now that I can look back over more than half a century as a student and teacher," I said in 1992,

> it seems clear to me that for those truly professional men and women I have admired most, there has been no essential dichotomy between their teaching and their scholarship, that scholarship meant for them not only distinguished original research but at the same time keeping abreast of the research and interpretations of others as well, and that their teaching and learning took place both in the classroom and beyond it, as they spoke to and wrote for members of the public as well as their students and professional colleagues.

I have tried to apply these words to my own teaching and learning. The writings in the present volume are sequels to those collected in *Pursuing Melville,* published at the time of my formal retirement. Almost all of these newer chapters and essays were first presented as public lectures before diverse audiences, both on college and university campuses and beyond: groups of students and teachers, college alumni, Wisconsin lawyers, church congregations, and a town-and-gown group, the Madison Literary Club. Five of the essays are published here for the first time; the others have appeared variously in pamphlets, as articles in magazines and scholarly journals, and as chapters in books, including the Emerson centennial volume and my own *Emerson on the Scholar* and *Melville's Reading* (1988). All of them reflect experience in the classroom and the scholarship that good teaching must depend on—meaning both original research and assimilation and application of the ongoing work of others.

Two of the papers were published in 1982. One of those, "Emerson as Teacher," had previously been read as a lecture on various campuses; it appeared by invitation in *Emerson Centenary Essays,* edited by Joel Myerson. The other, "Melville and Whitman," was written as a report on an innovative course I had taught shortly before I retired. In 1982 I met with a group of Wisconsin lawyers for an all-day seminar on Melville's "Bartleby," and in 1983 a similar group discussed *Billy Budd, Sailor.* The materials I prepared for each of the two seminars were then published in pamphlet form for wider dissemination; they have also been used, along with a lecture on "Benito Cereno," in several classrooms. During the 1980s I was a frequent traveler, speaking on both Melville and Emerson on a number of campuses in the East, Midwest, and Southwest. New material for these engagements included "Mulberry Leaves and Satin: Emerson's Theory of the Creative Process," an essay not in the present volume which was published in 1985 and later incorporated in *Emerson on the Scholar,* and an early version of a paper that is included here, "Whose Book Is *Moby-Dick?*" In 1986 my earlier paper on *Billy Budd,* augmented with material from a later, unpublished lecture, "Melville's Sense of the Past," appeared by invitation in *A Companion to Melville Studies,* edited by John Bryant for students and teachers of Melville.

Following an interval in the mid-1980s when I was recovering from surgery, I worked to complete a revised and enlarged edition of my *Melville's Reading* in order to bring together new information that had become available since the 1966 edition of this standard reference work. Part I, "Melville as Reader," comprises an "Introduction, Melville's Library," and nine chapters on the course of his reading over the years that are new to the 1988 edition. "An Author's Self-Education: Herman Melville's Reading" is the final version of a lecture based on the book that I read to various nonspecialized audiences; "Melville's Reading, 1853–1856," is a representative chapter of the book itself. Both selections convey something of what I have learned during my long engagement with Melville about a man who loved books and drew on them in his own writing for both inspiration and information.

Like the lecture on Melville's self-education, the papers on the railroad in American literature and on the course of Emerson's changing reputation were written with the aim of sharing a personal interest with nonspecialist listeners and readers. Along with my teaching of American authors and my research on both Melville and Emerson, I have long been interested in railroads, including an O-gauge operation in my own basement, and my essay " 'Pulse of the Continent': The Railroad in American Literature" exemplifies my attempts to follow Frost's injunction to combine one's vocation and avocation—in this case my teaching and my hobby. I like to think that teachers of literature generally are fortunate in being able to pursue what they do and what they love at one and the same time.

These three pieces first appeared in print while I was awaiting publication of *Emerson on the Scholar* in 1992. My interest in Emerson, like my interest in Melville, began in 1940 when I was a graduate student; the book gradually took form over the years during my service as an editor of Emerson's *Journals and Miscellaneous Notebooks* and my concurrent work on Melville. "The Scholar Idealized" includes passages from the introduction to *Emerson on the Scholar* and the concluding pages of its final chapter. Another essay, "Emerson Then and Now," first published in 1992, considers shifts in Emerson's reputation over the years. An invited lecture of 1991 on Melville that appears here, " 'The Flower of Fame,' " is a tribute to him on the hundredth anniversary of his death; it too was first published in 1992.

The four essays of the mid-1990s that follow deal with a group of Emerson's contemporaries who in their writings responded in quite different ways to his teaching and his example: Thoreau and Whitman, whose responses were positive; Hawthorne, who wrote in 1846 that he admired Emerson as a poet "but sought nothing from him as a philosopher"; and Melville, whose reaction was decidedly mixed, as I sought to demonstrate some years ago in "Melville and Emerson's Rainbow" (1979, 1982). The common theme of the four essays in this section is the matter of authorial voice: the writers' use of either the first person, as with the "I" of Thoreau, Whitman, Hawthorne's prefaces, and the Ishmael of *Moby-Dick,* or the third person, as in most of Hawthorne's fiction. (The "I" of Emerson's journals commonly became "we" in his essays or was changed to third person.) These five authors are those whose writings I taught most often between 1946 and my retirement from the classroom; I taught them again, using "Emerson as Teacher" and these four more recent essays, in an Elderhostel course during the summer of 1995. I shall never tire of such writers, nor absorb all that they have to teach.

For permission to reprint previously published essays I am grateful to the Wisconsin Humanities Council; to Greenwood Press, Southern Illinois University Press, the University of Missouri Press, and the University of South Carolina Press; and to the editors of *A Companion to Melville Studies, Emerson Centenary Essays, Melville Society Extracts,* and the *Wisconsin Academy Review.* I thank John Russell, executor, and also Little, Brown and Company, Henry Holt and Company, New York University Press, and Random House UK Limited for permission to quote other published material. The staff of the University of Missouri Press have again been most helpful—notably Gloria Thomas, the kind of editor every author needs!

And for more than a half century of encouragement, needed assistance, and—above all—patience, I thank the beloved dedicatee of this book, long my devoted partner in all this and in much, much more.

Abbreviations

Apart from minor alterations and standardization of page references in parenthetical citations and footnotes, all previously published material appears here in the version originally printed unless otherwise indicated in notes to the selections affected. Quotations from and citations to the works of Herman Melville are from named individual volumes of the Northwestern-Newberry Edition: *The Writings of Herman Melville,* edited by Harrison Hayford, Hershel Parker, and G. Thomas Tanselle, 15 vols. (Evanston and Chicago: Northwestern University Press and the Newberry Library, 1968–   )—unless another text is specifically cited. The following numbered volumes have been published to date: 1. *Typee: A Peep at Polynesian Life* (1968); 2. *Omoo: A Narrative of Adventures in the South Seas* (1968); 3. *Mardi and a Voyage Thither* (1970); 4. *Redburn: His First Voyage* (1969); 5. *White-Jacket: Or The World in a Man-of-War* (1970); 6. *Moby-Dick: Or The Whale* (1988); 7. *Pierre: Or The Ambiguities* (1971); 8. *Israel Potter: His Fifty Years of Exile* (1982); 9. *"The Piazza Tales" and Other Prose Pieces 1839–1860* (1987); 10. *The Confidence-Man: His Masquerade* (1984); 12. *Clarel: A Poem and Pilgrimage in the Holy Land* (1991); 14. *Correspondence* (1993); 15. *Journals* (1989).

In addition to shortened titles, the following abbreviations appear parenthetically throughout the text and notes to identify primary texts that are cited repeatedly:

CEC   *The Correspondence of Emerson and Carlyle.* Ed. Joseph Slater. New York and London: Columbia University Press, 1964.

CW   *The Collected Works of Ralph Waldo Emerson.* Ed. Alfred R. Ferguson et al. 5 vols. to date. Cambridge: The Belknap Press of Harvard University Press, 1971–   .

EL   *The Early Lectures of Ralph Waldo Emerson.* Ed. Stephen E. Whicher, Robert E. Spiller, and Wallace E. Williams. 3 vols. Cambridge:

Harvard University Press, 1959; The Belknap Press of Harvard University Press, 1964, 1972.

J   *Journals of Ralph Waldo Emerson.* Ed. Edward Waldo Emerson and Waldo Emerson Forbes. 10 vols. Boston and New York: Houghton Mifflin Co., 1909–1914.

JMN   *The Journals and Miscellaneous Notebooks of Ralph Waldo Emerson.* Ed. William H. Gilman, Ralph H. Orth, et al. 16 vols. Cambridge: The Belknap Press of Harvard University Press, 1960–1982.

L   *The Letters of Ralph Waldo Emerson.* Ed. Ralph L. Rusk. 6 vols. New York: Columbia University Press, 1939.

Log   Jay Leyda. *The Melville Log: A Documentary Life of Herman Melville, 1819–1891.* 2 vols. New York: Harcourt, Brace and Company, 1951; reprinted with a new supplementary chapter, New York: Gordian Press, 1969.

W   *The Complete Works of Ralph Waldo Emerson.* Ed. Edward Waldo Emerson. 12 vols. Boston and New York: Houghton Mifflin Co., 1903–1904.

Part One
1982–1986

1.

Emerson as Teacher

"To every serious mind," Ralph Waldo Emerson liked to say, "Providence sends from time to time five or six or seven teachers."[1] Emerson was a graduate of Harvard College, in the class of 1821, but there was not a single Harvard professor on the private list of personal benefactors he drew up in 1836, when he was thirty-three (*JMN* 5:160). And though Emerson was no professor himself, many other men and women of the nineteenth century, in all walks of life and with varying amounts of schooling, looked on him as their teacher and benefactor, known to them either through his published writings or by his appearance on local lecture platforms.

Considering Emerson in the role of teacher is not the customary approach to this "man without a handle," as the elder Henry James once addressed him.[2] Indeed, the problem of what to *call* Emerson has bothered critics and historians ever since his death in 1882. Matthew Arnold, when he came to lecture in America soon afterward, spoke of Emerson as one of the great "voices" heard in England during his youth and affirmed that "snatches of Emerson's strain" had continued to haunt his memory ever since. But though he warmly praised this "friend and aider of those who would live in the spirit" and singled out his *Essays* as "the most important work" written in English prose during the nineteenth century, Arnold found himself finally unable to categorize Emerson or to celebrate his achievement as that of "a great poet," "a great writer," or even "a great philosophy-maker."[3]

Arnold's difficulty has persisted down to our own day: we too are uncertain how to classify Emerson, how to deal with his poetry, or even in what course or department to consider his *Essays*. As Arnold recognized, they are not exactly *philosophy.* Indeed, few professional philosophers later than William James and George Santayana have looked in a kindly way on Emerson, any more than professional historians of recent years have been hospitable to Henry Adams. Like Teufelsdröckh in his friend Carlyle's *Sartor Resartus,* Emerson was a "Professor of Things in General"—*Allerley Wissenschaft*[4]—and was rightly suspicious of all compartmentalizing and departmentalizing. Indeed, he looked on specialization as necessary enough, but as a kind of necessary evil, or evil necessity. In an age of increasing specialization his American Scholar should be "Man Thinking," speaking for Man to men—as a generalist rather than a specialist or narrow advocate; we might well say that the substance of the Scholar's discourse would be the substance of a liberal education. The Scholar as teacher, having access to what Emerson calls "this original unit, this fountain of power," is one who can help others to "possess" themselves—the phrase turns up again in Emerson and also in Arnold—by returning to the same fountain, the common source accessible to every one of us (*CW* 1:53).

Here is a clue not only to Arnold's response to Emerson but also to Emerson's admiration for Milton: "Better than any other," Emerson said in a lecture of 1835, Milton "discharged the office of every great man, namely, to raise the idea of Man"—capital *M*—"in the minds of his contemporaries and of posterity." Milton was thus a master teacher of true humanism, "foremost of all men . . . in the power *to inspire*" (*EL* 1:148–49), and for Emerson the great business of books and teachers alike was "to inspire" rather than merely to instruct (*CW* 1:56). "Truly speaking," he said at Harvard in 1838, "it is not instruction, but provocation, that I can receive from another soul" (*CW* 1:80). The teacher may inspire or provoke; in the last analysis the student, responding actively and not passively, must finally *learn* for himself.

The occasion for Emerson's remark about "provocation" was a memorable one in his early career. He had been invited to address the graduating class of 1838 at Harvard Divinity School, not by the reverend professors on the faculty but by some of the senior students themselves—young men who had been visiting Concord to talk theology with this sometime clergyman, a Harvard product who had resigned his own pulpit six years before. What Emerson said in his address at Cambridge was provocative enough to shock old-guard Unitarians, men who looked on his liberal ideas about preaching and teaching as "the latest form of infidelity";[5] it would be thirty years before he was again invited to speak at Harvard. Having in effect left the ministry, Emerson would have welcomed a professorship, as he freely admitted in his journal—if not at Harvard, then perhaps in one of the "country colleges" such as Dartmouth, where he sometimes spoke; it would serve as a base of operations, he thought, and challenge him with "a stated task" (*JMN* 10:28).⁶ But no such post was offered him, and in the absence of other opportunities he continued lecturing and writing, not to enrolled students in college classrooms but to a whole generation of general listeners and readers at home and abroad, inspiring and provoking an ever-widening audience as his reputation steadily grew. Like all teachers of power, moreover, he attracted a broad spectrum of students, not all of whom liked what they read and heard or stayed to finish the course.

In Cambridge and Concord, Emerson was able to teach directly—face to face. "What are you doing now?" he asked young Henry Thoreau of Concord in 1837. "Do you keep a journal?" Thoreau's response was prompt: "So I make my first entry today."⁷ A Brooklyn newspaper editor, Walt Whitman, first knew Emerson indirectly, through his books: "I was simmering, simmering, simmering," Whitman reportedly said of the years before *Leaves of Grass;* "Emerson brought me to a boil."⁸ But though Emerson heated up some students like Thoreau and Whitman, others who sampled his offerings were cooled off or turned off. Nathaniel Hawthorne, his neighbor in Concord, was never sympathetic to Emerson's teachings; he wrote with amusement of how the village was "infested" by the "variety of queer, strangely dressed, oddly behaved mortals" who pursued Emerson to his home.⁹ Herman Melville, whose New York friends had warned him against Emerson's supposed obscurity, was pleasantly surprised on hearing Emerson lecture in Boston in 1849; "they told me that that night he was unusually plain," he explained. For years to come, both in private jottings and in published works, Melville alternately praised and damned "this Plato who talks thro' his nose."¹⁰ Had Emerson "not been there both to stimulate and exasperate Herman Melville," Perry Miller once remarked, "*Moby-Dick* would have emerged as only another sea-story."¹¹ Miller no doubt exaggerated, but his basic point was well taken: Emerson could indeed both inspire and provoke—in every sense of the two words. "Emerson was their cow, but not all liked the milk." So ran a caption in *Time* magazine some years ago under a panel of photographs of Hawthorne, Thoreau,

Whitman, and Melville, in that order, with Emerson gazing benignantly from one side.[12]

It was not only literary figures of the day who responded to Emerson. "His works, other men found, were in many respects diaries of their own which they had not kept," as Lyon Richardson has finely said.[13] A good example is Rutherford B. Hayes, lawyer, soldier, congressman, thrice-elected governor of Ohio, and finally president of the United States. As a young attorney in Cincinnati, Hayes helped to arrange for Emerson's first lectures there in 1850. Emerson remained his favorite author; in Hayes's judgment he had "the best mind of our time and race."[14] As Emerson continued distilling his lectures into published essays and as his readers in distant places grew increasingly eager to see and hear him, like Hayes in Ohio, his field of operations as itinerant teacher inevitably expanded. By the 1850s he was in steady demand as a lecturer, not only along the eastern seaboard as far south as Baltimore but across the Atlantic to England and Scotland in 1847–1848 and also beyond the Hudson into what was then "the West."[15] The vogue of the popular lecturer and the growth of the lyceum movement in the United States during the second quarter of the nineteenth century reflected the prevalent desire for self-improvement and the widespread interest in adult education that accompanied westward expansion and growing national prosperity. By the 1860s Emerson was making annual western tours: to Ohio, Indiana, and Illinois; to Michigan and Wisconsin; and eventually across the Mississippi to Iowa and Minnesota. In 1868 James Russell Lowell called him "the most steadily attractive lecturer in America."[16]

Emerson traveled west by train, stage, carriage, and boat, often under the most trying conditions; during one bitterly cold winter he crossed the frozen Mississippi four times on foot. When he made his first trip to Ohio in 1850 for his engagement in Cincinnati, he was en route by Lake Erie steamer to Sandusky when the vessel caught fire off Cleveland, where it made port safely in time for local Emersonians to assemble for an unscheduled lecture he was persuaded to give.[17] The lecture in Cleveland was free; by the 1860s the going rate for a one-night stand in the larger western cities had risen to fifty dollars. Thus Emerson's contemporary T. Starr King, when asked what he lectured for, answered: "FAME—Fifty and My Expenses."[18] Emerson wrote of lecturing in the West as an annual wager: " 'I'll bet you fifty dollars a day for three weeks, that you will not leave your library

& wade & freeze & ride & run, & suffer all manner of indignities, & stand up for an hour each night reading in a hall': and I answered, 'I'll bet I will,' I do it, & win the $900" (*JMN* 15:457).[19] Early in January of 1856, after a week of temperatures "varying from 20 to 30 degrees below zero," he observed that the climate and people of the West "are a new test for the wares of a man of letters. . . . At the lyceum, the stout Illinoian, after a short trial, walks out of the hall. The Committee tell you that the people want a hearty laugh, and [those] who give them that, are heard with joy. . . . [T]hese are the new conditions to which I must conform. . . . And Shakspeare or Franklin or Aesop coming to Illinois, would say, I must give my wisdom a comic form, instead of tragics or elegiacs" (*JMN* 14:27–28). Emerson's words seem prophetic of Mark Twain, who in the late 1850s, as Samuel L. Clemens of Missouri, was learning to be a riverboat pilot on the Mississippi, his other vocation as lecturer and writer being still some years before him.

In the course of a long career Emerson filled nearly fifteen hundred lecture engagements in twenty-two states and Canada plus his lectures in England and Scotland. Some cities and towns brought him back repeatedly. He spoke on many subjects, from popular science, biography, and literature in the early 1830s to an address on Carlyle in 1881, the year before his death. During the 1850s, when he appeared most often, he was giving more than fifty lectures every winter; in the 1860s both his platform reputation and his fees reached their peak. Apart from local newspaper reviews, which varied widely in tone, some of the best testimony about what it was like to hear Emerson speak comes from younger contemporaries who attended his lectures repeatedly from their student days into middle age— men of letters such as Lowell, George William Curtis, and E. P. Whipple. With younger listeners in the early years, if not with their elders or the authorities of Harvard, Emerson was immediately popular: for Lowell and his generation he became "our favorite teacher."[20] An older man once told Curtis that though *he* couldn't understand "Mr. Emerson," "my daughters do."[21] Emerson himself quickly recognized the difference in generations. He remembered a question his uncle Samuel Ripley had asked him years before, when as a boy of thirteen he had done his first actual teaching in his uncle's school: "How is it, Ralph, that all the boys dislike you & quarrel with you, whilst the grown people are fond of you?" "Now am I thirty six," Emerson reflected in the year after the Divinity School affair, "and the fact

is reversed,—the old people suspect & dislike me, & the young love me"
(*JMN* 7:253).

What the young people liked and understood in their teacher was less
the explicit message than the spirit of the man who spoke it; as Lowell
explained, "We do not go to hear what Emerson says so much as to
hear Emerson."[22] Certainly they did not go for cheap popularization or
sidewinding oratory, though both were common enough at a time when
public speakers customarily performed with all stops out. Emerson seldom
spoke extemporaneously or even from notes; he customarily read from a
prepared manuscript, though in his later years he had a disconcerting habit
of shuffling his pages about while he was talking. His delivery was simple
and even conversational; in speaking he was "apt to hesitate in the course
of a sentence," according to the senior Oliver Wendell Holmes, as though
"picking his way through his vocabulary, to get at the best expression of his
thought."[23] "There was no rhetoric, no gesture, . . . no dramatic familiarity
and action," said Curtis, "but the manner was self-respectful and courteous
to the audience, and the tone supremely just and sincere."[24]

Moncure Conway agreed: Emerson depended not on "tricks of any kind"
but rather on "clearness of thought and simplicity of statement."[25] Henry
James the elder emphasized his modesty on the platform, recalling

> his deferential entrance upon the scene, his look of inquiry at the desk
> and the chair, his resolute rummaging among his embarrassed papers,
> the air of sudden recollection with which he would plunge into his
> pockets for what he must have known had never been put there, . . .
> his uncertainty and irresolution as he rose to speak, his deep, relieved
> inspiration as he got well from under the burning-glass of his auditors'
> eyes, and addressed himself at length to their docile ears instead. . . .
> And then when he looked over the heads of his audience into the dim
> mysterious distance, and his weird monotone began to reverberate
> in your bosom's depths, and his words flowed on, now with a river's
> volume, grand, majestic, free, and anon diminished themselves to the
> fitful cadence of a brook . . . , and you saw the clear eye eloquent with
> nature's purity, and beheld the musing countenance turned within,
> as it were, and hearkening to the rumour of a far-off but on-coming
> world. . . .

It was all "intensely personal," James continued, and also "exquisitely
characteristic" of Emerson the man.[26]

Audiences everywhere were particularly struck with Emerson's voice, which Holmes described as "never loud, never shrill, but singularly penetrating."[27] It had "a strange power," said E. P. Whipple, "which affected me more than any other voice I ever heard on the stage or on the platform."[28] But however entranced they were by Emerson's way of speaking, few of his auditors followed everything they had listened to or even agreed with what they thought he had said. Hawthorne's son, Julian, recalled leaving the lecture-room in Concord one evening when he overheard "Prescott, the grocer, say to Jonas Hastings, the shoemaker, 'Did you get that about the Oversoul?' . . . Jonas . . . shook his head: 'No use wondering what he means; we know he's giving us the best there is.' "[29] At the other end of the spectrum there was downright hostility, particularly when Emerson ventured outside New England. In Wisconsin, for example, the *Kenosha Democrat* stigmatized him in 1860 as "an infidel—an abolitionist—a monarchist—all these, though he talk as musically as any dying swan."[30] Some unenthusiastic listeners, like the "stout Illinoian" Emerson himself mentioned, simply walked out of the hall. Those who stayed enjoyed Emerson's quiet humor, more characteristic of his lectures than of his published essays.[31] They especially liked the illustrative anecdotes "that sparkled for a moment upon the surface of his talk," as Curtis remarked, "and some sat inspired with unknown resolves, soaring upon lofty hopes."[32] By the 1860s, when Emerson had become something of an institution, Lowell felt that younger members of the audience were taking him for granted, failing to realize what they owed to him; their elders, Lowell said, better recognized "how much the country's intellectual emancipation was due to the stimulus of his teaching and example."[33] Curtis, who was a successful lecturer himself, put the same idea somewhat differently. Emerson, he said, "was never exactly popular, but always gave a tone and flavor to the whole lyceum course. . . . 'We can have him once in three or four seasons,' said the committees. But really they had him all the time without knowing it. He was the philosopher Proteus, and he spoke through all the more popular mouths. . . . They were . . . the middle-men between him and the public. They watered the nectar, and made it easy to drink."[34]

Like all teachers, especially those who teach other teachers, Emerson thus reached students even at second or third hand. "A teacher affects eternity," said Henry Adams; "he can never tell where his influence stops."[35] The thought is disturbing, since "when?" and "how?" and "by what channels?"

and "to what effect?" are questions difficult to answer on any chart or evaluation, however well intentioned. Doubtless Emerson himself, who thought a discourse should have some edge to it, was not too troubled when the response of listeners and readers was not unanimously favorable, though the outburst occasioned by the Divinity School Address proved more than he had quite bargained for. Religious conservatives then and now have protested against his liberal theology. When he lectured in Scotland in 1848 he was accused of being a pantheist.[36] At Columbus, Ohio, in 1867, a local Presbyterian minister preached against his appearance there, saying that "he had not expected to live to see the time when a Presbyterian pulpit would be disgraced by Ralph Waldo Emerson lecturing from it."[37] Among twentieth-century critics, Yvor Winters called Emerson and the Transcendentalists "moral parasites upon a Christian doctrine which they were endeavoring to destroy,"[38] and Randall Stewart stigmatized him as "the archheretic of American literature."[39] On the other extreme, the obvious vestiges of clericalism in Emerson have always offended the secular-minded. D. H. Lawrence, for example, admired "Emerson's real courage," but disliked the limitations of his idealism. In Lawrence's words, "all those gorgeous inrushes of exaltation and spiritual energy which made Emerson a great man, now make us sick,"[40] and some contemporary readers agree.

There has been a similar difference of opinion about Emerson's political and social views, which have also offended the extreme Left and the extreme Right of two centuries. In the 1840s he inclined toward the principles of what he called "the movement party" (*CW* 3:155) rather than toward the conservatism of "the establishment" (*CW* 1:190, 195), but he was never a partisan in the conventional sense. His increasing antipathy to slavery led him to support Free Soil candidates and later to gravitate toward the new Republican party, though for a long time he resisted identification with the Abolitionist movement. But believing as he did that slavery was flatly wrong and seeing its evil increasingly compounded by abridgment of the right of free speech and by coercion of Northern freemen as well as of Southern slaves, he ultimately found himself endorsing even John Brown's use of violence in retaliation. And so during the 1850s the peace-loving teacher became a militant activist, remaining so for the duration of the Civil War. If his moral activism seems inconsistent with his vocational role, it was not altogether out of character for a man who had insisted in his first published book that "the moral law lies at the centre of nature and radiates to the circumference" (*CW* 1:26). To condone slavery was unnatural and immoral, a denial of human worth and dignity and freedom; he *must* stand up and be counted with the opposition. "I divide men as aspirants & desperants," he once told Holmes. "A scholar need not be cynical to feel that the vast multitude are almost on all fours; that the rich always vote after their fears[;] that cities churches colleges all go for the quadruped interest, and it is against this coalition that the pathetically small minority of disengaged or thinking men stand for the ideal right, for man as he should be, & . . . for the right of every other as for his own" (*L* 5:17). And in 1863 he told a college audience that "a scholar defending the cause of slavery, of arbitrary government, of monopoly, of the oppressor, is a traitor to his profession. He has ceased to be a scholar" (*W* 10:247).

However one may judge Emerson's reluctant foray into public affairs,[41] his prolonged engagement with moral issues at considerable cost to his own peace and prosperity illustrates what he liked to call "the Scholar's courage" (*JMN* 10:28; 12:607), a form of his cardinal principle of self-reliance. In David Riesman's phrase, he was an *inner-directed* man, living from within. What he regarded as "the moral law of human nature" he had enunciated as early as 1833, when he was thirty: "A man contains all that is needful to his government within himself. He is made a law unto himself. All real good or evil that can befal him must be from himself. He only can do himself any good or any harm. . . . The purpose of life seems to be to acquaint a man with himself. . . . The highest revelation is that God is in every man" (*JMN* 4:84).

On this moral and religious basis Emerson deplored imitation of any model however fine and refused conformity to all wholly external patterns, rituals, creeds, sects, parties, precedents, curricula, or institutions of any kind, including churches, colleges, and governments. The law he followed, though wholly internal, was rigorous; "If any one imagines that this law is lax," as he said in "Self-Reliance," "let him keep its commandment one day" (*CW* 2:42). When a man can look within and "read God directly," as "The American Scholar" has it, the hour is too precious for secondhand readings (*CW* 1:57). On this same basis, looking back with a measure of detachment on the Divinity School controversy—that "storm in our washbowl," as he called it (*CEC* 196), he could write in 1840 that "In all my lectures I have taught one doctrine, namely, the infinitude of the private man. This, the people accept readily enough, & even with loud commendation, as long as I call the lecture, Art; or Politics; or Literature; or the Household; but the moment I call it Religion,—they are shocked, though it be only the application of the same truth which they receive everywhere else, to a new class of facts" (*JMN* 7:342).

The "one doctrine" that Emerson specifies lay at the vital center of his teaching over a lifetime, whether the subject addressed was religion, morality, or teaching itself. His conception of "the private man" was essentially religious, idealistic, and optimistic. Where "desperants" such as his Puritan forebears and his less sanguine contemporaries stressed the finite limitations of humanity, as in the fiction of Hawthorne and Melville, his own abiding impulse, like that of Thoreau and Whitman, was to emphasize mankind's infinite potential, though the experience of his middle years brought him to an increasing realization of the limiting power of circumstance. By temperament Emerson was an idealist, an "aspirant." But as his journals reveal, he was forever being reminded of that "yawning gulf" that stretches "between the ambition of man and his power of performance," and it is this disparity between desire and capacity that for him "makes the tragedy of all souls" (*CW* 4:103), a tragedy all too frequently compounded by distorted aims and wasted forces.

If the purpose of life, as Emerson thought, is "to acquaint a man with himself," the purpose of a teacher should be to foster a student's full realization, in every sense, of his or her own worth and potential. This is the burden of the lectures and addresses in which Emerson touches in some way on learning and teaching: the Address on Education and "The American Scholar" of 1837, the Divinity School Address and "Literary Ethics" of 1838, the lecture on "Education" of 1840, and the addresses to college audiences of the 1850s and 1860s, notably "The Celebration of Intellect." Relevant too are such essays of 1841 and 1844 as "Self-Reliance," "Spiritual Laws," "The Over-Soul," "Intellect," and "The Poet," this last with its Emersonian emphasis on the human need for self-expression—"It is in me, and shall out" (*CW* 3:23)—that not only brought Walt Whitman to a boil but also anticipated the teachings of John Dewey. Emerson's thinking about education, being of a piece with his general ideas, was essentially religious in character, though it has obvious secular implications and applications. To educate means *to draw out;* Emerson complained that "We do not believe in a power of Education. We do not think we can call out God in man and we do not try" (*EL* 3:290; cf. *CW* 2:158). His own basic objective, to "call out God in man," was not inherently different from that of the builders of medieval universities or nineteenth-century church-related colleges. Like them, he believed that religion and learning spring from a common source. He delighted to celebrate that source, that "original unit" and "fountain of power," as he called it in "The American Scholar," common to all individuals and linking them both with Man—again, capital *M*—and also with nature.

Every human being, Emerson believed, stands "in need of expression," students and teachers included: "In love, in art, in avarice, in politics, in labor, in games, we study to utter our painful secret" (*CW* 3:4). It is no different in teaching, though what a teacher expresses, he felt, is less what he *knows* than what he *is*. For him there were two kinds of teachers: those who "speak *from within*," and therefore teach with firsthand knowledge and authority; and those who speak only "*from without*, as spectators merely," on the basis of secondhand evidence (*CW* 2:170). For him, only the former—Emerson's "true scholars"—deserve the name of teacher. Like Alfred North Whitehead in our own century, Emerson protested against dead knowledge—what Whitehead in *The Aims of Education* (1929) would call "inert ideas."[42] "Life, authentic life, you must have," Emerson insisted, "or you can teach nothing" (*JMN* 7:27).[43] If life and power are present within, they will manifest themselves outwardly, whether by our conscious intention or otherwise. "That which we are, we shall teach," he wrote, "not voluntarily but involuntarily. . . . Character teaches over our head" (*CW* 2:169). "If a teacher have any opinion which he wishes to conceal, his pupils will become as fully indoctrinated into that as into any which he publishes" (*CW* 2:85). Again: "The man may teach by doing, and not otherwise. If he can communicate himself he can teach, but not by words. He teaches who gives, and he learns who receives" (*CW* 2:88).

Since for Emerson a student's self-realization meant self-reliance, he reminded himself of "the cardinal virtue of a teacher" exemplified by Socrates: "to protect the pupil from his own influence" (*JMN* 10:471). Neither teachers nor parents, he cautioned, should try to make duplicates of themselves. " 'Get off that child!' he said in a lecture; 'One is enough.' "[44] His friend Moncure Conway, writing of Emerson's powerful stimulation of a variety of writers differing in both their aim and their style, rightly observed that "they who came to his fontless baptism were never made Emersonians."[45] His words would have pleased Emerson himself, who in his later years remarked in his journal, "I have been writing & speaking what were once called novelties, for twenty five or thirty years, & have not now one disciple. Why? Not that what I said was not true; not that it has not found intelligent receivers but because it did not go from any wish in me to bring men to me, but to themselves. I delight in driving them from me. . . . This is my boast that I have no school & no follower. I should account it a measure of the impurity of insight, if it did not create independence" (*JMN* 14:258).

Independence, self-reliance, self-knowledge, self-expression, self-fulfillment—these were the "novelties" that Emerson taught as writer and lecturer, whatever his subjects and courses, and the lesson was heard and repeated. "I would not have any one adopt *my* mode of living on any account," wrote one of his alumni, Henry Thoreau, in *Walden*. "I desire that there may be as many different persons in the world as possible; but I would have each one be very careful to find out and pursue *his own* way."[46] "Not I, nor any one else can travel that road for you," Walt Whitman responded in *Leaves of Grass*. "You must travel it for yourself."[47] Even Melville chimed in, though with a note of warning, in *Moby-Dick:* "the only mode in which you can derive even a tolerable idea of [the whale's] living contour, is by going a whaling yourself; but by so doing, you run no small risk of being eternally stove and sunk by him."[48] So Emerson, by recurrent challenge and by cumulative example, provoked and inspired and *educated* his students—and in turn his students' students—to walk on their own feet, to work with their own hands, to speak their own minds (cf. *CW* 1:70), just as every great teacher invariably does. Indeed he is no teacher unless, like Emerson, he truly creates independence.

2.

Melville and Whitman

One of the standard course offerings each semester in my department at the University of Wisconsin–Madison has been a multiple-section "course for majors," each version of which concentrates on the work of one or two British or American writers who can thus be studied more intensively than is possible in the survey, period, and genre courses usually offered to undergraduates. In the fall of 1981, when my turn to teach the course came around, I decided on selected writings of Herman Melville and Walt Whitman—two authors not usually paired as are Emerson and Thoreau, for example, or Poe and Hawthorne, Hawthorne and Melville, Whitman and Dickinson, or Mark Twain and Henry James. By associating Melville and Whitman, I thought, we would be doing something out of the ordinary that would be challenging for both the class and the instructor.

Melville and Whitman were exact contemporaries with a good many affiliations in common, although they apparently never met. Each man was largely self-educated, in terms of both the world of books and the world of experience, and each broke new ground as a literary artist. Each was at once a realist and a romantic, and like Melville's Ishmael they demonstrated in a number of their most characteristic writings how meditation and water are wedded forever. Although Melville is remembered primarily for his fiction and Whitman for his poetry, the author of *Moby-Dick* wrote poems that deserve to be better known, and reading Whitman's distinctive prose as well as his verse is essential to a full understanding of his thought and art.

The course as I offered it in 1981 attempted to address these general considerations. Section i below reprints the handout I prepared at the outset as a supplement to standard biographical information about the two men; it brings together for the first time the few known facts concerning their limited knowledge of one another. Section ii discusses the course itself. As with most courses, the semester took some surprising turns, and as a learning experience the readings and discussion that engaged us succeeded in enlightening the instructor along with other students in our group.

i. Biographical

As editor of the *Brooklyn Daily Eagle* in the mid-1840s, Walt Whitman briefly reviewed Herman Melville's first two books, *Typee* (1846) and *Omoo* (1847). He found *Typee* "strange, graceful, most readable. . . . As a book to hold in one's hand and pore dreamily over of a summer day, it is unsurpassed."[1] *Omoo* he thought "the most readable sort of reading. The question whether these two stories [*Typee* and *Omoo*] be authentic or not has, of course, not so much to do with their interest. One can revel in such richly good natured style, if nothing else." He recommended the new work "as thorough entertainment—not so light as to be tossed aside for its flippancy, nor so profound as to be tiresome."[2]

"Probably Whitman read nothing else by Melville," Thomas L. Brasher has concluded, "since in commenting to [Horace] Traubel in 1889 on Edmund C. Stedman's *Library of American Literature* and on its engraved portraits of authors [including both Melville and himself], he said of Melville, 'I know little about him but they say much of him here.' So far as I know, this remark, along with the reviews of *Typee* and *Omoo,* is all Whitman ever said about Melville."[3] Certainly there are no references to Melville or his works in Whitman's published correspondence. In 1889 he had probably been hearing of Melville from their mutual friend Stedman and his son Arthur; the Stedmans had been in touch with both writers concerning their portraits and the selections from their writings used in *A Library of American Literature,* published in eleven volumes between 1888 and 1890 by the New York firm of Charles L. Webster & Co.—Mark Twain's publishing house.

By the time of the Civil War, Melville's earlier fame had suffered eclipse and Whitman's reputation was still to be won, especially in the United States. Both writers were read and appreciated abroad, however, and their

British admirers liked to couple their names together—sometimes going on to deplore their neglect by their fellow Americans. One of these admirers from overseas, Robert Buchanan, a Scot who visited the United States in 1884, called on Whitman in Camden but failed to find Melville in New York. In the following year he published a poem, "Socrates in Camden," that speaks of Whitman as a "sun-like music-maker" who "Shines solitary and apart," and calls Melville the "sea-compelling man" who "Sits all forgotten or ignored, / While haberdashers are adored!" In New York, he added in a footnote, "No one seemed to know anything of the one great imaginative writer fit to stand shoulder to shoulder with Whitman on that continent."4

Both Melville and Whitman must have seen copies of Buchanan's poem. Melville was sent a copy by an English correspondent, James Billson of Leicestershire, to whom he wrote in acknowledgment that "for more than one reason, this Piece could not but give me pleasure. Aside from its poetic quality, there is implyed in it the fact, that the writer has intuitively penetrated beneath the surface of certain matters here. It is the insight of genius and the fresh mind. The tribute to Walt Whitman has the ring of strong sincerity. As to the incidental allusion to my humble self, it is overpraise, to be sure; but I can't help that, tho' I am alive to the spirit that dictated it" (*Correspondence*, 489).

Buchanan had more to say of Melville in 1889, when, in a note to his "Imperial Cockneydom," recalling once again his visit to the United States in 1884, he wrote that E. C. Stedman had "seemed much astonished" at his interest in Melville. Stedman, he went on to explain, told him "that Melville was dwelling 'somewhere in New York,' having resolved, on account of the public support of his works, never to write another line."5 Buchanan's remarks raise certain questions. First, Melville had in fact continued to write, both in prose and in verse, during his so-called "silent years," and during the late 1880s was to publish two privately printed volumes of poetry and to write *Billy Budd, Sailor*, which remained in manuscript until 1924. Second, Stedman and Melville were near neighbors on East Twenty-sixth Street in 1884, and two years before that, Stedman had joined with founding members of the Authors Club in an unsuccessful attempt to persuade Melville to become a member. Stedman's son Arthur, who became Melville's literary executor after Melville's death in 1891, referred to Buchanan as merely a literary adventurer who "apparently 'sought everywhere' except in the one place where all of Mr. Melville's contemporaries made their search when they had occasion to visit him—the City Directory."[6]

By 1888 both Stedmans had made their way to Melville's home, and after one of his visits the elder Stedman remarked in a letter to Melville that, "as you said so much of Whitman," he would send a "chapter" on Whitman for Melville to read, "—not that it is of any great importance" (*Correspondence*, 741). Unless Stedman was referring to an unpublished manuscript, as Jay Leyda conjectured in *The Melville Log* (*Log*, 2:805), the "chapter" was probably his discussion of Whitman in *The Poets of America*, published in two volumes in 1885. Arthur Stedman visited both Whitman and Melville, and the two authors became fond of him; Whitman called him a "dear good invalid, consumptive y'ng fellow,"[7] and his friendship with Melville "grew fast," as a niece of Stedman's recalled, having been "enthusiastically encouraged" by Stedman's father as an old admirer of *Moby-Dick*.[8] In 1891 and 1892 the younger Stedman wrote biographical sketches of both Melville and Whitman for periodicals and for *Appleton's Annual Cyclopaedia*; in 1892 he published *Selected Poems of Whitman* and *Autobiographia: The Story of a Life*, consisting of selections from Whitman's prose writings, and new editions of Melville's *Typee, Omoo, White-Jacket*, and *Moby-Dick*, contributing a biographical and critical Introduction to *Typee*.

ii. The Course

Since there was not time enough to cover all of Melville, I rather arbitrarily chose to read only *Typee, Mardi, Moby-Dick*, and *Pierre*, the posthumously published *Billy Budd, Sailor*, and a generous selection of the poetry. We were able to study proportionately more of Whitman, using the Comprehensive Reader's Edition of *Leaves of Grass* plus reprints of the 1855 and 1860 editions. The opening selection was *Typee*, Melville's readable first book, which I expected to follow with *Mardi* before turning to the 1855 *Leaves;* by that time, I thought, the group would be acclimated to one another and to the kind of open discussion I wished to foster. But because of some delay in getting textbooks, we were obliged to take up Whitman's "Song of Myself" immediately after *Typee* and before turning to *Mardi*. This fortuitous change was all to the good. "Song of Myself" and

Mardi, though different in form, are alike in one sense: they are works of subjectively oriented young writers exploring new and different territory, each in his own way, and for students reading them in juxtaposition they proved to be immediately engaging.

Frankly, the warm response to *Mardi* surprised me. Many readers find the book confusing and unsatisfying, but this group did not, for they applied to Melville's poetic prose—so different from that of *Typee*—what they had learned in reading Whitman's verse. They quickly responded to the musical rhythms of *Mardi,* to its abundant images and symbols, and to Melville's frequent use of what Lawrence Buell has aptly called "Transcendentalist catalogue rhetoric,"[9] which had become familiar to them in "Song of Myself." Dealing with *Mardi* in turn prepared them for *Moby-Dick* (which many of the group already knew but had not read closely) and especially for *Pierre,* a complex book that isn't likely to interest those who read only for the story line. I have never had more success in discussing these three books with undergraduates.

The later works of both Melville and Whitman, including *Billy Budd, Sailor,* also proved to be interesting and provocative. As I expected, we found that Whitman's *Drum-Taps* and Melville's *Battle-Pieces* illuminated one another in many ways and revealed much about their authors as the two writers reflected on the course of our Civil War. Whitman's war poems were immediately moving and easier for the students to grasp in terms of both technique and tone; Melville's were more difficult and evidently more challenging. I remarked about the different ways in which both writers drew upon Emerson, with Whitman following Emerson's thinking in "The Poet" and Melville his actual practice as a versifier, and I said something about differing attitudes toward the aftermath of war in Melville's "Supplement to *Battle-Pieces*" and Whitman's *Democratic Vistas.* But I saw no need to send class members to the several scholars and critics who have published detailed comparisons and contrasts of *Battle-Pieces* and *Drum-Taps;* in class discussion they readily identified the principal points at issue, as good students usually manage to do for themselves if adequately prepared and duly encouraged.

Teaching Whitman either with or before Melville is of course not the only way to introduce students to these authors, but in this one instance it certainly worked well for both my students and myself. I can confidently recommend the general principle of devoting a semester to an in-depth reading of two authors whose respective thought and style can thus be closely examined, understood, and appreciated by able undergraduates. And in approaching Melville's challenging trilogy of *Mardi, Moby-Dick,* and *Pierre* with any group that is already familiar with "Song of Myself," it might be salutary to remind them of the rhetorical elements common to both Whitman's poetry and Melville's best prose.

3.

Herman Melville's "Bartleby"

"Bartleby, the Scrivener: A Story of Wall-Street" was first published anonymously in 1853, in the November and December issues of *Putnam's Monthly Magazine,* and was reprinted three years later as "Bartleby" in *The Piazza Tales* (New York: Dix & Edwards, 1856), the only collection of Herman Melville's magazine pieces to appear during his lifetime. Although the story was not again reprinted until 1922, when it was published in a new English edition of Melville's works at the outset of the modern Melville revival, it has since become widely known through its appearance in college anthologies, in subsequent editions of Melville's writings, and through its dramatization for both television and opera.

Most twentieth-century readers are likely to think of Melville primarily as the author of *Moby-Dick* (1851), but in his own day he was repeatedly tagged as the author of *Typee* (1846) and *Omoo* (1847), his first two books, which were based on his adventures of earlier years in the South Pacific. In his later writings Melville sought another kind of fame, and with *Moby-Dick* he hoped at last to gain it. "What 'reputation' H.M. has is horrible," he wrote to his friend Nathaniel Hawthorne in 1851 while that book was in progress; because of *Typee,* which told of his life among a savage tribe in the Marquesas Islands, he predicted that he would "go down to posterity" only "as a 'man who lived among the cannibals'" (*Correspondence,* 193). Even *Moby-Dick,* the book now regarded as his masterpiece, failed to impress either contemporary critics or the reading public as he had hoped, and his next book, *Pierre* (1852), was an out-and-out disaster that threatened to end his career as a writer. After his publishers refused his next book-length manuscript in the spring of 1853, Melville turned to magazines as a source of income, and over the next three years he completed fifteen stories and sketches plus a serialized novel, *Israel Potter* (1855). Some of these pieces, "Bartleby" among them, are now ranked with his finest work.

Since *Pierre* had prompted some critics to question not just Melville's talent, but even his sanity, he must have been attracted by the cloak of anonymity provided by magazine publication, along with the needed money it earned for him: five dollars per printed page, well above the average for authors of that period. But his authorship was not long a secret in New York literary circles, and one weekly journal cited "Bartleby" in remarking that authors of "such clever articles . . . have become perfectly well known." When "Bartleby" was reprinted as Melville's in *The Piazza Tales* it was called "a portrait from life" by one reviewer and said by another to be "based on living characters," but no critic of the time identified its supposed originals.[1] More recent commentators have sought among Melville's several relatives who were lawyers for some model for the attorney who tells the story: his uncle Peter Gansevoort in Albany; his father-in-law, Lemuel Shaw, Chief Justice of the Supreme Court of Massachusetts, in Boston; and his brothers, Gansevoort and Allan Melville in New York, Allan's office being located at No. 10 Wall Street. One study argues that the narrator's profession and his particular duties as Master in Chancery, involving an old distinction in Anglo-Saxon jurisprudence between Chancery (or Equity) and common law, are important to a full understanding of the story. Whether or not Melville intended to portray in his narrator some individual attorney of his acquaintance, he was obviously familiar with such legal distinctions as well as with the operations of a contemporary Wall Street law office.

Readers of "Bartleby" will notice that there are several allusions in the story to actual persons, places, and events associated with New York City in the 1840s and 1850s: John Jacob Astor; the murder of Samuel Adams by John C. Colt in January of 1842; the career of the notorious swindler Monroe Edwards; the streets of the city and its prison known as The Tombs. One of Melville's biographers, Leon Howard, noting that the story "was supposedly based upon a certain amount of fact," speculates that "some anecdote concerning a lawyer's clerk" may have suggested "Bartleby." Such an anecdote appears in the first chapter of a novel of 1853, *The Lawyer's Story,* by James C. Maitland, which Melville would have seen advertised. The novel begins: "In the summer of 1843, having an extraordinary quantity of deeds to copy, I engaged, temporarily, an extra copying clerk, who interested me considerably, in consequence of his modest, quiet, gentlemanly demeanor, and his intense application to his duties." Melville's own development of his lawyer's "extra copying clerk," or scrivener, as copyists were called in the nineteenth century, possibly involved recollections of such friends as George J. Adler, whose symptoms of agoraphobia may have suggested Bartleby's preference for seclusion, or Eli James Murdock Fly, who had once been a New York scrivener. Melville had known Fly since his boyhood in Albany and had traveled with him to Illinois in 1840; in New York Fly did "incessant writing from morning to Eve[nin]g" for a Mr. Edwards, but in more recent years he had been living in Vermont as "a confirmed invalid." The "rumor" that Bartleby had lost his place as a "subordinate clerk in the Dead Letter Office at Washington" (*Piazza Tales,* 45) is probably traceable to a journalistic fad in the years just before the story was written, when a number of American newspapers carried sentimental accounts of the Dead Letter Office.

Recent scholarly studies of "Bartleby" have emphasized its relation to the contemporary scene in the 1840s and 1850s rather than the supposed autobiographical implications of the story that had attracted Melville's biographers and critics between the 1920s and the 1960s. Some readers have compared Bartleby's fellow employees with characters in Dickens and Bartleby himself with eccentrics drawn by Washington Irving and Charles Lamb; still others have seen Bartleby as a Christ figure. But the most interesting development in twentieth-century criticism of the story has been the pronounced shift in focus from Bartleby to his employer, who in trying to come to terms with the moral and ethical problem posed by the scrivener's recalcitrance manages to reveal more of his own character to the reader than he does that of Bartleby.

To date there have been four book-length publications devoted to this single story: *A Symposium: Bartleby the Scrivener,* edited by Howard P. Vincent in 1966 (Kent, Ohio: Kent State University Press), which included a bibliography of 117 items; *Bartleby the Scrivener: A Casebook for Research,* edited by Stanley Schatt in 1972 (Dubuque, Iowa: Kendall-Hunt Publishing Company); *Bartleby the Inscrutable: A Collection of Commentary,* edited by M. Thomas Inge in 1979 (Hamden, Conn.: Archon Books), which includes an annotated bibliography of 262 items; and *The Silence of Bartleby,* by Dan McCall in 1989 (Ithaca and London: Cornell University

Press). The outpouring of published essays has continued unabated, with still no consensus concerning either Bartleby or the lawyer through whose eyes we see him.

Melville and the Magazines

What I have to say about Herman Melville and "Bartleby" will not constitute an interpretation of Melville's story, but rather an effort to place it for the reader in the context of Melville's career immediately following the appearance of *Moby-Dick* and *Pierre*. I must declare at the outset that we don't know how Melville himself may have spoken of the story, or what he thought privately about either Bartleby or the attorney who employed him; there is no discussion of it in his surviving correspondence, and, with the exception of a single discarded leaf (numbered "36"),[2] neither a manuscript nor working notes have come down to us. We have only the published text, comprising the attorney's words about Bartleby, about the other characters, about what takes place in the story, and about himself.

It will be in order to look at the four stories of 1853, "Bartleby" included, that constituted Melville's first work for the magazines and then to examine two specific images in "Bartleby" that relate the story directly to Melville's earlier books, *Moby-Dick* included. I hope that these comments will contribute to discussions of the story and, beyond that, will give readers some idea of how literary scholars go about their business, not only in the classroom but also in the research and analysis that are part of our preparation for day-to-day teaching. A word of caution: not all of us in this multifaceted profession work in the same way, even within the discipline of literary study, or think in the same way—more than 250 published comments on "Bartleby" alone have accumulated over the years, with more still appearing! No two works of literature will present exactly the same problems to a scholar or teacher, and what I am about to do with Melville and with "Bartleby" isn't necessarily what I or any other scholar-teacher in the field would do with Milton or Shakespeare, or Wordsworth or Whitman, or Mark Twain or James Joyce—just to mention a very wide range of writers.

It is well to remember that in the early 1850s Melville was caught in an economic squeeze not untypical of American authors today but even more common for writers in the nineteenth century. Before the adoption of international copyright in 1891, the year of Melville's death, the serious writer in this country had to compete on his own level with "pirated" editions of British authors, such as Thackeray and especially Dickens, on which American publishers paid no royalties. Then there were equivalents of today's Gothics, romances, and pulps, turned out for a mass audience in this country by what Melville's friend Hawthorne called "a d——d mob of scribbling women."[3] (I quote Hawthorne with my fingers crossed!) Melville himself knew well enough that professional writers cannot ignore popular taste, and he soon learned that what he "felt most moved to write" was in effect "banned" because it would not pay. "Dollars damn me," was his phrase. He tried to compromise, he told Hawthorne, but "the product is a final hash, and all my books are botches" (*Correspondence,* 191). So he declared in a letter written in June of 1851—just at the time when he was putting the final touches on *Moby-Dick.* Melville was only thirty-two when he published *Moby-Dick,* his sixth book in five years. In the course of writing it he had moved his family from New York to a farm near Pittsfield, Massachusetts, that he called "Arrowhead"; Hawthorne was his neighbor in Lenox, some seven miles away.

In the spring of 1853 Harper & Brothers, Melville's American publisher, compounded his recurrent financial problems by refusing his latest book-length manuscript, "The Isle of the Cross." He had gone into debt to purchase his Pittsfield farm, he was overdrawn in his royalty accounts with the Harpers, and his health was another cause for worry. For the next three dark years, while his relatives were trying unsuccessfully to secure a consular appointment for him in the Pacific islands or in Italy, Melville supported his family chiefly by writing anonymously for the two best American periodicals of the day, *Harper's New Monthly Magazine* and *Putnam's Monthly Magazine.* By the spring of 1856 he had written fifteen shorter magazine pieces and the one longer serial, *Israel Potter;* some of his stories, including "Bartleby," were about to appear in the collected *Piazza Tales,* and he had begun another new book, *The Confidence-Man* (1857). Although the work of these years was long neglected, both the best of the magazine pieces and *The Confidence-Man* are now seen as worthy successors to *Moby-Dick,* but their cost in terms of mental stress and physical effort was heavy.

Four Stories of 1853

Let us now look more closely at the story of "Bartleby" in its immediate context: that critical year of 1853 in which Melville turned from book-length fiction to writing for magazines. On the basis of my own research, published in 1980 as "The Chronology of Melville's Short Fiction, 1853–1856," we know that "Bartleby" is not Melville's first magazine story, as some scholars formerly thought it to be, but more likely his fourth. His initial pieces for *Harper's* were probably two brief stories called "The Happy Failure" and "The Fiddler," which were long supposed to be of later composition simply because they weren't actually published until the summer of 1854; a third story was "Cock-A-Doodle-Doo!," which appeared in December of 1853. Meanwhile, Melville had sent "Bartleby" to *Putnam's*, where it appeared in November and December of 1853. It is my own conviction that "Bartleby" will seem even more interesting if it is read not simply as an isolated story but rather as the most complex narrative of this group of four. As a comparison of their common elements will show, all of these tales are concerned with the common theme of failure, to which their respective protagonists have made a response in terms either of conventional piety, realistic self-appraisal, transcendent enthusiasm, or—in Bartleby's case—apathetic withdrawal: "I would prefer not to."

As Lewis Mumford remarked years ago, Melville had a habit of "playing with his own fate" in the stories he wrote,[4] and in reading a piece such as "The Fiddler," where a failed poet whose work has just been damned learns that it is possible to live "*with* genius and *without* fame" (*Piazza Tales*, 267),[5] it is easy to think of Melville recalling the reception of *Moby-Dick* and the absolute disaster of *Pierre*. But what strikes me is that in the other three stories, "Bartleby" in particular, Melville is approaching his failed protagonist in terms of a first-person narrator who is detached from that protagonist, and as he moves from story to story his interest seems to lie increasingly with the narrator as an independent observer trying to understand the other character's failure. A biographer or biographical critic might well see Melville doing something almost therapeutic here, especially in "Bartleby," where the self-satisfied lawyer who tells the scrivener's story seems far removed in every way from the character and personality of Herman Melville himself.

Melville's Stories of 1853: An Analytical Table

	"The Happy Failure"	*"The Fiddler"*	*"Cock-A-Doodle-Doo!"*	*"Bartleby"*
	Rural setting	Urban setting	Rural setting	Urban setting
	Narrator an anonymous nephew, uncharacterized	Narrator a failed poet named Helmstone	Narrator an anonymous farmer, in debt and given to "doleful dumps"	Narrator an anonymous attorney, safe, prudent, methodical, given to "the easiest way of life"
	Protagonist an anonymous uncle, with an invention to drain swamps and marshes	Protagonist a once-famous violinist, Hautboy, who now teaches fiddling for a living	Protagonist a wood-sawyer, Merrymusk, who was once a sailor	Protagonist a scrivener, Bartleby, who *may* have once worked in the Dead Letter Office
	Central symbol is the uncle's unsuccessful invention	Central symbol is Hautboy's fiddle, plied with "the bow of an enchanter" though the tunes are common	Central symbol is the cock's triumphant crow—even in the face of death	Central symbol is "the dead brick wall"—duplicated in The Tombs
	Protagonist praises God for his failure, which "has made a good old man of me"	Protagonist *a realist*, hitting "the exact line between *enthusiasm* and *apathy*," who has learned to be happy *with* genius and *without* fame"	Protagonist *an enthusiast*—even in the face of death (he, his family, and the cock all *die*)	Protagonist *apathetic* ("I would prefer not to"); like Melville's Pierre, he dies in The Tombs
	Narrator says that his uncle's example "did for me the work of experience"	Narrator burns his manuscripts, buys a fiddle, and takes "regular lessons of Hautboy"	Narrator freed of his "doleful dumps"; "under all circumstances crow[s]" late and early with a continual crow"	Narrator seems noncommittal on seeing Bartleby sleeping "with kings and *counselors*" ("Ah, Bartleby! Ah, humanity!")

Both in these early tales and in several later pieces the character who observes the action is a bachelor—and for Melville, bachelors, along with college sophomores, were type figures whose lack of worldly experience made their judgment suspect in his eyes. In chapter 115 of *Moby-Dick,* for example, the captain of a ship aptly named *The Bachelor* responds to Captain Ahab's inquiry about the White Whale by saying that he simply doesn't believe in any such creature (*Moby-Dick,* 494), and in a sketch called "The Paradise of Bachelors" (1855) there is a group of unmarried London barristers to whose "bachelor imaginations" all "legends" about "the thing called pain, the bugbear styled trouble," likewise seem merely "preposterous" (*Piazza Tales,* 322). The list of impercipient observers could be continued with the sanguine Amasa Delano, captain of the ship *Bachelor's Delight* in "Benito Cereno" (1855), described as "a person of a singularly undistrustful good nature" (*Piazza Tales,* 47) who never understands or appreciates the suffering undergone by the story's title character. The narrator of "Bartleby," that "eminently *safe* man" given to "the easiest way of life" (14), makes no reference to either wife or children, and his judgment of another character outside his obviously limited world must be discounted accordingly.

Two Images in "Bartleby"

Now, having placed "Bartleby" in its immediate context, the stories of 1853, let us relate certain elements in the narrative to Melville's earlier development. I want to look backward from "Bartleby" to the three books sometimes regarded as a trilogy, *Mardi* (1849), *Moby-Dick,* and *Pierre,* in terms of two recurrent figures: the image of *the wall* and the image of *the soul's ship.* Let's begin with this passage in "Bartleby":

> I now recalled . . . that for long periods [Bartleby] would stand look-
> ing out, at his pale window behind the screen, upon the dead brick
> wall. . . . And more than all, I remembered . . . an austere reserve
> about him, which had positively awed me into my tame compliance
> with his eccentricities, when . . . behind his screen he must be stand-
> ing in one of those dead-wall reveries of his. (28–29)

This comment takes on far more meaning if one reads it with reference to a series of related passages in *Moby-Dick,* all having to do in some way with the White Whale. Consider first this exchange between Ahab and Starbuck, his first mate:

> "But what's this long face about, Mr. Starbuck; wilt thou not chase the white whale? art not game for Moby Dick?" . . .
> "Vengeance on a dumb brute!" cried Starbuck, "that simply smote thee from blindest instinct! Madness! To be enraged with a dumb thing, Captain Ahab, seems blasphemous."
> "Hark ye yet again,—the little lower layer. All visible objects, man, are but as pasteboard masks. But in each event—in the living act, the undoubted deed—there, some unknown but still reasoning thing puts forth the mouldings of its features from behind the unreasoning mask. If man will strike, strike through the mask! How can the prisoner reach outside except by thrusting through the wall? *To me, the white whale is that wall, shoved near to me.* Sometimes I think there's naught beyond. But 'tis enough. He tasks me; he heaps me; I see in him outrageous strength, with an inscrutable malice sinewing it. That inscrutable thing is chiefly what I hate, and be the white whale agent, or be the white whale principal, I will wreak that hate upon him. Talk not to me of blasphemy, man; I'd strike the sun if it insulted me." (*Moby-Dick*, 163–64, emphasis added)

> . . . you must now have perceived that the front of the Sperm Whale's head is *a dead, blind wall*, without a single organ or tender prominence of any sort whatsoever. (Ishmael, in "The Battering Ram," *Moby-Dick*, 336–37, emphasis added)

> "*The dead, blind wall* butts all inquiring heads at last." (Ahab, in *Moby-Dick*, 521, emphasis added)

What I'm suggesting, of course, is that the lawyer-narrator in "Bartleby" stands in somewhat the same relation to the scrivener as the conventionally minded Starbuck in *Moby-Dick* stands to Captain Ahab: Bartleby, like Ahab, has somehow met his White Whale; what remains to him within the action of the story proper is simply that "dead, blind wall" that he confronts "in one of those *dead-wall* reveries of his." The lawyer, on the other hand, is as much outside Bartleby's range of experience as Starbuck is outside Ahab's, though ironically he is as much a prisoner of the encapsulating walls in this "story of Wall Street" as is Bartleby himself. Indeed our lawyer is one of that extended line of bachelors in Melville who, safe in their snug retreats, believe in no White Whales and scoff even at pain and trouble—until, of course, a Bartleby comes into the "safe" attorney's business and bosom.

In turning to the second image, that of the soul's ship, I begin with a remark of the lawyer's:

> If [Bartleby] would but have named a single relative or friend, I would instantly have written, and urged their taking the poor fellow away to some convenient retreat. But he seemed *alone, absolutely alone* in the universe. *A bit of wreck in the mid Atlantic.* (32, emphasis added)

To anyone who knows *Mardi, Moby-Dick,* and *Pierre,* those words should start all manner of echoes. Bartleby's cosmic loneliness, for instance, is like that of Pip in *Moby-Dick,* who has jumped out of a whale-boat in fear for his life:

> Now, in calm weather, to swim *in the open ocean* is . . . easy. . . . But the awful *lonesomeness* is intolerable. The intense concentration of self in the middle of such a heartless immensity, my God! who can tell it? ("The Castaway," *Moby-Dick,* 414, emphasis added)

As for Bartleby as "a bit of wreck," look at this sequence of passages from the trilogy:

> But . . . if after all . . . , the verdict be, the golden haven was not gained;—yet, in bold quest thereof, better to sink in boundless deeps, than float on vulgar shoals; and give me, ye gods, *an utter wreck,* if wreck I do. (*Mardi,* 557, emphasis added)

> "For the third time *my soul's ship* starts upon this voyage, Starbuck." (Ahab, in "The Chase—Third Day," *Moby-Dick,* 565, emphasis added)

> [Pierre's] *soul's ship* foresaw the inevitable rocks, but resolved to sail on, and make a courageous *wreck.* (*Pierre,* 339, emphasis added)

To the degree that Melville's writing represents a continuous voyaging through the world of mind first envisioned in *Mardi,* the soul's ship by the time of "Bartleby" has indeed struck the rocks, the explorer's vessel has broken up, and Bartleby himself is "alone, absolutely alone," as "a bit of wreck in the mid Atlantic." Small wonder that he is beyond the reach of our bachelor lawyer!

In thus relating "Bartleby" to the uneasy course of Melville's career up to 1853, I have tried to show that it repeats certain patterns and recapitulates certain images and themes of earlier works that in turn throw light upon the story. I do not consider "Bartleby" to be autobiographical in the transparent sense, though I believe that Melville has drawn upon his own experience as writer and thinker in the same way that he has drawn upon his knowledge of lawyers, on his knowledge of the New York scene, and on characters that he probably knew, for all of these are components that went into the story in one way or another. I'm not saying, moreover, that the story *solves* anything. Great literature, I think, does not offer solutions or answers, though it may yield considerable illumination of our problems; it is like that art which Picasso had in mind when he reportedly said that art is a lie that tells the truth.

Here in conclusion is an anecdote from Melville's *Pierre,* which is the story of a young man undergoing initiation into the problems of mature existence. Pierre comes across a pamphlet by a mysterious philosopher named Plotinus Plinlimmon which purports to solve the dilemma facing Pierre himself: how to live by the standard of absolute truth in a disconcertingly relative world. Reading avidly, Pierre comes to the final pages, where the solution is presumably offered—only to find that there the pamphlet is torn! As Melville's narrator says wryly about Plinlimmon's pamphlet, "to me it seems more the excellently illustrated restatement of a problem, than the solution of the problem itself" (*Pierre,* 210). Let these words serve as my own concluding comment on the story of "Bartleby."

4.

Melville's "Benito Cereno"

erman Melville's "Benito Cereno," first published serially in *Putnam's Monthly Magazine* in October, November, and December 1855, was subsequently included in his *Piazza Tales* (1856). Although it is a story of the sea, like so much of his earlier writing, it differs from most of its predecessors in being based on a single source—the American Captain Amasa Delano's first-person account, in *A Narrative of Voyages and Travels* (Boston, 1817), of events that had taken place off the coast of South America in 1804. Melville's story, however, is narrated in the third person and the time of the events as he describes them is shifted from 1804 to 1799. The rationale for this change in time is a matter I shall return to.

Like the actual Delano, Melville's fictional Delano must *act* in a situation new to his experience, and to act he needs first of all to interpret that situation: he must *appraise* the other two principal figures, Benito Cereno, captain of the Spanish ship that Delano has boarded, and Babo, Cereno's apparently devoted body servant. One of the two is white, the other black. One is free, the other a slave—or are *both* in some way enslaved? One is presumed to be good, the other evil—or are *both* in some way corrupted? Such a triad is familiar to readers of Melville's books, from *Typee* ("Typee or Happar?" asks narrator Tommo) through *Pierre* (Lucy or Isabel? good angel or bad?) to *Billy Budd, Sailor,* where Captain Vere must evaluate the character and testimony of antagonists Billy Budd and John Claggart.

Even though "Benito Cereno," like *Billy Budd, Sailor,* is a third-person narrative, told by a narrator who is not a participant in the action, we as readers are made to see and experience what Captain Delano sees and experiences, and consequently to become as uneasy, as troubled, as he is. The very atmosphere of the story is indeterminate, beginning with the prevalent "grayness" of the opening paragraphs. Aboard the *San Dominick,* Cereno's ship, Delano is repeatedly puzzled by the poor condition of the vessel itself, by the very appearance of the characters he encounters there, and by what both Spanish sailors and black slaves say and do. Suspense slowly builds, for the reader as well as for Delano, as the narrative proceeds through a series of his hard-to-interpret encounters with Cereno, Babo, and both sailors and slaves to a striking and unexpected climax.

In a moment of physical action, the real situation aboard ship becomes clear at last to both Delano and the reader. As the American captain prepares to leave for his own vessel aboard its small boat, Cereno, whose demeanor at their parting has baffled Delano, suddenly leaps into the boat and Babo follows him, dagger in hand. Seeing the dagger, the American at first supposes that he is its intended target, but when Babo attempts to stab not Delano but the hapless Benito Cereno, "across the long-benighted mind of Captain Delano, a flash of revelation swept" (*Piazza Tales,* 99). What he has heretofore been given to see was in truth an elaborate charade: the blacks, not the whites, were actually in control of the *San Dominick* under Babo's leadership, and Benito Cereno had been forced to deceive Delano by acting as though he were still in command. Delano's men subdue Babo as Delano himself, heretofore the outsider, now becomes directly involved in the action. As he stands with his foot grinding the prostrate Babo he unconsciously assumes the exact attitude of the "dark satyr" carved on the *San Dominick*'s elaborate stern-piece (49).

What follows this denouement is a pitched battle between Delano's men and the rebellious blacks, with the Americans victorious; a voyage to Peru, where the Spanish colonial authorities conduct an elaborate investigation of the slave mutiny; and a brief conclusion telling what becomes of both Cereno and Babo. More than one critic has raised questions about Melville's handling of this part of the story, particularly his inclusion of long legal documents which tend to slow the reader's responses, coming as they do before the reported conversation between Delano and Cereno that took place while they were en route to Peru. These documents, which include a deposition by Cereno himself, tell a horrifying tale not only of mutiny but of cannibalism. Observe the narrator's carefully qualified comment: "*If* the Deposition have served as the key to fit into the lock of the complications which precede it, then, as a vault whose door has been flung back, the San Dominick's hull lies open today" (114; emphasis added).

But these revelations do not end the story or explain Delano's part in it. When you as reader come at last to consider the narrative as a whole, you will inevitably be led to ask yourself whether what has transpired has in any way *changed* Amasa Delano—just as one asks whether the lawyer's encounter with the scrivener in "Bartleby" has in any way changed *him*. Consider first Delano's conversation with the Spanish captain whose life he has saved—and who has saved his own life as well. "I know not," Cereno tells him,

> "whether desire for my own safety alone could have nerved me to that leap into your boat, had it not been for the thought that, did you, unenlightened, return to your ship, you, my best friend, with all who might be with you, stolen upon, that night, in your hammocks, would never in this world have wakened again. Do but think how you walked this deck, how you sat in this cabin, every inch of ground mined into honey-combs under you. Had I dropped the least hint, made the least advance towards an understanding between us, death, explosive death—yours as mine—would have ended the scene." (115)

When the two captains agree that all that has happened to save them both "is owing to Providence," Delano goes on to say that "the temper of my mind . . . , added to my good nature, compassion, and charity, . . . enabled me to get the better of momentary distrust, at times when acuteness might have cost me my life, without saving another's" (115). But what are we to make of this subsequent exchange?

> [Delano:] "[T]he past is passed, why moralize upon it? Forget it, See, yon bright sun has forgotten it all, and the blue sea, and the blue sky; these have turned over new leaves."
> [Cereno:] "Because they have no memory; because they are not human."
> [Delano:] "But these mild trades that now fan your cheek, do they not come with a human-like healing to you? Warm friends, steadfast friends are the trades."
> [Cereno:] "With their steadfastness they but waft me to my tomb, Señor."
> [Delano:] "You are saved; you are saved: what has cast such a shadow upon you?"

[Cereno:] "The negro." [Or, in Spanish, "the blackness."]
There was silence, while the moody man sat, slowly and uncon-
sciously gathering his mantle about him, as if it were a pall.
There was no more conversation that day. (116)

So the dialogue ends, as with Paolo and Francesca in the *Divine Comedy:*
"And that day they spoke no more."

Cereno's reply—"The negro"—to Delano's question "What has cast such
a shadow upon you?" is in keeping with the play upon color throughout
the story, with its grays, its blacks and whites, and the brighter colors of
the Spanish flag. One line of interpretation holds that "blackness" here
has religious and even metaphysical implications. Here the "shadow" over
Cereno echoes the concluding sentence of the story's third paragraph:
"Shadows present, foreshadowing deeper shadows to come" (46), and
"blackness" itself is in keeping with what Melville had written in 1850,
commenting in "Hawthorne and His Mosses" on light and shade in
Hawthorne's stories: there he had found both an "Indian-summer sunlight"
and a "blackness ten times black." "This great power of blackness" in
Hawthorne, Melville had speculated, "derives its force from its appeals
to that Calvinistic sense of Innate Depravity and Original Sin, from whose
visitations, in some shape or other, no deeply thinking mind is always
and wholly free. For, in certain moods, no man can weigh this world
without throwing in something, *somehow like* Original Sin, to strike the
uneven balance" (*Piazza Tales,* 243, emphasis added). Delano, it is said, is
obviously not a "deeply thinking mind"; therefore he is simply incapable of
appreciating the metaphysical blackness—the "sense of Innate Depravity
and Original Sin"—that so appalls Benito Cereno.

But there is an opposing line of interpretation that has been gaining more
currency in recent years among critics of Melville who take his "blacks"
and "whites" more literally, in terms simply of race. Delano, they argue,
has stumbled upon the reality of racial conflict between Spaniards and
Africans, whites and blacks, free men and slaves, but the American captain
shows little understanding of either side. The blacks he thinks of as docile
and good-natured enough, but "stupid" (75); the Spaniards are "as good
folks as any in Duxbury, Massachusetts" (79). What, then, were Melville's
own opinions about race and about slavery? Critics are divided in their
answers. Some have called him anti-black, a racist—even those who have

reached that conclusion reluctantly. At the other extreme are some who have seen him as pro-black. Citing his championing of Polynesians and native Americans—"so-called savages"—in his earlier writings, they say that here he is really on the side of the oppressed slaves, and that Babo is the real hero of the story.

As you weigh these conflicting readings, let me throw these related issues open for consideration. Specifically, whose story is "Benito Cereno"? Is it the title character's? Is it Babo's, as the pro-black interpreters would have it? Or is it Amasa Delano's, whose gropings for the truth influence our own shifting approach to the other members of Melville's triad? Who among all the characters, blacks and whites, are the good guys and the bad guys? And what is the story's primary focus? Is that focus on race and slavery, on Innate Depravity, or on some other element? How can Delano *act*—or the reader *judge*—when he cannot *know*? Is Delano more or less wise— or more or less foolish—than the average man or woman?

To be more specific, what are we to make of Melville's inclusion of the long legal documents—not simply the depositions of the whites but the fact that the blacks, by contrast, remain altogether *silent?* Are the documents really the "key" to the situation aboard the *San Dominick?* What about its grisly figurehead, which turns out to be the skeleton of Cereno's friend Don Alessandro Aranda (107)—evidently the victim of cannibalism? Or the carved stern-piece, where the depiction of one figure with its foot on the neck of another is replicated in Delano's spurning of Babo? Or above all, the recurrent phrase *"Follow your leader,"* the motto chalked below the figurehead, revealed to Delano following the denouement (99), repeated by Delano's mate to the American boarding-party (102), mentioned once more in the deposition (107), and repeated again in the conclusion, where we are told that the title character, Benito Cereno himself, "did, indeed, follow his leader" in death (117).

Given these significant patterns within the narration, let me suggest some possible inferences about Melville's story and his objectives in writing and publishing it in 1855. First, I find a touchstone for judging all three of the principal characters in the narrator's words at the outset, where he leaves it "to the wise to determine" whether Amasa Delano, "a person of a singularly undistrustful good nature," is perceptive enough to recognize "malign evil in man," which is to say, depravity (47)—not only in blacks or Spaniards, slaves or slaveholders, but in mankind generally. For whatever the color

of their skin, we are reminded in the course of the story that all men—
and women too—are capable of "malign evil": witness the Spaniards, who
traffic in slaves; the black men, who practice cannibalism on Alessandro
Aranda; and witness too Amasa Delano's white American crew when they
subsequently attack the blacks. As Mark Twain's Huck Finn rightly says,
"Human beings *can* be awful cruel to one another."

Let us recognize, moreover, that this is a story that operates on several
levels, like so much of Melville's writing. I myself think that slavery is the
immediate, or topical, issue, with implications for both Northerners and
Southerners in the United States of 1855, but I also think that it serves to
bring out what I regard as Melville's ultimate subject, *the human potential
for malevolence*—that "something, *somehow like* Original Sin," as he had
put it in "Hawthorne and His Mosses," that must, "in *some* shape or other,"
visit *every* "deeply thinking mind." This is that "power of blackness" that
eludes "bachelors" like Amasa Delano even as it obsesses Benito Cereno—
and, as Melville feared, that somehow failed to touch most of his fellow
Americans, Yankees or Southerners, whether in 1799 or in 1855.

Why, then, did he move the action back to 1799? Because, I would
suggest, there are still other implications in his story that I would term
historical. Here as elsewhere the respective ships are microcosms, and as such
they are representatives of still larger worlds. Delano's ship, the *Perseverance*
in the narrative Melville drew upon, has been rechristened the *Bachelor's
Delight* in "Benito Cereno." In Melville's other writings, including *Moby-
Dick,* "Bartleby," and "The Paradise of Bachelors," unmarried men such
as the lawyer in "Bartleby" and the fictional Delano in "Benito Cereno"
repeatedly display—along with "sophomores"—a characteristic lack of
maturity and understanding. The *San Dominick,* as Cereno's vessel is called
here, was actually the *Tryal* in Melville's source; the new name is a reminder
to Melville's contemporaries of an infamous uprising in the island of Santo
Domingo that had taken place in—yes, 1799. One of the ships, Amasa
Delano's, is an example of Yankee enterprise; the other, Cereno's, coming
as it did from the Old World to the New, is associated with such European
institutions as the imperialistic Spanish government, the military, and the
church; significantly, the Spanish ship is shown here as fallen into decay. In
its voyage to South America the *San Dominick* brought with it slaves and
slavery. Its original figurehead, as we learn from the deposition, had been
"the image of Christopher Colon, the discoverer of the New World" (107);

after the blacks seized the ship they substituted the skeleton of Aranda, a dealer in slaves.

When Amasa Delano finds himself in the very posture of the masked figure on the stern-piece, with *his* foot on the prostrate Babo, he too has become enmeshed in the struggle of blacks versus whites—on the side of white repression, we must note. The devices of the figurehead, the carved stern-piece, and even the flag of Spain, insultingly converted by Babo into a barber's apron, are obviously allegorical touches reminiscent of Gothic devices in Hawthorne and Poe; I take them to be Melvillean signs to more percipient Yankee readers to be wiser than Delano, lest America in the troubled decade before the Civil War follow *its* leaders, as Benito Cereno followed slaveholder Aranda, into some untimely fate. Here again, however, he is characteristically setting forth for readers of *Putnam's*, a magazine with an antislavery orientation, a problem—or rather, a series of interrelated problems—rather than offering any ready-made solutions. And for "deeply thinking minds" of the twentieth century, the larger issues remain: not only of race and racism but also of humanity's innate capacity for evil and its equally deplorable incapacity for perceptive understanding. They are as pressing today as they were for Herman Melville in 1855.

5.

Innocence and Infamy

Melville's *Billy Budd, Sailor*

A s Melville's *Moby-Dick* (1851), *The Confidence-Man* (1857), and *Clarel* (1876) recapitulate in large measure the writings that immediately preceded them, so *Billy Budd, Sailor* not only sums up the thought and art of Melville's last years but also looks back in setting, characterization, and theme over his writing as a whole.[1] Left in manuscript at his death in 1891 and unpublished until 1924, *Billy Budd* has since appeared in many editions and printings, including more than twenty translations. It has generated an extensive body of strikingly divergent commentary whose opposite poles are readings in terms of either personal tragedy or ironic social commentary.

The manuscript of *Billy Budd,* which Melville's widow, Elizabeth Melville, described as "unfinished,"[2] comprises 351 leaves in her husband's crabbed hand, written partly in ink and partly in pencil, with some passages heavily revised; no printer could have worked directly from such disordered copy. The Genetic Text published by the University of Chicago Press in 1962 is now considered the standard transcription; other versions, especially those published in earlier years, differ significantly in their readings. Analysis of the manuscript has disclosed that Melville's story evolved in three major phases of composition, together with other, less clearly defined stages and substages. In general terms, the first phase involved concentration on Billy himself as protagonist, the second phase either introduced John Claggart or at least brought him to the fore as Billy's antagonist, and the third phase developed Edward Fairfax Vere as the sea commander under whom Billy is tried, convicted, and executed. This order of development, it might be noted, anticipates that of later critical discussion of the story, which also con-centrated first on Billy, then on Claggart, and ultimately on Captain Vere.

Synopsis

Melville's title character is a handsome sailor "aged twenty-one, a foretop-man of the British fleet toward the close of the last decade of the eighteenth century" (44), when Great Britain was at war with postrevolutionary France. We see him first aboard a homeward-bound English merchant ship, the *Rights-of-Man,* which is stopped by a British naval vessel seeking additional crewmen through forcible impressment. The warship bears another allegor-ical name: H.M.S. *Bellipotent,* or "war-power." The boarding officer selects Billy Budd, who is immediately transferred from the *Rights-of-Man* to the *Bellipotent* and inducted into the King's service. Already an accomplished seaman, Billy attracts favorable notice from both officers and sailors, with a single exception: John Claggart, master-at-arms, who serves aboard the ship as a nautical chief of police. Claggart's inherently evil nature is both drawn to and repelled by Billy's "good looks, cheery health, and frank enjoyment of young life" (78). The two men stand in sharp contrast as types of innocence and worldly experience. Billy, in the "simplicity" of his youthful goodness, has never willed malice nor been inflamed by the jealousy that possesses the master-at-arms as he looks enviously upon the Handsome Sailor.

After failing in an attempt to entrap Billy through an intermediary, who is sent to offer Billy money if he will turn mutineer, Claggart goes to the *Bellipotent*'s captain, falsely charges Billy with fomenting mutiny, and repeats the accusation to Billy himself during a confrontation in Captain Vere's cabin. Amazed and horrified by the groundless charge, Billy is unable to speak and defend himself as the captain urges him to do; a vocal impediment that afflicts him in time of stress produces only "a convulsed tongue-tie" (98), and he lashes out with his fist, striking his accuser dead with a blow to Claggart's forehead. Vere, disbelieving Claggart's charge against Billy, is nevertheless aware that the young sailor, while innocent of mutiny, has in fact struck and killed a superior officer. In the captain's own words, Billy's deed is "the divine judgment on Ananias" delivered by "an angel of God"—yet that angel "must hang" (100–101). Death by hanging is the sentence subsequently imposed upon Billy by the drumhead court that Vere quickly convenes, and the Handsome Sailor is hanged at dawn from a yard-arm of the mainmast before the entire ship's company. "At the penultimate moment, his words, his only ones, words wholly unobstructed in the utterance, were these: 'God bless Captain Vere!'" (123).

Although the *Bellipotent*'s crew involuntarily echo Billy's blessing, their first response soon gives way to a threatening murmur that is promptly quelled by a strategic command from the quarter-deck. A similar murmur that arises following Billy's burial is also quieted by a drumroll to quarters, "and toned by music and religious rites subserving the discipline and purposes of war, the men in their wonted orderly manner dispersed to the places allotted them when not at the guns." "With mankind," Vere would say, "forms, measured forms, are everything" (128). Both Billy and Claggart are dead, and Vere's death is soon to follow. In an encounter between the *Bellipotent* and a French warship, the *Athée* (or *Atheist*—a third allegorical name), the captain receives a fatal wound and dies ashore at Gibraltar, "cut off too early" for a part in Horatio Nelson's memorable victories over the French at the Nile and Trafalgar. Not long before his death he is heard to murmur "words inexplicable to his attendant: 'Billy Budd, Billy Budd'" (129).

Among contrasting references to Billy and his fate that conclude the story, one, a journalistic account purportedly appearing in "a naval chronicle of the time" (130), exactly reverses the truth, calling Billy the ringleader of a mutiny who, when arraigned before his captain by the master-at-arms, stabs his accuser to the heart and subsequently pays the penalty of death for his crimes. The other, a sailor's ballad entitled "Billy in the Darbies," expresses in rough but eloquent verse "the general estimate" among Billy's own shipmates of "his nature and its unconscious simplicity" (131). These contradictory verdicts on the Handsome Sailor are summed up in a brief comment that Melville himself wrote in and then deleted from his manuscript. Such a story, he observed, is "not unwarranted by what sometimes happens" in the actual world—a world which, like the writer in the "naval chronicle," cannot distinguish between "Innocence and infamy, spiritual depravity and fair repute."[3]

Even in the world where literary critics live and move and have their being, there have also been and continue to be fundamental differences of opinion about the characters and characterizations of the two antagonists and also of Captain Vere, whose problematic role in the story has come to be the primary focus of much recent criticism. Each of the three figures has been singled out as a hero by at least one commentator—Vern Wagner, for example, finds even Claggart "spiritually heroic"[4]—and as a villain by others. Where did Billy and Claggart err in their appraisals of one another? Was there in fact some supporting evidence or testimony unfavorable to Billy that Claggart could have cited when he accused him of fomenting mutiny? Was Billy in any sense justified when he replied to Claggart's accusation with a blow, whatever his actual intention? Given the situation in the British fleet at the time of the Great Mutiny of 1797, with an engagement with the French always imminent, did Vere act responsibly or precipitously in immediately trying Billy aboard the *Bellipotent?* Was the trial conducted fairly, and were the verdict and the sentence properly arrived at—in terms not only of military necessity but also of law, of justice, and of morality? And where did Melville himself stand with respect to these questions and to their larger ethical and philosophical implications?

Since Melville's twentieth-century critics disagree so strongly over such issues, one may ask further about the basis for their disagreements. Are the characters and events of the story ambiguous in themselves? Is Melville's narrative willfully equivocal? Are modern readers perhaps over-subtle, projecting their own contrasting values onto a relatively straightforward nineteenth-century fiction? Or do *all* of these elements contribute in some degree to the difficulty? These are among the problems one faces in studying Melville's *Billy Budd, Sailor* and in surveying the extensive body of criticism that has grown up about it. In addressing these issues one needs first of all to understand when and how Melville came to write the story and what subsequent scholarly analysis of the manuscript has revealed about its growth and development.

Genesis and Growth

"Billy in the Darbies" and *Billy Budd, Sailor*

The retrospective and even elegiac tone that marks Melville's last prose narrative also characterizes his third published volume of poetry, *John Marr and Other Sailors,* completed after his retirement from the customs service at the end of 1885 and privately printed in 1888. As we now know, Melville began *Billy Budd, Sailor* in the course of his work on the *John Marr* volume, for which the ballad entitled "Billy in the Darbies" that now concludes *Billy Budd* was originally intended, and indeed the entire story has much in common with the sailor verse.

In describing the speaker of "John Marr," the title poem in that volume, Melville wrote an introductory prose sketch, similar to those he had composed in the 1870s and after for his "Burgundy Club" poems, "At the Hostelry" and "Naples in the Time of Bomba." Like Melville himself, John Marr is a former sailor; like Jack Centian, dean of the Burgundy Club, he also bears some resemblance to Thomas Melvill, Jr., Melville's paternal uncle: both spend their last years on a remote frontier prairie, lacking that "common inheritance" that would serve as a basis for mutual communication with their neighbors. "Whether as to persons or events, one cannot always be talking about the present, much less speculating about the future," Melville's headnote observes; "one must needs recur to the past, which . . . supplies to most practical natures the basis of sympathetic communion." But "the past of John Marr was not the past of these pioneers," and when he "naturally" speaks to them of "some marine story or picture" he finds "no encouragement to proceed." As one of them finally tells him, "Friend, we know nothing of that here" (*Poems,* 160- 61).

So Marr, like Herman Melville himself in his so-called silent years, breaks off his attempts to communicate with his contemporaries and turns instead to his own private memories, recalling his shipmates of former days as though they were "phantoms of the dead":

> As the growing sense of his environment threw him more and more upon retrospective musings, these phantoms . . . became spiritual companions, losing something of their first indistinctness and putting on at last a dim semblance of mute life; and they were lit by that aureola circling over any object of the affections in the past for reunion with which an imaginative heart passionately yearns. (*Poems,* 164)

The shipmates John Marr remembers in the verse which follows—first "merchant-sailors," then "huntsman-whalers," and finally "man-of-war's men"—appear in the chronological order of Melville's own experiences at sea: first aboard a Liverpool packet in 1839, then during his whaling years that began in 1841, and finally on the American warship that brought him home from the Pacific in 1844. Other poems in the volume make more explicit references to associates of Melville's own past. Two of them go back to the long-remembered visit of 1842 by Melville and Toby Greene (here called "the Typee-truants") to the Marquesas Islands, seen now in retrospect as "Authentic Edens in a Pagan sea" (*Poems,* 20). "To the Master of the 'Meteor'" honors Melville's seagoing brother Thomas, who had died in 1884. Another, "Jack Roy," is clearly a tribute to the admired Jack Chase, "that great heart" to whom *Billy Budd, Sailor* is dedicated. The speaker in the dramatic monologue "Bridegroom Dick" recalls still other seamen Melville himself had known, including his cousin Guert Gansevoort, a naval officer who appears in the poem both as a hero of the Mexican War and as a key figure who keeps his own counsel concerning the *Somers* mutiny affair of 1842, a controversial event which is also "cited," though "without comment," in *Billy Budd* (114).

Bridegroom Dick goes out of his way to voice the same dislike of ironclad warships expressed earlier in Melville's poetry of the Civil War, notably "A Utilitarian View of the Monitor's Fight," and again in the fourth chapter of *Billy Budd,* which deals with the "change in sea warfare" brought about by such "inventions of our time" (56). As steam power took over from the sailing ships Melville had known and loved in his youth, and as ironclads like the *Monitor* and the *Merrimac* rendered the old oaken warships both vulnerable and obsolete, he came to think of vessels out of the past, such as Nelson's *Victory* and the ships depicted by the artists Turner and Haden, as symbolizing cherished qualities and values that to the modern world seemed superannuated—like a once well-known author fallen out of communication with his contemporaries. As Edward Stessel has aptly said, "the wooden ships" in Melville's writing "were of his time of promise and their obsolescence was his own."[5]

Another poem of the *John Marr* volume, the short sea-ballad "Tom Deadlight," is set aboard one of these old ships: a British man-of-war "homeward-bound from the Mediterranean" in the year 1810 (*Poems,* 182). As with "John Marr" and those still earlier poems that Melville had attributed to the Marquis de Grandvin and Jack Gentian in his Burgundy Club manuscripts, a prose headnote introduces the speaker: in this instance a seaman facing death who is saying farewell to his messmates, like the speaker of "Billy in the Darbies." That ballad in its original form was a companion-piece to "Tom Deadlight." Its setting too was aboard a British warship "in the time before steamships" (*Billy Budd, Sailor,* 43)—

presumably in 1797, the year of the "Great Mutiny" referred to in *Billy Budd;* Melville, as we now know, first thought of his speaker in the ballad not as young Billy but as an older man apparently guilty of fomenting mutiny, the crime for which he has been condemned to hang.

As with both "John Marr" and "Tom Deadlight," Melville drafted a prose headnote to the ballad "Billy in the Darbies"—and as with the earlier Burgundy Club pieces, the headnote grew in length until it far overshadowed the short verse it was intended to introduce. Removing the ballad from his projected volume, Melville then developed the burgeoning headnote into what became *Billy Budd, Sailor,* his final venture in prose fiction, with the ballad headed "Billy in the Darbies" standing as its conclusion. The narrator of *Billy Budd,* it may be observed, sounds very much like the authors of these several earlier headnotes—which is to say, like Melville himself. Twice he recalls specific incidents of Melville's own visits to England: at Liverpool in 1839 (43: "now more than half a century ago") and at Greenwich in 1849 (66: "now more than forty years ago"); he also alludes habitually to figures of history and literature that had long engaged Melville. But his guarded allusion to the *Somers* mutiny of 1842, like his reference in the *John Marr* volume, contrasts strikingly with the impassioned discussion of the case in Melville's earlier *White-Jacket* (1850). Although Charles Anderson, Newton Arvin, and various later critics have taken *Billy Budd* as his further comment on the *Somers* affair, it is clear from what is now known about the genesis and growth of the story that Melville did not begin writing it with the *Somers* case specifically in mind, though in the last phase of its composition that case "was certainly a cogent analogue."[6]

Billy and Claggart

As Melville's narrative of the condemned sailor developed apart from the *John Marr* volume, he altered his original conception of his title character as an older man, laying particular stress on a younger Billy's lack of worldly experience and delineating his appearance and character accordingly. In the story he is presented as "much of a child-man" (86); the old Dansker's nickname for his young friend is "Baby" (70). To the reader who knows Melville's earlier works Billy recalls unsophisticated youths such as Redburn and Pierre, or the young soldiers of *Battle-Pieces* (1866) whom Melville had seen as fated for tragic enlightenment. "All wars are boyish, and are fought by boys," Melville wrote in "The March into Virginia," and many youthful warriors, beginning as "Moloch's uninitiate," must ultimately "die, experienced" and "perish, enlightened" (*Poems*, 10–11). Here Captain Vere terms Billy a "fated boy" (99); in another of the war poems, "On the Slain Collegians," Melville had written of "striplings" and their "fated parts," and—in lines that seem to anticipate the very name of Billy *Budd*—compared them with

> plants that flower ere comes the leaf—
> Which storms lay low in kindly doom,
> And kill them in their flush of bloom.
> (*Poems*, 105)

In the expanded story young Billy appears as a fine physical specimen—a "Handsome Sailor"—but an inexperienced moral innocent, one who on either count might well have "posed for a statue of young Adam before the Fall" (94). He is repeatedly likened both to other "young" figures of antiquity—Alexander, Achilles, David, Joseph, and Isaac—and to the sailor companions of Melville's own youth. The reminiscing John Marr regards all sailors as "Barbarians of man's simpler nature" (*Poems*, 166); Billy too has a "simple nature" (52), and the narrator twice calls him a "barbarian" (52, 120), implicitly associating him not only with sailors but also with those uncivilized and un-Christianized Polynesians described in *Typee* and *Omoo*, victims of what passes for Christian civilization. Melville, it has been aptly said, "had thought of unspoiled barbarians at every stage of his writing since *Typee*,"[7] and in *Billy Budd* he specifically compares Billy's attitude toward the Chaplain's religion to that of a "superior savage, so called—a Tahitian, say, of Captain Cook's time or shortly after that time" (121). In both his appearance and his character, Billy with his "simple nature" is thus reminiscent of all youthful, unenlightened, and even "savage" characters in Melville's writings from *Typee* onward.

When Melville turned from Billy to Claggart, the second of his major characters to emerge as the story developed, he in a sense moved from the world of *Typee* and *Omoo* to that of *Redburn* and *White-Jacket*, for Claggart is a further development of such figures in the latter books as Jackson and

Bland. Thematically, he is the antithesis of Billy, for he is a man "dominated by intellectuality" who finds civilization "auspicious" (75); the two of them are paired as Jackson is paired with young Redburn, or Radney in *Moby-Dick* with Steelkilt, and to think of the one figure apparently led Melville to conceive of its opposite as well.

Claggart and his "mystery of iniquity" (108) presented more difficulty in characterization than did the simpler Billy. "His portrait I essay," the narrator remarks of Claggart, "but shall never hit it" (64), and as the manuscript reveals, Melville was still in the process of retouching that portrait when he put work aside during his last illness. In seeking to get at Claggart's hidden nature he made explicit reference to both the Bible and Plato, and in writing of the man's mixture of envy and antipathy with respect to Billy he drew as well on such literary analogues as Shakespeare's Iago and Milton's Satan. Within the compass of Melville's own works, Claggart climaxes that long line of monomaniacs—men obsessed with one passionately held idea—that runs from Ahab in *Moby-Dick* through the subordinate characters in *Clarel,* to all of whom Melville had extended his sympathetic understanding, if not his approval.

Captain Vere

As in *Moby-Dick* he had ascribed "high qualities" and "tragic graces" to "meanest mariners, and renegades and castaways" (117), so in *Billy Budd,* with Billy and Claggart, Melville initially created a drama played "down among the groundlings," its stage "a scrubbed gun deck" (78–79). Insofar as *Billy Budd* is the story of these two antagonists, it has the democratic implications of Melville's earliest books, but with the emergence of Captain the Honorable Edward Fairfax Vere, the last to develop of the story's three principal characters, the dramatic focus of its central chapters shifts from the gun deck to the captain's cabin.

Unlike Billy and Claggart, deriving as they do from antecedents in Melville's early books, Vere is the creation of an older writer—and a more conservative thinker, in the view of critics such as Milton R. Stern, Thomas J. Scorza, and Michael Paul Rogin; his affiliations are chiefly with the work of Melville's later years. The sea-captains of the earlier fiction, Ahab included, are typically autocrats; the occasional exceptions, like Amasa

Delano and Benito Cereno, are special cases. During the Civil War, when Melville visited the battle-front and came to know senior military men, he seems to have formed a higher opinion of the officer class; his sketches of the 1870s concerning Major Jack Gentian and his depiction of Captain Turret in "Bridegroom Dick"—much less the martinet than Vere—are indications that he had indeed done so. But Captain Vere, it must be remembered, was created to fulfill the demands of Melville's plot, which required a senior officer to preside over young Billy's condemnation and to carry out the sentence of death by hanging. Melville must therefore have asked himself the obvious question: what kind of man could and would do what Vere must do?

In his efforts to answer this question Melville was led into even more troublesome psychological probing than his analysis of Claggart entailed. Late revisions in those manuscript passages that deal with Vere's state of mind at the time of Billy's fatal blow testify that he was still retouching Vere's portrait as well as Claggart's when his last illness prevented further work on the story. As the manuscript stands, Vere appears, for good or for ill, as a supremely dedicated servant of king and country, first and foremost an officer enrolled in "the host of the God of War—Mars" (122). Along with Melville's Jack Gentian, another patrician figure with a background of military service, Vere might well be called "an old-fashioned Roman," not only for his patriotism and devotion to duty but also for his regard for established principles and values that have come down to him from the past. As Vere is "allied to the higher nobility," so Melville, like Ishmael, is descended from "an old established family in the land" (*Moby-Dick*, 6); Michael Rogin's *Subversive Genealogy* interprets Vere's role as a reaffirmation of Melville's own familial values.[8] Emphasis on the contrast between Vere's private feelings for Billy and the rigorous demands of his profession has reminded other critics—notably Brook Thomas— of the situation repeatedly faced by Melville's father-in-law, the eminent Massachusetts jurist Lemuel Shaw, who in more than one critical case ruled contrary to his own sympathies in order to uphold the letter of the law as he understood it.[9]

As a defender of the old order against modern innovation, Vere again has much in common with Melville, as can be seen in the writings of Melville's later years: he was a man disenchanted with the prevailing faith in humanity's so-called progress—"Adam's alleged advance," as he had called it in the Burgundy Club sketches (*Great Short Works*, 406)—who believed instead that human nature is essentially the same from age to age, regardless of superficial changes such as modern inventions and other supposed improvements. Both Vere and the reclusive Melville of the last decades of his life take more satisfaction in reading than in "social converse"; Vere loves "history, biography, and unconventional writers like Montaigne" (416) as did Melville himself, and he too is "as apt to cite some historic character or incident of antiquity" (originally "cite some allusion to Plutarch, say, or Livy") "as he would be to cite from the moderns" (63).[10]

Another possible analogy between Vere and Melville turns on the captain's relation to Billy Budd. Given his favorable impression of the young sailor, he clearly disbelieves Claggart's charge that Billy has been fomenting mutiny, but he nevertheless arranges a confrontation between them. In a "fatherly" tone he encourages the vocally hesitant Billy to reply to Claggart (99), thus helping to precipitate the fatal blow by which Billy strikes Claggart dead. From then on, however, "the father" in Vere is "replaced by the military disciplinarian" (100), but after the trial it is Vere himself, "old enough to have been Billy's father" (115), who tells the young sailor of the verdict.

The narrator's repeated references to Vere as a kind of "father" to Billy, figurative or otherwise, have prompted biographically oriented critics such as Robert Penn Warren and Edwin Haviland Miller to recall that in February of 1886, when Melville was presumably at work on the poem and headnote that evolved into *Billy Budd*, his son Stanwix died in San Francisco at the age of thirty-five. Stanwix Melville, we would say today, had never found himself, and his death may also have brought back to mind the earlier loss of Melville's first child, Malcolm, who in 1867 had ended his life at age eighteen with a pistol shot. Accidental or otherwise—the circumstances are cloudy—the death of Malcolm had been traumatic for the Melvilles, who were already experiencing other domestic difficulties, and was at least partly responsible for their virtual withdrawal from New York society during the later years of their marriage.

As the head of his family Herman Melville was a strict disciplinarian, given to a moodiness and irascibility that some of his relatives by marriage came to interpret as outright insanity. When he began to develop the story that became *Billy Budd*, Peter L. Hays and Richard Dilworth Rust conjecture, he identified Billy with his lost sons and the bookish, moody, and sometimes irascible Vere with their strict father.[11] Vere's actions, it will be remembered, appear irrational to the "prudent surgeon" in the story, whose supposition that the captain may actually be "unhinged" leads the narrator to speculate on the difficulty of drawing a line between sanity and insanity (100, 102). This controversial father-and-son hypothesis has fascinating implications for interpreting the characters of both Billy and Vere—specifically for evaluating both the narrator's remarks about their private farewell (which he does not render dramatically) and the tone of Billy's final words, "God bless Captain Vere!"

Although this provocative theory remains one that can neither be proven nor yet disproven, it would seem to be in consonance with the retrospective character of so much of Melville's writing, especially that of the latter half of his life. With particular reference to the *John Marr* volume and the "inside narrative" that Melville then went on to write (41), one might add the further adjective *elegiac;* the ultimate subject of *Billy Budd,* it may well be, is death. But how to read that final story, as its narrator pointedly declares, "every one must determine for himself" (102), and it is tempting to say that as many interpretations have been advanced as there have been readers and critics. In opposition to anyone expressing sympathy for Vere and his conservative values—especially if he or she sees either Vere or the narrator as a projection of the older Melville—stand those who take the book as reaffirming the iconoclastic ideas they attribute to the younger author who wrote *Typee, Omoo,* and *White-Jacket.*

Other Sources and Analogues

In addition to broad resemblances in setting, theme, and characterization between *Billy Budd, Sailor* and Melville's earlier writings, specific verbal parallels suggest that Melville may have been rereading his earlier works at the time he was composing both *John Marr* and *Billy Budd;* his *White-Jacket, Israel Potter,* and "Benito Cereno" come readily to mind. He may also have read, or reread, material on the *Somers* case, which was under renewed discussion in American magazines in 1887 and 1888, but there is no evidence to establish whether or how such recent analyses may have influenced his late writings.[12] For the immediate historical background of *Billy Budd, Sailor* he is known to have consulted at least two sources:

The Naval History of Great Britain, by the British historian William James, quoted briefly in chapter 3 of the novel (55), and Robert Southey's *Life of Nelson,* which Elizabeth Melville described as "kept for reference" for the story.[13] B. R. McElderry, Jr., and Richard and Rita Gollin have noted parallels in Douglas Jerrold's *Black-Ey'd Susan* and *The Mutiny at the Nore* and Captain Marryat's *The King's Own;*[14] John Bryant adds *Working a Passage* by Charles F. Briggs.[15] Hayford and Sealts cite James Fenimore Cooper's *The Two Admirals* and *Wing-and-Wing* and point to possible "unsuspected analogues" in American naval history, Melville's own experience in the American navy, and various pieces of minor sea literature.[16]

With regard to Vere's conduct of Billy's trial and execution, Hayford and Sealts concluded—perhaps somewhat hastily—that Melville "simply had not familiarized himself with statutes of the period concerning administration of British naval justice,"[17] for in terms of historical fact neither a drumhead court nor a hanging could legally have taken place aboard a British warship on detached service in 1797. No naval officer of Vere's rank and assignment was authorized to try a seaman for a capital offense. Moreover, both the size and the composition of the drumhead court that Vere appoints are contrary to statute, and the British Mutiny Act, which the captain cites as justification for his actions, actually applied only to land forces of the period rather than to the navy. Finally, even were the court's proceedings in order, its resulting sentence of death should not have been carried out before the findings in Billy's case were submitted to higher authority for review.[18] Was Vere then deliberately violating established procedures, as anti-Vere critics have charged? Or did he act out of sheer ignorance of the law? Or was it Melville himself who either did not know or for some reason chose to disregard what he had learned—or should have learned—from naval and legal history?

"Melville's expertise in naval law and history" must indeed be assumed, according to Richard H. Weisberg, a man trained both in literature and in jurisprudence, who adds that in view of "the extreme accuracy of so much of the legal detail in the story" the burden of proof must therefore be on anyone who thinks differently. Weisberg contends "that Captain Vere's articulation and application of the law in many respects were erroneous, and that Melville intended his reader both to realize this fact and to consider its broader implications."[19] Stanton Garner, who has taught naval science as well as literature, takes this line of reasoning even further. Melville, he holds, "did not simply make some mistakes in handling the facts of history." Instead, through the mouth of a designedly unreliable narrator, "he deliberately introduced errors" in order to undercut his narrator's statements.[20]

These two commentators are positing a norm, grounded on the specifics of naval law and history, against which Melville's supposed narrative strategy as an historical novelist and also Captain Vere's actions as a naval commander can both be evaluated. But in view of the actual development of the *Billy Budd* manuscript, the informed critic must keep in mind that from its very beginnings, in the original ballad, the central figure of Melville's story was a condemned man; neither his subsequently conceived antagonist nor the captain as agent of his condemnation was initially present, and indeed Vere did not emerge as a distinct character until a relatively late phase of composition. Whatever Melville may have ultimately come to think of the *Bellipotent*'s captain, he obviously did not begin his narrative with the intention of either attacking or defending Vere's decisions.

Who then was responsible, Vere or Melville, for the captain's departures from legal orthodoxy? Within the narrative itself, taken altogether on its own terms, the testimony of Vere's fellow officers is especially pertinent. Although these experienced professionals voice reservations about the captain's handling of Billy's case, their comments are all based on pragmatic rather than legal considerations, as though they were wholly unaware of any provisions to the contrary in British naval law. As their several remarks about Vere are plainly meant to suggest, they feel that he moved hastily and secretly to try Billy aboard the *Bellipotent* when he might better have referred the whole affair to the admiral, but not one of them charges him with acting illegally rather than imprudently in assuming responsibility in so crucial a matter.

By introducing the other officers' testimony, Melville is inviting his reader to examine Vere's actions in the context of the story as he himself conceived it, not with strict reference to naval law and history. He allows Vere himself to say that he has both the option and the obligation to act, and that his appointment of a summary court "would not be at variance with usage" (104). To account to the reader for Billy's trial, conviction, and execution it was imperative for Melville to allow Vere that option but to require him to choose as he did. To argue that a British captain of 1797 should have declined, on statutory grounds, to try Billy is really to say that

Melville should have written an altogether different story. What readers and critics must deal with, therefore, is the story as he actually composed it: as fiction with an historical setting—as in the earlier *Israel Potter*, for example, another eighteenth-century narrative that takes place partly on shipboard—but not with the historian's fidelity to fact.

The internal logic of *Billy Budd, Sailor*, both as Melville first conceived its basic situation and as he later developed its action, not only turned on Billy's condemnation but also required an immediate trial for a capital offense, an unqualified verdict of guilty as charged, and a prompt carrying out of the sentence. The closest analogue yet suggested for a story with these requirements involves a visit that Melville himself had made during the Civil War to the Union front, a visit that provided the basis for one of the poems in *Battle-Pieces*. While in a Virginia camp, as Stanton Garner reports, Melville or perhaps his brother Allan, a New York lawyer, "may well have been told" of a recent incident involving a Union picket who had deserted his post, joined a Confederate battalion, and then been captured by his former comrades. His brigade commander promptly convened a drumhead court, which found the soldier guilty of desertion and sentenced him to be shot on the following day. The entire brigade was drawn up to witness his execution, which was said to have made a strong impression on the troops. "It is difficult to doubt that Herman heard this story," Garner writes, noting that "the entire drumhead court and execution sequence is too close to the action of *Billy Budd, Sailor* to ignore. If he heard it, he was profoundly affected by it."[21]

How *Billy Budd, Sailor* should be read and interpreted in relation to these various analogues and possible sources in its author's experience, his reading, and his previous writing remains an open question among present-day critics, who disagree over such fundamental issues as the tone of the story and Melville's possible intentions in composing it. Apart from the manuscript itself there is no reference to *Billy Budd* among his surviving papers or in any of the biographical sketches published after his death in 1891 by Arthur Stedman, his literary executor. When Stedman, with the encouragement and support of Elizabeth Melville, prepared four volumes of his fiction for new editions in 1892 he did not include *Billy Budd*, though bringing out a previously unknown story might well have furthered their objective of keeping Melville's name and fame alive; the obviously unfinished state of the manuscript may have dismayed one or both of them. After Elizabeth Melville's death in 1906 the Melville papers passed in turn to her daughters, Elizabeth and Frances, and then to the eldest granddaughter, the late Eleanor Melville Metcalf. The manuscript of *Billy Budd* is now in the Melville Collection of the Houghton Library, Harvard University, a gift from Eleanor Metcalf.

Editions

The first mention of *Billy Budd* in print came in Raymond Weaver's pioneering biography of 1921, *Herman Melville: Mariner and Mystic;* the first published text of the story appeared in 1924 in *"Billy Budd" and Other Prose Pieces,* edited by Weaver as volume 13 of the Standard Edition of Melville's *Complete Works.* Weaver's freely edited transcription was republished in 1928, with numerous modifications, in his *Shorter Novels of Herman Melville.* Neither text is free of error, and each silently introduces grammatical and stylistic emendations. Weaver's intention as editor was to provide a text for general readers rather than for scholars; "the state of the manuscript," he declared in his Introduction of 1928, prevented his offering a version that would be "adequate to every ideal."[22] F. Barron Freeman's scholarly edition of 1948, *Melville's "Billy Budd,"* sought to provide in a single text both a literal transcription of the manuscript (including variants) and a reading version, but his valuable contributions to an understanding of the story were offset by his inadequate analysis and transcription, resulting in a mistaken account of the manuscript's genesis and growth.[23]

The Chicago edition of 1962 is based on a new and independent transcription and analysis of the *Billy Budd* manuscript. Recognizing the impossibility of providing a single text equally suitable for scholars and general readers, its editors prepared both a Genetic Text—a literal transcription of the component manuscript leaves as Melville left them— and a Reading Text; the latter, based on the Genetic Text, embodies the wording of the story

> that in the editors' judgment most closely approximates Melville's final intention had a new fair copy of *Billy Budd, Sailor,* been made without his engaging in further expansion or revision. His inconsistent spelling, capitalization, hyphenation, paragraphing, and punctuation . . . have here been standardized—within the limits imposed by his own char-acteristic syntax—in accordance with present-day usage.[24]

The Editors' Introduction surveys the growth of the manuscript, the history of the text, and perspectives for criticism. Editorial Notes & Commentary, a Bibliography, and Textual Notes accompany the Reading Text; a detailed analysis of the manuscript introduces the Genetic Text. The University of Chicago Press has issued convenient paperback editions of both the Reading Text (1962) and the Genetic Text (1978), each including relevant apparatus along with the Editors' Introduction in full. Although no scholar has challenged the accuracy of the transcription constituting the Chicago Genetic Text or taken issue with either the editors' analysis of Melville's manuscript or their account of its genesis and growth, some reviewers and commentators—notably Milton R. Stern, Stanton Garner, Thomas J. Scorza, and Brook Thomas—have disagreed with the editorial principles followed in establishing the Chicago Reading Text; in 1975 Stern published a somewhat different version based on the genetic transcription in the Chicago edition, and it is his text that Scorza and Thomas have elected to cite.[25] The Chicago Reading Text has been widely reprinted in college anthologies, however. It is also used in the third volume of Melville's prose works issued by the Library of America (1984), where a textual note by the volume editor, Harrison Hayford, observes that the *Billy Budd* manuscript had not yet been prepared for publication by the editors of the Northwestern-Newberry edition of *The Writings of Herman Melville*.

With respect to plans for treatment of *Billy Budd* in the new edition, Hayford explained that divergences between the principles followed in the Chicago Reading Text and those established in the completed volumes of the Northwestern-Newberry edition are "minor as to treatment of wording; thus differences in the wording of the eventual Northwestern-Newberry edition are likely to result merely from normal and necessary judgmental differences in the application of principles to individual problems. There will be greater divergences in the treatment of the spelling and punctuation."[26]

Reception and Interpretation

Beginning with Raymond Weaver in 1921, the first critics to deal with *Billy Budd, Sailor* treated the story as an allegorical conflict between good and evil, resolved only in tragic terms; some writers associated Billy with Christ and Claggart with Satan. J. Middleton Murry and E. L.

Grant Watson, who read the narrative as Melville's spiritual autobiography, went on to call it his "last will and spiritual testament" and, in Watson's celebrated phrase, his "testament of acceptance."[27] With the writings of Lewis Mumford, Yvor Winters, and Charles Weir, Jr., critical attention began to shift from Billy and Claggart to Captain Vere, and by 1946 Raymond Short had identified Vere as "the true hero of the novel."[28] Meanwhile, George Arms also raised the possibility that *Billy Budd* might be "more concerned with social repercussions" than previous discussion had implied,[29] and other critics began exploring it as social and political commentary rather than religious allegory or spiritual autobiography; some followed the lead of Anderson and Arvin in taking the story as Melville's oblique comment on the *Somers* mutiny. During the late 1940s, moreover, Herbert Schneider, Richard Chase, and Charles Olson were challenging the older view that the story and its title character are genuinely "tragic."

Vigorous reassessment of *Billy Budd* marked the decade following publication of Freeman's edition in 1948. By 1950 Joseph Schiffman, acting on a suggestion by Gay Wilson Allen, declared that the story is neither a tragedy nor a "testament of acceptance" but "a tale of irony."[30] "Ironist" readings of literary works were much in fashion during the 1950s, and to other critics of the ironist persuasion (Harry M. Campbell, Arthur Sale, Karl E. Zink, Lawrance Thompson, Vern Wagner, and their successors) young Billy is a passive victim of injustice whose final words—"God bless Captain Vere!"—must be read ironically, and Vere himself, with his devotion to "forms, measured forms," is a reactionary authoritarian, as Leonard Casper argued in "The Case against Captain Vere."[31] A literal reversal of values evidently took place in discussion of Billy Budd: in 1959, a quarter-century after Watson had called the story a "testament of acceptance," Phil Withim rechristened it Melville's "testament of resistance."[32]

In 1962, when the Chicago edition of *Billy Budd, Sailor* appeared, its two editors expressed the hope "that a comprehensive scholarly edition of the work will narrow the ground of disagreement and widen that of understanding."[33] This still remains a hope unfulfilled, however, for advances in literary scholarship do not necessarily produce corresponding advances in literary criticism. The critical reassessments of the 1950s, signalized by new readings not just of Melville but of literature generally, were relatively quiet preludes to the social and political upheavals on college and university campuses during the Vietnam years. Like their antiwar students, some academic professionals displayed little interest in the findings of textual scholarship, for those were times when imaginative literature—if it was to be read at all—had either to be politically "relevant" or had to be made to seem so.

How relevance was demonstrated in *Billy Budd* can be illustrated by two essays of 1968. For Kingsley Widmer in "The Perplexed Myths of Melville," Vere is "the second-rate mad Captain"; Billy and Claggart are "stupid goodness versus depraved rationality, a cut-down Christ against a hopped-up Satan." The story itself "often shows infelicities," its concluding ballad is "not a very good poem," and only readers "confused" by Melville's emphasis on Vere's "decent and serious qualities" and "their own acceptance of arbitrary authority" will excuse the captain's "outrageous and immoral behavior."[34] In Charles Mitchell's "Melville and the Spurious Truth of Legalism," Billy and Claggart appear as doubles of Vere who mirror the submerged moral conflict within him between heart and intellect. Mitchell asserts that "Vere becomes a Claggart by killing Billy," thus placing reason and the law above "the moral majesty of human feeling" and so exemplifying "the principle of evil within the organization man—lawyer, captain, chief of police."[35]

One response open to a troubled reader was to go on liking Melville but to reject *Billy Budd* as an aberration, just as earlier critics such as Richard Chase and Charles Olson had already done. Another was to find a more sophisticated way of interpreting the story that would dissociate Melville from what Widmer condemned as Vere's "outrageous and immoral behavior" and from that pervasive "principle of evil" which Mitchell saw contaminating "the Establishment." Such a way had in fact been opened a decade earlier with the emergence of ironist criticism, which in turn was an offshoot of the still earlier "New Criticism" of Richards, Eliot, and Brooks and Warren. The New Critics had taught the importance of close reading and analysis of literary texts; some of the ironists, in their zeal for just such analysis, went on to distinguish Melville's opinions not only from Vere's but from those of his narrator as well, basing their whole methodology on the premise that the "I" who is speaking in *Billy Budd* cannot be trusted.

Those who assume that Melville's narrator is biased or even obtuse, as Thompson and other ironists would have it, agree that he must be regarded as *unreliable*. Melville, they contend, is using all the devices of the accomplished ironist to undercut the narrator's version of events in order to give us the real "inside narrative" promised in his subtitle. An ironist is one who is aware of discrepancies between appearance and reality—between outward dissembling and inward intention, for example, or between what words seem to say and what they truly mean. An ironist *writer* plays upon and uses these very discrepancies so as to reveal inner truth; an ironist *reader* is one capable of responding in kind. Melville is just such a writer, the argument runs; his earlier works attest it. *Billy Budd* must, therefore, be read ironically—if only by the few who are percipient enough to do so.

That there is irony in *Billy Budd, Sailor* is not denied by other readers, although they see the story in different terms—*tragic* irony, for example, as Richard Harter Fogle contends.[36] Critics such as Edward H. Rosenberry also take issue with the idea of dissociating Melville so completely either from his narrator or from Vere; the captain has attracted defenders once again in the cooled-down 1970s and 1980s. Both "straight" and "ironist" readings have continued to appear over the years, with the ironists disagreeing not only with the opposition but also among themselves: just what is the *real* "inside narrative"? Such disagreement may reflect an inherent instability, either in Melville's text (Paul Brodtkorb, Jr., emphasizes its unfinished state)[37] or in the nature of the critical enterprise itself.

Attempts to account for that instability have been made by a number of analysts in recent years, some with regard to changing fashions of criticism or of whatever deeper historical or sociological forces may underlie such changes. In the 1980s *Billy Budd, Sailor* attracted the special attention of critics schooled in semiotics, structuralism, and poststructuralism—or "deconstruction." Barbara Johnson, who is well versed in these matters, observes that the continued critical debate over the story simply recapitulates an opposition within *Billy Budd* "between two conceptions of language, or between two types of reading": literal-minded Billy "reads everything at face value, never questioning the meaning of appearances," while the worldly-wise Claggart, himself "a personification of ambiguity and ambivalence," is "properly an ironic reader." It is "precisely this opposition between the literal reader (Billy) and the ironic reader (Claggart)," she holds, that has been reenacted in the persistent division among the critics between "the 'acceptance' school and the 'irony' school," a dichotomy "already contained within the story."[38] But one may also argue, with considerable historical justification, that "the real focus" of critical disagreement "lies less within Melville's text than in some extraliterary universe of discourse, be it semantic, philosophical, or political" and conclude that the contending critics have seen in his story, given its ambiguities, very much what their own predispositions and allegiances conditioned them to see.[39] So by "selecting and combining as he pleases" (to borrow Melvillean language), each commentator tends to read "his own peculiar lesson according to his own peculiar mind and mood" (*Pierre*, 342).

Problems for Future Study

Scholars and critics wishing to minimize the subjective element in their approach to *Billy Budd, Sailor* will need to devote more attention than their predecessors to the story as the work of an older Melville—"the Melville who awaits discovery," in Stanton Garner's phrase.[40] As the author of *Battle-Pieces* (1866) and *Clarel* (1876) he had already given much thought to issues that also arise in *Billy Budd:* war and peace, religion and philosophy, indeed the whole course of human history. *Billy Budd* ought not to be read as an immediate sequel to *White-Jacket* (1850), as it has sometimes been taken, nor should Captain Vere be treated like the two-dimensional Captain Claret. Coming between them are such subtle accounts of military and naval figures as those of General Glendinning in *Pierre*, of Paul Jones and Ethan Allen in *Israel Potter*, of both Northern and Southern officers in *Battle-Pieces*, and of Major Jack Gentian in the Burgundy Club sketches.

Many of the books that survive from Melville's library were acquired during the last quarter-century of his life, and both his reading and his writing during these years may well have more bearing on *Billy Budd* than has yet been recognized. Critics should consider, along with possible new sources and analogues, the relation of *Billy Budd* to other late Melville manuscripts (some of them still unpublished), especially the prose-and-verse experiments scheduled for collection in a future volume of the Northwestern-Newberry edition. With regard to the *Billy Budd* manuscript itself, scholars and critics have too often neglected to go behind any and all reading texts of the story; they still need to acknowledge and assimilate what the Chicago Genetic Text and the accompanying editorial analysis have to tell them about Melville's art and Melville's thought as his story gradually took form.[41]

As for interpretation and criticism, with its recent concentration on Captain Vere and his actions rather than on other elements of the story, it would be well for future commentators to approach Vere less as the object of ideological attack or defense and more as a dramatic character. Once Melville himself had proceeded far enough with the story to look at his captain not merely as a functional figure—one needed to turn the wheels of an already determined plot—he began to treat him as a character in his own right, one who demanded to be fleshed out and made credible as a human being. The man Melville ultimately presented to us is not necessarily the cardboard figure that opposing critics have continued to treat as either a paragon of virtue or an utter monster; he is a fallible mortal, forced to make a judgment that would give pause to Solomon. And as Leon Howard once wrote with reference to Melville's Ahab, it may well have been "the author's emotional sympathy for a character of whom he intellectually disapproved" that gave his story "much of its ambiguity and dramatic intensity."[42]

Rather than seeking either to praise Vere or to blame him—a choice explicitly left to the reader—Melville's narrative accounts for what Billy's captain is and does in terms of his class and military vocation. At the same time it places Vere as the pivotal point of the dialectic that runs throughout the story, whether one looks at its characterization—Billy versus Claggart—or its themes: not only good and evil, but also innocence and experience, frankness and concealment, nature and society, barbarism and civilization, heart and head, love and justice, what is right and what is legal, peacemaking and warmaking, the *Rights-of-Man* and the *Bellipotent.* For Melville and his art, as he himself acknowledged, such "unlike things must meet and mate" (*Poems*, 231).

Vere, after all, is captain of the *Bellipotent,* not of the *Rights-of-Man,* with the *Atheist* waiting just over the horizon. His name, like those of the ships and of Billy Budd himself, has allegorical overtones: *vir* in Latin is *man.* The best thumbnail sketch of the captain outside Melville's own narrative describes him in the way just suggested, defending not Vere and his actions but the author's impressive work of characterization. Joyce Adler's *War in Melville's Imagination* (1981) takes Vere as

> the symbolic figure—not crudely, but finely and fairly drawn—of civilized man: learned, but not sufficiently imaginative; not devoid of the ability to love, but not allowing this capacity to develop; sensitive

to the difference between the good and evil signified by Billy and Claggart, but the puppet of the god he has been trained to think must rule in this world. His ultimate faith is in Force, not only against the enemy, but in dealing with his own side—utilizing impressment, flogging, and hanging—and in dealing violently with his own heart.[43]

There is a subject for future critics. The proper study of mankind, for us in our century as for Melville in his, is still man, and we too must live in what his *White-Jacket* called "this man-of-war world"—the world of the *Bellipotent,* where innocence and infamy are not always discernible for what they really are. Like Vere and like Melville, we also must walk its deck.[44]

Part Two
1988–1992

6.

An Author's Self-Education

Herman Melville's Reading

Among our most prominent nineteenth-century American authors, four in particular were largely *self-educated:* Walt Whitman, Herman Melville, Emily Dickinson, and Mark Twain. None of the four was a college graduate—though Mark Twain received honorary degrees —and perhaps coincidentally, none of the four was seriously regarded as a major author until our own century.

How such writers learned about the world, about themselves, and about their own craft is always a fascinating story, involving a varied combination of personal experience and later reflection upon it—reflection commonly abetted by the perspective they gained through the vicarious experience of reading. Like the four authors I have named, most of the principal figures in American literature, whatever their formal training, were great readers, men and women who schooled themselves for authorship by studying the works of other writers as they sought to perfect their own literary skills and to develop their individual idioms and styles.

Much has been done to identify and locate the books, magazines, and newspapers that our writers owned and borrowed. A useful survey of this work can be found in the fascinating article "Private Libraries of American Authors: Dispersal, Custody, and Description," by Alan Gribben, who is also the author of a monumental two-volume work of 1980 entitled *Mark Twain's Library: A Reconstruction.*[1]

Very few authors have taken the trouble to catalog the books on their own shelves. Most of them are no more specific about their holdings than was Henry Thoreau in this much-quoted remark from his journal of 1853: "I have now a library of nearly nine hundred volumes, over seven hundred of which I wrote myself." His wry reference was to the unsold copies of *A Week on the Concord and Merrimack Rivers,* his first book, composed in part during his famous two years at Walden Pond, from 1845 to 1847, and published in 1849. Yet Thoreau too was an avid reader of other writers, ancient and modern; Robert Sattelmeyer has recently published a four-hundred-page study of his reading.[2]

My own research labors concerning an individual author began with my doctoral dissertation at Yale, "Herman Melville's Reading in Ancient Philosophy," completed in 1942. The dissertation included an appendix listing books Melville had bought from his publishers, as noted on their successive statements of account that are preserved in the Melville Collection at Harvard's Houghton Library. Out of this beginning came a long article published serially in the *Harvard Library Bulletin* from 1948 to 1950, with later supplements, entitled "Melville's Reading: A Check-List of Books Owned and Borrowed." In this study I first surveyed the records of Melville's reading and then listed all the titles he was recorded as owning or borrowing; Melville himself never undertook his projected catalog of his personal library. Publication of this article was instrumental in turning up additional Melville association volumes, as they are known in the trade, leading to the appearance in 1966 of an expanded version of my work, this time in book form, that has been widely used by other scholars. In the spring of 1988, with the accumulation of much additional evidence, both internal and external, and the emergence of still more books from Melville's library, I published *Melville's Reading: Revised and Enlarged Edition.* A reviewer once delighted me by calling the 1966 edition a study of the self-education of a major author; the new volume of 1988 carries that study even further. Let me turn now to some of its major findings.

i

In Herman Melville's case, he could say with his own Ishmael, the narrator of *Moby-Dick,* that "A whale-ship was *my* Yale College and my Harvard" (*Moby-Dick,* 112). Indeed, Ishmael's words have often been quoted by those who assume that Melville's education was gained largely at sea. But this is to overlook his own statement to Nathaniel Hawthorne, in a letter of 1851 written while *Moby-Dick* was in progress, that until he *left* the sea in 1844 he "had no development at all. From my twenty-fifth year I date my life. Three weeks have scarcely passed, at any time between then and now, that I have not unfolded within myself" (*Correspondence,* 193).

Between the ages of twenty-five and thirty-two, from 1844 to 1851, Melville had written and published five books and was finishing his sixth, *Moby-Dick.* These books, the tangible evidence of his "unfolding," were the product not only of their author's personal experience before the mast, but also of his wide and deep reading and reflection. Until he had gained perspective on his adventures, to adapt a line from T. S. Eliot, he had had the experience but largely missed the meaning. Like Mark Twain, Melville was an omnivorous reader, thoroughly at home in libraries both public and private, and a buyer as well as a borrower of books. As with one of his own protagonists, the title character of *Pierre* (1852), "A varied scope of reading, . . . randomly acquired by a random but lynx-eyed mind, . . . poured one considerable contributary stream into that bottomless spring of original thought which the occasion and time had caused to burst out in himself" (*Pierre,* 283).

Like Emerson's idealized "American Scholar," Melville was "a creative *reader*" as well as a creative writer. Or, to cite Eliot once again, good poets *borrow* but great poets *steal,* and as a creative reader *and* writer Melville learned to supplement what he had learned from experience by extracting and appropriating whatever he needed from an increasing variety of books and authors, and so to put his experience in perspective. A recent scholar, Nancy Craig Simmons, characterized what he did in these words: "Melville's genius lay . . . in his ability to transform and complicate borrowed materials in ways that simultaneously explore the recesses of his own mind, his problems as a writer, and the culture in which he lived."[3] In the process of using his reading in this way he also succeeded in speaking to countless other readers and writers—across the years and around the globe. Now, long after his death, his achievement is at last fully acknowledged.

Melville's success in his own time began with his *Typee* (1846) and *Omoo* (1847), primarily based on his experiences at sea and in the Pacific islands but greatly enriched by his reading in other men's books on the South Seas. For later writings he also turned to specialized works: books on whaling for *Moby-Dick,* books of poetry when he was writing verse in the mid-1850s and after, and books on Palestine when he wrote *Clarel* (1876), a long narrative poem, based partly on the journal of his earlier travels in the Holy Land, that reflects his own search for religious faith.

Equally important was his wide general reading: his boyhood devotion to Cooper and Byron, his mature knowledge of poetry and drama from the Greeks and Romans to Shakespeare and Milton and their contemporaries—he responded with special enthusiasm to seventeenth-century writers—and his growing familiarity with authors of his own century. Among his contemporaries he read Hawthorne, Emerson, Thoreau, and later Whitman at home; Wordsworth, Coleridge, Lamb, Hazlitt, De Quincey, Carlyle, Dickens, Tennyson, Arnold, and the Brownings in Great Britain; and Goethe, Schiller, Richter, and Madame de Staël on the continent. He had a strong interest in philosophy, beginning with his exposure to Plato and Seneca in 1847 and 1848 and continuing throughout his life; during his last illness, along with "the Mermaid Series of old plays," he was reading Schopenhauer. And always the most abiding and pervasive influence was the King James Bible, which he obviously knew almost by heart and quoted in nearly everything he wrote.

ii

Like many great readers, Melville came from a family that loved books. His father, an importer of French goods, books included, seems to have had an extensive library. His mother established a custom of reading aloud in the evening that was continued in the homes of her children, Herman among them. His brothers and sisters, readers all, exchanged books and their opinions about books among themselves and their friends, both in their early years and in later life. Moreover, as we have learned only recently, Melville had a better preparatory schooling—in New York City and in Albany—than had long been supposed. In Albany, for example, he studied ancient history, biography, and literature at the Albany Academy, acquiring a limited knowledge not only of Latin but even of Greek, and at the Albany Classical School he exhibited a talent for original composition.

When his father's business reverses and subsequent death brought an end to Herman's formal schooling, he continued to read on his own, making use of the libraries of an Albany uncle, Peter Gansevoort, of the Albany Young Men's Association, and of another uncle in Pittsfield, Massachusetts,

Thomas Melvill, Jr., with whose family he lived for the better part of a year. Later, when hard times led him to become a sailor, he read whatever came to hand in ships' libraries.

Melville's really intensive reading, however, belongs to the years of his "unfolding." For his first books, as I have noted, he began both to borrow and to buy works on the South Seas. With his initial success as an author, as he married and settled in New York City and came to move in literary circles, his reading markedly broadened, with consequent effect on his writing. In New York he had access to the extensive private library of his friend Evert Duyckinck, a prominent editor, and, through Duyckinck, to the resources of the New York Society Library, a private institution where both he and his brother Allan held membership. "By the way, Melville reads old Books," Duyckinck reported. "He has borrowed Sir Thomas Browne of me and says finely . . . that Browne is a kind of 'crack'd Archangel'" (*Log*, 1:273).

It was Browne who in turn led Melville to read the dialogues of Plato, which greatly influenced both the form and the content of Melville's third book, *Mardi* (1849). *Mardi* is a philosophical romance, quite unlike *Typee* and *Omoo*, that prepared the way for *Moby-Dick*. Meanwhile, Melville was beginning to build an extensive library of his own. His significant purchases of Dante, Milton, Shakespeare, Wordsworth, and Coleridge all date from the late 1840s. So too does his first reading of Emerson, whom he had heard lecturing in Boston. In 1849, on a trip to Europe, he bought still more books, ranging from the plays of Marlowe and Jonson to the writings of Goethe and De Quincey.

In 1850 the Melvilles moved from New York City to a farm near Pittsfield that Herman called "Arrowhead." In addition to Melville's old associations with the area there was his developing friendship with Hawthorne, who was then living nearby at Lenox; the older writer exerted a powerful influence on *Moby-Dick*, both directly and through his writings. At Pittsfield Melville missed the resources of New York's libraries and bookstores—its "long Vaticans and street-stalls," as he called them (*Moby-Dick*, xvii). Though he had access to the shelves of the Pittsfield Library Association, "They have no Vatican (as you have)," he wrote ruefully to Duyckinck (*Correspondence*, 209), from whom he continued to borrow books—notably the writings of Thomas Carlyle, another major influence on *Moby-Dick*. At this same time he was also collecting works on whales and whaling that he needed for the more technical aspects of *Moby-Dick*, being aided by relatives who bought books for him and by at least one New York bookseller who imported a volume from London.

Moby-Dick, now considered Melville's masterwork, was not the immediate success he had hoped for. He wanted to escape the reputation he had gained with *Typee* as the "man who lived among the cannibals" (*Correspondence,* 193); contemporary readers and critics, however, wanted more books like *Typee* and *Omoo* and deplored what Melville offered them in *Mardi,* in *Moby-Dick,* and especially in his seventh book, *Pierre* (1852). As a result, his career as a professional author virtually ended during the later 1850s, when, after the utter failure of *Pierre,* he first wrote magazine fiction and then tried his hand at lecturing. (Early in 1859 he came to the Midwest, giving a lecture called "The South Seas" in Chicago, Rockford, Quincy, and Milwaukee.) In 1863 he left Pittsfield for New York City, where he lived until his death in 1891. He published four volumes of verse during these years, two of them privately printed. From 1866 until 1885 he supported his family by working as a customs inspector on the city's docks. After his retirement in 1885, in addition to writing verse he composed his last prose work, *Billy Budd, Sailor,* which was not published until long after his death.

Most of the books that survive from Melville's library date from the New York years. He visited bookstores in both New York and Philadelphia, reportedly spending more than his family liked, although his wife's receipt of an inheritance led her to allow him $25 a month for buying books and prints. His purchases included volumes of poetry and criticism by various hands (notably Matthew Arnold), the works of Balzac, and many books on fine art, a major interest along with his continuing fondness for both drama and philosophy. The Berkshire Athenaeum, Pittsfield's public library, holds many prints from Melville's collection, the gift of one of his granddaughters.

A current subject of lively investigation, I might note, is Melville's sensitive response to pictorial art, as provocative as his response to books and abundantly evident from the time of his early works through the writing of *Billy Budd, Sailor* during his last years. Three recent illustrated volumes represent this new interest. *Herman Melville's Picture Gallery* (1986), by Stuart M. Frank, identifies and comments on the numerous prints and other images of whales and whaling that Melville refers to in *Moby-Dick,* to the great enrichment of that mighty work. Christopher Sten has assembled a gathering of critical essays in *Savage Eye: Melville and the Visual Arts* (1991). Robert K. Wallace, who has cataloged several collections of Melville's prints, has explored relations between Melville's works and British art and art criticism in *Melville and Turner: Spheres of Love and Fright* (1992); a sequel is in prospect.[4]

During Melville's later years in New York he continued borrowing books: from Duyckinck, until his friend's death in 1878, and from various institutional collections—especially the New York Society Library, where he again held membership in 1890 and 1891 and from which he drew extensively, both for himself and for his wife and their unmarried daughter. He was reading contemporary authors such as Howells and Kipling and becoming acquainted with Schopenhauer; they preferred lighter fiction.

Epilogue

When Melville died in September 1891, by then a forgotten figure among American authors, the inventory of his estate valued at $600 his "Personal books numbering about 1,000 volumes." Some of these books were kept by his widow, passing after her death to a married daughter and later to four granddaughters. Three of the granddaughters in turn gave most of the books they had inherited to Harvard, where, along with various family papers, they now constitute the Melville Collection, housed in Houghton Library. A fourth granddaughter presented most of her books to the New York Public Library, where they constitute the Osborne Collection. Other books and papers kept by relatives of Melville are also in the New York Public Library as part of its extensive Gansevoort-Lansing Collection, which was recently augmented by the additional Melville Family Papers— a literal "find" that was purchased for the library after making a wholly unanticipated appearance in upstate New York. Many references to books and reading occur throughout the family correspondence.

The books that Melville's widow did not keep were sold to various book dealers in New York and Brooklyn when she moved to smaller quarters in 1892. No record was made of their titles, either by Mrs. Melville or by the dealers concerned, though we do know some of the individuals who bought from the Brooklyn shop. However, those books that had once been Melville's were not commonly identified in sale catalogs until the 1920s, when the first wave of the modern Melville revival began and the presence of Melville's autograph in a book came to enhance its worth substantially.

Since then, the value of Melville association volumes has steadily escalated. In 1945 a single heavily annotated book that Melville had used in writing *Moby-Dick*—the *Narrative* of Owen Chase, where Melville found the suggestion for the ramming and sinking of the *Pequod* by a whale— brought $2,100 at auction in New York. In the 1980s, when a whole cluster of books has come onto the market, two individual sales at auction are especially noteworthy: Melville's copy of Dante brought $16,000 and his Milton a cool $100,000! All this out of a personal library once valued at a mere $600. As Melville's Ishmael would put it, "Oh, Time, Strength, Cash, and Patience!" (*Moby-Dick,* 145).

In the 1940s, when I first began tracking the books Melville had owned, 210 surviving titles were known, of which 191 had then been located; by 1995 these totals had increased to 273 known survivors, of which 247 had been located.[5] Fortunately, most of these are available to scholars, either in New York or Cambridge, at the Berkshire Athenaeum, at various institutional libraries holding one, two, or three books, or in the hands of cooperative private collectors. Others, however, have disappeared from sight after being listed in auction catalogs.

Still other titles of books read by Melville are known because records of his buying or borrowing have survived: the accounts with his publishers at Harvard; Duyckinck's notebook of "Books Lent," now in the Duyckinck Family Papers at the New York Public Library; the charging records of the New York Society Library, which is still flourishing; and other references to books and reading in the correspondence of the Melvilles and their relatives and friends, some published and some still in manuscript.

All of these available books and records are open to the Melville scholar because Melville himself was a book lover who bought and borrowed books, because many of those books and the records concerning them were kept in the family or elsewhere, and because modern libraries have the facilities to treasure what has come their way, either by good fortune or through enlightened acquisition.

In lieu of a final summation, here are two apposite comments on Melville's reading, the first by the late F. O. Matthiessen and the second by Melville himself: "The books that really spoke to Melville," Matthiessen finely observed in his *American Renaissance,* "became a part of him to a degree hardly matched by any other of our great writers in their maturity."6 Those of us who have closely followed Melville's absorption and transformation of what he read—a study in itself—will wholeheartedly agree with these words. A passage from Melville's *White-Jacket* (1850) nicely captures his own attitude toward books and reading. It is "a fact which every book-lover must have experienced before me," he wrote, "that though public libraries have an imposing air, and doubtless contain invaluable volumes, yet, somehow, the books that prove most agreeable, grateful, and companionable, are those we pick up by chance here and there; those which seem put into our hands by Providence; those which pretend to little but abound in much" (*White-Jacket*, 169). Melville's own writings, we have found, fully support his affirmation here, to which most of us, whether authors or readers, would probably subscribe; I surely do myself.

7.

Melville's Reading, 1853–1856

elville's decision to become a magazine writer, made chiefly out of his pressing need for money after the Harpers declined his eighth book-length manuscript,[1] opened a new chapter in his professional career. From 1844 until the summer of 1853, except for his occasional pieces for the *Literary World* and *Yankee Doodle,* he had been a writer only of books. In 1851 he had refused his friend Evert Duyckinck's request that he contribute to *Holden's Dollar Magazine,* and in 1852 he had evidently not responded to other invitations from the publishers of *Putnam's Monthly Magazine* in New York and *Bentley's Miscellany* in London. At the same time, however, he was well aware that the American reading public preferred those authors "who write those most saleable of all books nowadays—ie—the newspapers, & magazines," as he remarked ruefully to Richard Bentley in his letter of 20 July 1851 (*Correspondence,* 198). Melville obviously had no objection to seeing long excerpts from his own works included in advance notices of his books and in later reviews. One example was the appearance in *Harper's* for October 1851 of an entire chapter of *Moby-Dick,* "The Town-Ho's Story" (chapter 54), a self-contained episode that served as an advertisement for the book a month before its American publication. Other segments of his earlier works could also have been printed as independent stories or sketches, as the Harpers may well have realized. Now, after the failure of *Pierre* (1852), it would be prudent for them to recruit Melville as an anonymous contributor to their new magazine rather than to risk bringing out another book with his name on the title page.

As for Melville, who had previously thought of publishing *Pierre* "anonymously, or under an assumed name," as he had suggested to Richard Bentley in his letter of 16 April 1852 (*Correspondence*, 228), the prospect of writing both anonymously and in shorter forms might well have seemed attractive by 1853, given the energy it had cost him to turn out eight book-length manuscripts in roughly as many years, plus the repeated disappointments he had suffered with *Moby-Dick*, with *Pierre*, and with his recently rejected work, *The Isle of the Cross*. By 13 August 1853 he had three new magazine pieces ready for the Harpers: probably "The Happy Failure" (1854), "The Fiddler" (1854), and "Cock-A-Doodle-Doo!" (1853). By September he had also completed a longer story, "Bartleby, the Scrivener" (1853), for *Putnam's Monthly Magazine*, a younger rival of *Harper's* that also published its contributions anonymously.[2] But he had not yet given up the idea of another still longer work, for on 24 November he wrote the Harpers to say that he had "in hand, and pretty well on towards completion, another book—300 pages, say—partly of nautical adventure, and partly—or, rather, chiefly, of Tortoise Hunting Adventure" (*Correspondence*, 250).

The Harpers responded favorably to Melville's request for an advance payment of $300 for the new book, but a disastrous fire at their New York publishing house seems to have interfered with further negotiations for the projected work. He may have adapted some of the material on "Tortoise Hunting" for "The Encantadas," which he sent to George Palmer Putnam in the following February (*Correspondence*, 256); the ten component sketches appeared serially in the issues of *Putnam's Magazine* for March, April, and May 1854. Between July 1854 and March 1855, *Putnam's* also serialized his *Israel Potter*, which was then reprinted as Melville's eighth published book (1855). By May 1856 a total of fourteen tales and sketches by Melville, apart from *Israel Potter*, had appeared in *Harper's* and *Putnam's* magazines; he had also written an additional piece, "The Two Temples," that remained unpublished after George Putnam and his editor, Charles F. Briggs, rejected it. In 1856 the new firm of Dix and Edwards, which had recently bought *Putnam's Magazine*, reprinted five of his contributions in *The Piazza Tales*, his ninth published book, along with a new title piece, "The Piazza," that Melville wrote especially for the volume.

Despite his uncertain health, Melville had worked productively for three years, earning an estimated total of $1,329.50 for his magazine writing alone, which yielded him $5.00 per printed page;[3] most contributors were paid a dollar or two less. But times were hard, and though reviews of the collected *Piazza Tales* were generally favorable, the receipts from sales failed to meet the costs of production.

Sources of the Magazine Pieces

One reviewer of *The Piazza Tales,* writing in the *Newark (N.J.) Daily Advertiser* for 18 June 1856, hailed Melville's book as a return to "the real Typee and Omoo vein," complaining that his more recent works had been "the fruits of his reading rather than of his imagination."[4] There was some justification for this last remark, as even Melville himself had admitted with respect to *Mardi* (1849), but it would be a mistake to suppose that his reading had not also contributed substantially to his magazine writing. Scholarly investigation of these pieces in recent years, as I have summarized it elsewhere,

> has now established Melville's principal sources in his own observation of the contemporary scene (some of it recorded in his earlier journal-entries), his wide knowledge of general literature, and his reading of more specialized materials ranging from narratives of Pacific voyages to newspaper and magazine articles of the day that added both substance and topical interest to his writing.
>
> The investigation of Melville's use of these varied source materials helps to explain what George William Curtis meant in 1855 when he applauded one of the stories as "thoroughly magazinish."[5]

Curtis's remark confirms the sagacity of George Putnam and the brothers Harper in soliciting manuscripts from Melville and paying for them at premium rates; it also suggests that Melville himself became a better judge of popular taste as a magazine writer than he had been as the author of *Pierre.* He evidently took profitable notice of what contemporary newspapers and magazines of the 1850s were carrying and learned to pattern his own pieces accordingly, with respect to both form and content. He began buying monthly numbers of *Harper's* when it first appeared in June 1850, and at Pittsfield in September 1851 he became a regular subscriber (Check-List, no. 240),[6] though there may have been some delay in receiving the magazine. In a letter of 5 November 1851 from his mother to his sister

Augusta, who was then living with Allan Melville's family in New York, it was reported that Herman had "bought at the Village"—Pittsfield— the October number, which included "The Town-Ho's Story," and that Allan had sent the November issue to Arrowhead. "We have up to May 1851," Maria Melville noted, but not the issues for June through September, "which we would like to have."[7] Melville presumably subscribed as well to *Putnam's,* which began publication in January 1853, though there is no record of his term of subscription (Check-List, no. 413).

Among other periodicals that Melville read at least occasionally is *Littel's Living Age,* an eclectic Boston weekly that reprinted fiction, poetry, and comment from foreign periodicals. In the summer of 1856 he spoke with his friend J. E. A. Smith about an article on Cooper, Dana, and himself, "A Trio of American Sailor-Authors," copied from the *Dublin University Magazine* in the *Living Age* for 1 March 1856 (Check-List, no. 327.1). The Melvilles probably saw some or all of the local Pittsfield newspapers: the *Sun* (see Check-List, no. 216), the weekly *Culturist and Gazette,* and the *Eagle,* for which Smith was a writer and—beginning in 1854—an editor. They also subscribed for a time to the *New York Herald;* Maria Melville, in her letter of 5 November 1851 quoted above, complained, "We have not had a Herald or any paper for ten days past," and Melville himself, in a later notation inside the front cover of his notebook of "Lecture Engagements" (now in the Harvard College Library), wrote, "Herald stops Jan 7th 1854." On occasion he read other metropolitan newspapers, at Pittsfield or elsewhere. The *New York Times* or *New York Tribune,* the *Springfield (Mass.) Republican,* and the *Albany Evening Tribune, Albany Evening Journal,* and *Albany Argus* all provided material at various times for one or another of the magazine pieces. Like the monthly magazines, with their comments on literature, art, and current events at home and abroad, the newspapers kept him abreast of what was taking place in the world beyond Berkshire.

What I have called Melville's "own observation of the contemporary scene" is evident in a number of these short pieces in his abundant references—overt and otherwise—to persons, places, and events he knew at first hand. As his relatives must have been aware and as some reviewers shrewdly guessed, many of the characters in his short fiction were based on men and women he knew at various times and places in his career. He himself was to remark in *The Confidence-Man* (1857) that any writer of fiction must necessarily "pick up" most of his characters "in town," for the city is "a kind of man-show" where he "goes for his stock, just as the agriculturist goes to the cattle-show for his" (238). And since Melville never excelled at originating plots, a number of his stories, like his earlier books, are elaborations of personal experience, sometimes as recorded in his journal and frequently supplemented by material drawn from his reading.

In this connection, several contemporary authors contributed in a special way to Melville's writing for the magazines. Both nineteenth-century reviewers of *The Piazza Tales* and twentieth-century critics have seen resemblances between his shorter fiction and the sketches and tales of Irving, Poe, Hawthorne, Lamb, and Dickens. Although no single work by any of these contemporaries can be considered a primary source of a given piece by Melville, he not infrequently followed the lead of others in terms of plotting, characterization, and technique of narration. As we know, Melville had been reading Hawthorne, Lamb, and Dickens since 1849. In 1850 his "Hawthorne and His Mosses" in effect dismissed Irving as merely an imitator of Goldsmith, but when he turned to shorter fiction in 1853 he himself found Irving a useful model. His friend Richard Lathers gave him a new set of Irving's works in June of that year; in August he reciprocated with an abridged version of Abraham Tucker's *Light of Nature Revealed* (Check-List, nos. 292a, 529). Melville's only known copy of Poe's works is a later edition acquired in 1860 and given to his wife in 1861 (no. 404a), but his caricature of Poe as the peddler in chapter 36 of *The Confidence-Man* shows his familiarity with the man and his writings.

A brief review of the stories and their sources, in the approximate order of their composition, will illustrate the foregoing generalizations. What seem to be Melville's first two magazine pieces of 1853 (although they were not published until 1854), "The Happy Failure" and "The Fiddler," are set, respectively, along the Hudson River—which Melville knew well from his years in Albany and Lansingburgh—and in New York City. The title character of "The Happy Failure," an unsuccessful inventor, has been said to resemble two of his kinsmen whose careers were relatively unsuccessful: Thomas Melvill, Jr., and Herman Gansevoort; the "uncle" of the story and his black servant, Yorpy, are like Poe's Legrand and Jupiter in "The Gold-Bug." An experience of failure also befalls the narrator of "The Fiddler," when his "poem" is "damned" and he must therefore learn to live "*with* genius and *without* fame" (*Piazza Tales,* 267).[8] According to Donald Yannella in a recent essay, "Writing 'the *other* way,'" the narrator's situation is like Melville's own after the mixed reception of *Moby-Dick* and the outright failure of *Pierre*, when he turned to magazine fiction much as the narrator takes up "fiddling"; Yannella also suggests that Standard and Hautboy, the supporting characters, may be patterned after Melville's New York friends Evert Duyckinck and Cornelius Mathews.[9]

The next two stories of 1853, "Cock-A-Doodle-Doo!" and "Bartleby, the Scrivener," are longer and more fully developed narratives; one is set in rural Berkshire and the other in a New York lawyer's Wall Street office—a locale Melville knew well, his brother Allan being a Wall Street lawyer. Both stories deal once more with characters out of step with their environments; both make knowing references to current events; both reflect Melville's general reading. The Berkshire narrator in particular alludes freely to classical and biblical topics, names *Tristram Shandy* and *The Anatomy of Melancholy*, parodies a poem by Wordsworth, and echoes *Hamlet* and *Paradise Lost*. As contemporary comment suggested, the lawyer-narrator in "Bartleby" and his forlorn clerk may have been patterned after living models; the supporting characters could easily have come from the pen of Dickens, Lamb, or Irving. The idea for "Bartleby" may have been suggested to Melville by an advertisement in the *New York Times* and *New York Tribune* for 18 February 1853 that quoted the first chapter of a novel by James A. Maitland: *The Lawyer's Story*, in which a lawyer hires an extra copying clerk. The concluding references in "Bartleby" to the Dead Letter Office in Washington pick up another topic of interest that had been featured in newspapers of the early 1850s.

Between the late summer of 1853 and the following spring, Melville composed three two-part sketches that Jay Leyda has called "diptychs": they all feature contrasting episodes, one American and the other English. The first part of "Poor Man's Pudding and Rich Man's Crumbs," which has a Berkshire setting like that of "Cock-A-Doodle-Doo!," may be a parody of Catharine Maria Sedgwick's *The Poor Rich Man and the Rich Poor Man* (1836). The second part is based directly on journal entries Melville had made in London in 1849. Both sections of "The Two Temples" come primarily out of Melville's personal observation: his familiarity with two New York churches and his acquaintance with the sexton of one of them, Isaac Brown, plus his rewarding visit to a theater while he was in London. "The Paradise of Bachelors and the Tartarus of Maids" begins with recollections of Melville's bachelor friends in London and closes with a graphic but symbolic description of an American paper mill, recalling an actual excursion to a paper factory that he had made in 1851 and revealing his close familiarity with Berkshire geography.

The ten sketches that make up "The Encantadas," written in 1854, are based primarily on Melville's recollections of his visit to the Galapagos Islands during his whaling years, supplemented by material drawn from at least six books of Pacific voyages written by David Porter, James Colnett, "that excellent Buccaneer" William Cowley, James Burney, the naturalist Charles Darwin, and Amasa Delano. Some or all of these works were in his library at Pittsfield. He had used Porter's *Journal* as early as *Typee* and bought Darwin's journal of his voyage on the *Beagle* in 1847 (Check-List, no. 175); he was to draw more extensively on Delano's *Narrative of Voyages and Travels* in "Benito Cereno" (1855) and on James Burney's five-volume *History of the Discoveries in the Pacific Ocean* in his lecture of 1858–1859, "The South Seas." The account in Sketch Eighth of the ordeal of Hunilla, the Chola widow, elaborates on reports carried in Albany and Springfield newspapers during November of 1853; Melville may have enriched his treatment of her story by recalling the case of Agatha Hatch Robinson, brought to his attention by Hawthorne and possibly used in *The Isle of the Cross,* which was apparently the book-length manuscript he had failed to place with the Harpers in 1853. Most of the poetic epigraphs for the sketches came from a still unidentified edition of the works of Edmund Spenser;[10] the others are from the poetry of William Collins and from Melville's surviving copies of Thomas Chatterton's works and the plays of Beaumont and Fletcher (Check-List, nos. 137, 53).

There are primary sources for two of Melville's longer contributions to *Putnam's: Israel Potter,* written in 1854, and "Benito Cereno," composed a year later, both being adaptations and expansions of narratives by other writers. For *Israel Potter* Melville used an 1824 pamphlet ascribed to the real-life Potter but presumably written for him by its publisher, Henry Trumbull (Check-List, no. 407). Melville had acquired the pamphlet before his European trip of 1849, when he bought an old map of London (no. 330a) for possible use in "serving up" Potter's story at some future time. When he came to construct his serialized novel, as Walter E. Bezanson has observed in his Historical Note to the Northwestern-Newberry edition of *Israel Potter,* he "moved in and out of his sources so frequently" that the finished story "offers a rare opportunity to watch him at work."

Four books were successively open beside him during the writing of thirteen of his twenty-six chapters: Henry Trumbull's *Life* . . . ; Robert C. Sands's compiled *Life and Correspondence of John Paul Jones* (New York, 1830); James Fenimore Cooper's *History of the Navy of the United States of America* (New York, 1853); and Ethan Allen's *A Narrative of Colonel Ethan Allen's Captivity* (first published in Philadelphia, 1779).

In addition, he read widely in Benjamin Franklin's collected writings, made minor use of a few other books, and refreshed his memory of England and Paris with his own journal.[11]

One of the "other books" was the two-volume *Life* of the painter Benjamin Haydon (Check-List, no. 262), which Melville bought on 7 April 1854 while in New York for his brother Allan's birthday; a passage in the first volume was the germ of chapter 23 of *Israel Potter* (*Log*, 1:486). For his adaptation of Trumbull's pamphlet, as Bezanson points out, he had already changed the narrative mode from first person to third and proceeded to move Potter's birthplace from Cranston, Rhode Island, to the Berkshire region of Massachusetts, thus preparing the way for his own "prelude of 'poetic reflection' on the Berkshire country" in chapter 1 and allowing for his further use of David Dudley Field's *History of the County of Berkshire* and J. E. A. Smith's *Taghconic*[12] (Check-List, nos. 216, 478; for chapters set in England, see nos. 304a, 330a).

At some time in 1854 Melville wrote two shorter pieces, "The Lightning-Rod Man" and "The 'Gees." As local newspapers testify, the Berkshires had been invaded by salesmen of lightning-rods in the fall of 1853; the late Helen Morewood, a descendant of Melville's neighbors in Pittsfield, repeated to Jay Leyda a story her father had told of an actual encounter between Melville and one of these itinerants.[13] "The Lightning-Rod Man" alludes to Cotton Mather's *Magnalia Christi Americana,* of which the Pittsfield Library Association had a copy; the late Margaret Morewood, Helen Morewood's sister, remembered another copy at Arrowhead.[14] In view of the narrator's satirical reference to his visitor as a "pretended envoy extraordinary" from the gods (*Piazza Tales,* 124), it may be significant that in the spring of 1854 Melville urged his sister Helen to read "Plutarch on the Cessation of the Oracles" (Check-List, no. 404.2). "The 'Gees," which draws on Melville's firsthand knowledge of Portuguese sailors during his years at sea, may have been suggested by a review article in *Putnam's Monthly* for July 1854 that dealt with supposedly fixed racial distinctions; Melville's satirical sketch anticipates his chapter on Indian-hating in *The Confidence-Man* (1857).

Perhaps the least characteristic of Melville's stories is "The Bell-Tower," submitted to *Putnam's* in the spring of 1855, which somewhat resembles the work of Hawthorne and Poe. Its setting in Renaissance Italy may reflect Melville's familiarity with Machiavelli's *Florentine Histories* (Check-List, no. 340a) and the *Autobiography* of Benvenuto Cellini. Other sources that have been suggested include articles on Albertus and Agrippa in Pierre Bayle's *Dictionary,* Mary Shelley's *Frankenstein,* and Hawthorne's "The Minotaur" in his *Tanglewood Tales* (nos. 51, 467, 256).

For "Benito Cereno," Melville enlarged upon chapter 18 of *A Narrative of Voyages and Travels in the Northern and Southern Hemispheres* (Boston, 1817), written by a Yankee sea captain, Amasa Delano; he had previously used this book in "The Encantadas." G. Thomas Tanselle has suggested that it may well have been called to Melville's attention in March 1853 by Henry F. Hubbard, who had been one of his shipmates aboard the *Acushnet* in 1841 and had since settled in California.[15] Hubbard came to Pittsfield for a reunion with his sister Sarah, who had married Amasa Rice, a Pittsfield farmer. The mother of Henry and Sarah Hubbard was a fourth cousin of Amasa Delano; since Melville presented a copy of *Moby-Dick* to Hubbard during his visit to Arrowhead, it is even possible that Hubbard returned the favor with a copy of *Voyages and Travels,* though the particular volume owned by Melville has not come to light. The Northwestern-Newberry edition of *The Piazza Tales,* which reproduces Delano's eighth chapter in facsimile, also discusses Melville's adaptation and enlargement of his narrative.

Three pieces written between the summer of 1854 and the summer or fall of 1855, "Jimmy Rose," "I and My Chimney," and "The Apple-Tree Table," are best discussed as a group. All three are domestic narratives related in the first person; all have settings in houses that Melville knew well, Broadhall and Arrowhead, though he shifted their locations for fictional purposes. The title character of "Jimmy Rose," another of Melville's worldly failures, has attributes of Melville's father, his grandfather, and especially his uncle Thomas Melvill, Jr. The features of Jimmy's old house in the city—notably the parlor adorned with "genuine Versailles paper" (137)—clearly identify it as a re-creation of Broadhall, where Major Melvill had lived during his Pittsfield years.[16] "I and My Chimney" describes the imposing central chimney of a farmhouse very much like Arrowhead, though the threatened removal of the chimney may have been suggested by a similar alteration at Broadhall in 1851 after its sale to Melville's friends the Morewoods.

The narrator of "I and My Chimney," who takes to "oldness in things" (361), is like the storytellers in works of Washington Irving, of George William Curtis, and perhaps of Hawthorne; his domineering wife could have come out of any number of Irving's writings. Essentially the same couple, along with their two daughters and "Biddy the girl," reappear as city dwellers in "The Apple-Tree Table," a story significantly subtitled "Original Spiritual Manifestations." But though the wife of "I and My Chimney" is interested in such current fads as "Swedenborgianism, and the Spirit Rapping philosophy, with other new views" (362), her skeptical counterpart in "The Apple-Tree Table" does not believe in "spirits" and spirit-rapping as her daughters do. Her husband, the narrator, half accepts what he reads in Cotton Mather's *Magnalia;* she, however, puts her trust in "Professor Johnson, the naturalist" (396).

"I and My Chimney" is especially interesting to students of both Melville's life and Melville's reading, since it effectively combines literary borrowings with personal experience to form a well-integrated narrative. Mrs. Melville later recalled that in February 1855 her husband "had his first attack of severe rheumatism in his back—so that he was helpless—and in the following June an attack of Sciatica—Our neighbor in Pittsfield Dr. O. W. Holmes attended & prescribed for him."[17] Similarly, the narrator-protagonist in "I and My Chimney" is "crippled up as any old apple tree" with sciatica (360), and there may be other biographical elements in the story as well—notably the question of the chimney's possible "unsoundness" because of some "secret closet" within it (375).[18] As for reflections of Melville's reading, his references to the pyramids in "I and My Chimney" show his knowledge of Giovanni Battista Belzoni, the Egyptologist whose machine for regulating the waters of the Nile may have previously suggested the uncle's "Great Hydraulic-Hydrostatic Apparatus" in "The Happy Failure" (255). The "secret closet" of the narrative may recall Irving's "Legend of the Arabian Astrologer" in *The Alhambra,* the evident source of a much-quoted image in book 21 of *Pierre:* the descent into the pyramid in search of its inmost chamber (*Pierre,* 285). The narrator's account of his pyramidal chimney also echoes what Henry Thoreau had written of the chimney he constructed at Walden, as Pamela Matthews has persuasively demonstrated.[19]

In the concluding chapter of *Walden* (1854), moreover, Thoreau mentioned "the story which has gone the rounds of New England, of a strong and beautiful bug which came out of the dry leaf of an old table of apple-tree wood"—the very story on which Melville based "The Apple-Tree Table." Reading *Walden* in 1854 or 1855 probably sent Melville back to at least one of two works associated with his stay at Broadhall in 1850: Timothy Dwight's *Travels in New England* and Field's *History of the County of Berkshire,* which offer versions of the same story. In his annotated copy of the *History* (Check-List, no. 216), a number of passages are marked, some used in "The Apple-Tree Table" and others in the earlier *Israel Potter.*

Recapitulation: "The Piazza"

The dialectic of old and new, spiritualism and naturalism, that runs through "I and My Chimney" and "The Apple-Tree Table" is a sign that in his magazine fiction of the mid-1850s Melville was doing more than merely writing to please the public. His earlier stories had expressed his concern for the poor and oppressed; "Temple First" and "The Lightning-Rod Man" satirize contemporary religionists of differing stripes; "The Tartarus of Maids" and "The Bell-Tower" show his distrust of industrialization and technology; "Benito Cereno," as commentators now recognize, is an oblique comment on those prevailing attitudes toward blacks and slavery in the United States that would ultimately precipitate civil war between North and South. Some modern readers take "I and My Chimney"—the very story that Curtis termed "thoroughly magazinish"—as an allegorical treatment of the divided state of the Union in the 1850s. But at the same time the chimney represents something very personal to Melville, and the search for some reputed "unsoundness" within it may recall the examinations, physical and mental, that he himself was reportedly obliged to undergo in the years after *Pierre.*

In late January or early February 1856, before "I and My Chimney" and "The Apple-Tree Table" appeared in *Putnam's,* Melville wrote "The Piazza" as a title piece for the five earlier stories from the magazine that are collected in *The Piazza Tales.* His narrator opens the story with an epigraph from Shakespeare's *Cymbeline* and specifically reminds the reader of *Hamlet, Macbeth,* and *A Midsummer Night's Dream.* Following a familiar Melvillean pattern, he employs numerous biblical and mythological references and alludes also to "old wars of Lucifer and Michael" in *Paradise Lost,* to Emerson's poem "The Problem," and to *Don Quixote*—Melville had bought a translation of Cervantes's work in September 1855 (Check-List, no. 125). The story of the narrator's disillusioned attempt "to get to fairyland" is counterpointed by his direct reference to "one Edmund Spenser, who had been there—so he wrote me" (6); the lonely girl Marianna whom he encounters on his journey recalls both Shakespeare's dejected Marianna in *Measure for Measure* and Tennyson's "Marianna" and "Marianna in the South."

The story's opening narrative, which uses both Arrowhead and the nearby Mount Greylock as its setting, establishes a characteristic tone for what is to follow, much as Hawthorne's account of the old manse at Concord prepares the reader for the tales collected in his *Mosses from an Old Manse.* Melville may well have been rereading both Hawthorne and his own "Hawthorne and His Mosses" when he made the decision to introduce his own collection with "The Piazza." One writer, Helmbrecht Breinig, takes "The Piazza" as Melville's new evaluation—even his parody—of Hawthorne and "a more skeptical revaluation" of what he had previously written about Hawthorne's tales in 1850 as he himself was working on *Moby-Dick.*[20] Certainly "The Piazza" reflects the altered tenor of his more recent reading and writing, looking forward to the chastened mood in which he was to compose *The Confidence-Man,* much as "Hawthorne and His Mosses" reflects the ebullience with which he began *Moby-Dick* six years before. The narrator of "I and My Chimney" closes his story "standing guard over [his] mossy old chimney" (377); the narrator of "The Piazza" walks "the piazza deck, haunted by Marianna's face, and many as real a story" (12).

8.

"Pulse of the Continent"

The Railroad in American Literature

L ong before twentieth-century Americans became entranced with space travel and space ships, both the lure of distant prospects and the urge to build machines to reach them were part of our national heritage. From the very beginnings of the nation our people have been travelers and explorers, whether bound toward some prospective haven ahead or rushing, like Melville's *Pequod,* from all havens astern. As our machines have grown ever larger and more complex, so mechanization and industrialization have increasingly modified and complicated the character and quality of American life itself. During the nineteenth century the harnessing of steam power for travel, first by water and later by rail, greatly accelerated the pace of westward movement across the continent. By the 1860s the greater concentration within our northern states of railroads and the factories they served had a significant economic, political, and ultimately military effect on relations between the American North and South.

Though development of the steamboat in the first decade of the century had been both exciting and profitable, the excitement it generated "was nothing compared to the railroad." So wrote Leo Marx in *The Machine in the Garden,* his provocative study of "technology and the pastoral ideal in America"—a book drawn upon here.[1] According to Marx, the Iron Horse became "a kind of national obsession" during the 1830s as railroad-building burgeoned along our eastern seaboard. Americans thought of it as "the embodiment of the age, an instrument of power, speed, noise, fire, iron, smoke," Marx tells us, "—at once a testament to the will of man rising over natural obstacles, and, yet, confined by its iron rails to a predetermined path, it suggested a new sort of fate." In *Walden* (1854) Henry Thoreau specifically called the steam locomotive "a fate, an *Atropos,* that never turns aside," proposing "Atropos" as a fitting name for an engine.

By the time of *Walden* the Iron Horse was "the 'industrial revolution incarnate'" for Americans, as Marx observes, noting that like most visible symbols of power, railroads and especially steam locomotives aroused varying reactions in the public at large. On the one hand they were hailed in the rhetoric of the day as "the triumphs of our own age, the laurels of mechanical philosophy, of untrammeled mind, and a liberal commerce," while on the other they were characterized with covert misgivings as "iron monsters" and "dragons of mightier power, . . . breathing smoke and flame through their blackened lungs." By the Civil War years modern technology had become a source of both pride and fear, of revulsion as well as excitement, among our forebears; a similar ambivalence toward technology is familiar in our own century.

Even Thoreau, who had little use for most of the mechanical gadgetry that so enthralled his countrymen, revealed contradictory feelings. "Our inventions," he charged in *Walden,* "are wont to be pretty toys, which distract our attention from serious things. They are but improved means to an unimproved end, an end which it was already but too easy to arrive at; as railroads lead to Boston or New York." Still, both sight and sound of the locomotive aroused Thoreau's undenied interest. He describes with evident pleasure the "golden and silver wreaths" of the steam cloud trailing behind it; he notes with admiration the regularity of its passage and acknowledges its tireless energy; he goes on to salute the "enterprise and bravery" of commerce generally—though not without significant qualification: "If all were as it seems, and men made the elements their servants for noble ends! . . . If the enterprise were as heroic and commanding as it is protracted and unwearied!" And finally, with particular reference to the machine itself, the veritable Iron Horse: "I will not have my eyes put out by its smoke and steam and hissing."

Emerson, Thoreau's Concord mentor, took a somewhat different view of the railroad. But as befitted a man carrying "a Greek head on stout Yankee shoulders," as James Russell Lowell said of him, he too, from the very beginning, had a double reaction to this latest means of travel. In the spring of 1834, meditating about an excursion by rail, when "our tea-kettle hissed along through a field of mayflowers," first the Yankee in him thought of its "hitherto uncomputed mechanical advantages"; then the philosopher took over, seeing "a practical confirmation of the ideal philosophy that Matter is phenomenal whilst men & trees & barns whiz by you as fast as the leaves of a dictionary. . . . The very permanence of matter seems compromised." So Emerson wrote in his private journal.

Like Wordsworth before him, who had described man's inventions as Nature's "lawful offspring," Emerson found no essential difference between the bounty of Nature herself and the artificial products of man's mind and hand. Moreover, with his dynamic conception of an inner life ever seeking to express itself outwardly in whatever form might readily serve, he made no hard-and-fast distinction between the so-called fine arts and those thought of only as useful. Thus he affirmed in "The Poet" (1844) that "the factory-village, and the railway" are, for the true poet, as much a part of nature as "the bee-hive, or the spider's geometrical web"; all are outward expressions of the Life Within that gave them birth and being.

Such an inclusive view of nature and art, such a poetic vision, Emerson readily acknowledged, was not yet that of his age, for all its confirmed interest in material things: "I look in vain for the poet whom I describe," he wrote. But "America is a poem in our eyes . . . and it will not wait long for metres."

Eleven years later, having received from an ex-newspaperman in Brooklyn a small volume of unconventional verse called *Leaves of Grass,* Emerson felt that his call for the poet and the poetry he wished for was being answered at last. Writing to Walt Whitman in 1855, he praised Whitman's new book as "the most extraordinary piece of wit and wisdom that America has yet contributed." Whitman's response to Emerson's fulsome comments was exuberant, though not exactly to the master's liking. Without asking permission, he passed the letter along for publication in the *New York Tribune,* he printed it again himself in the 1856 edition of *Leaves of Grass,* and he had stamped on the spine of the book one of Emerson's most generous sentences: "I greet you at the beginning of a great career. R. W. Emerson."

For Whitman, who in "Song of the Exposition" (1876) was to call on his special Muse to "migrate from Greece and Ionia" to "a better, fresher, busier sphere" in the New World, the Emersonian regard for modern inventions as fit subjects for modern poetry was welcome confirmation of his own taste and inclination, which was unreservedly given to what Emerson had termed "the barbarism and materialism of the times." Unlike his more genteel Bostonian contemporaries, Whitman discerned that the poetic Muse—that "illustrious emigré"—was manifestly answering his own invitation to migrate by "making directly" for nineteenth-century America,

> By thud of machinery and shrill steam-whistle undismay'd,
> Bluff'd not a bit by drain-pipe, gasometers, artificial fertilizers,
> Smiling and pleas'd with palpable intent to stay,
> She's here, install'd amid the kitchen ware![2]

It was probably inevitable that Whitman should repeatedly work locomotives into such later verses as "A Song of Joys" (1860) and "Passage to India" (1871), feeling as strongly as he did about the poetic qualities of machinery and the sound of steam whistles. "To a Locomotive in Winter" (1876) directly addresses his "fierce-throated beauty," the basic intention being (according to his preliminary note) to "Ring the bell all through & blow the whistle." In the poem, rich in both auditory and visual imagery, he calls on the machine itself to "serve the Muse and merge in verse, even as here I see thee":

> Thee in the driving storm even as now, the snow, the winter-day
>   declining,
> Thee in thy panoply, thy measur'd dual throbbing and thy beat
>   convulsive,
> Thy black cylindric body, golden brass and silvery steel,
> Thy ponderous side-bars, parallel and connecting rods, gyrating,
>   shuddering at thy sides,
> Thy metrical, now swelling pant and roar, now tapering in the
>   distance,
> Thy great protruding head-light fix'd in front,
> Thy long, pale, floating vapor-pennants, tinged with delicate purple,
> Thy dense and murky clouds out-belching from thy smoke-stack,
> Thy knitted frame, thy springs and valves, the tremulous twinkle of
>   thy wheels,
> Thy train of cars behind, obedient, merrily following,
> Through gale or calm, now swift, now slack, yet steadily careering;
> Type of the modern—emblem of motion and power—pulse of the
>   continent. . . .

"To a Locomotive in Winter" has had an indifferent reception, both popular and critical, since Whitman's day. I happen to like it, though, honestly, I'm not sure whether I respond in my vocational capacity as a sometime teacher of literature or simply as a railroad buff of long standing. I applaud Whitman's effort, being mindful not only of Emerson's teaching in "The Poet" but also of Hart Crane's warning that "unless poetry can absorb the machine, i.e., *acclimatize* it as naturally and casually as trees, cattle, galleons, castles," it has "failed of its full contemporary function." If Whitman, obeying the Emersonian injunction to translate modern America into poetry, has even partially succeeded in realizing the locomotive as "Type of the modern—emblem of motion and power—pulse of the continent," he has to that degree countered an assumption of traditional artists noted in *The Education of Henry Adams* (1907): "The power embodied in a railway train could never be embodied in art."

Few poets of the nineteenth century even attempted such an embodiment, as Adams was well aware, although there is another surprising exception besides Whitman: Emily Dickinson, in a playful poem that has been called "her cartoon of a railway train":

> I like to see it lap the Miles—
> And lick the Valleys up—
> And stop to feed itself at Tanks—
> And then—prodigious step
>
> Around a Pile of Mountains—
> And supercilious peer
> In Shanties—by the sides of Roads—
> And then a Quarry pare
>
> To fit its Ribs
> And crawl between
> Complaining all the while
> In horrid—hooting stanza—
> Then chase itself down Hill—
>
> And neigh like Boanerges—
> Then—punctual as a Star
> Stop—docile and omnipotent
> At its own stable door—[3]

These lines may have been suggested in part by a "remarkable truth" that Dickinson had presumably come across in a newspaper: that every locomotive "has a distinct individuality of its own." A related idea, that of an interpersonal relationship between man and machine, is illustrated in certain versions of the ubiquitous popular ballad of "Casey Jones," that "brave engineer" who had his own unmistakable way with the Iron Horse and with its steam whistle—the feature so beloved of Whitman. "All the switchmen knew by the engine's moans, / That the man at the throttle was Casey Jones." When Casey "Took his farewell journey to the Promised Land" aboard his doomed locomotive, his "Fireman jumped off" safely before the final crash, "but Casey stayed on," like the traditional captain going down with his ship, with the engine's whistle screaming forth his warning to the endangered train ahead.

Among more finished works by such recognized American poets as Carl Sandburg and William Carlos Williams, it is the sense of movement through space and time that they celebrate in their verse dealing with railroads; their fascination is with the movement that the power of the locomotive made possible rather than with the Iron Horse itself. So in literature as in life, the railroads carried immigrants and easterners to the West and Midwest. Often the moving train becomes a symbol of escape from the ordinary life of farms and small towns, like Melville's ships leaving the land behind and heading for the open sea. So it is for Sandburg's "Mamie," whose romantic dreams of escape to the big city from her Indiana home are nourished as she sees the morning papers brought by train from far-off Chicago and watches the dwindling trail of smoke as a locomotive disappears down the tracks. (Poor Mamie! She finally *goes* to Chicago, where—disillusioned, but still a dreamer—she wonders about some even bigger city to which the railroad might yet take her.)[4]

In American prose, long before Mamie's escape by train from Indiana, Hepzibah and Clifford Pyncheon, in what Nathaniel Hawthorne called "The Flight of Two Owls," had also chosen the railroad in a desperate effort to get away from their ancestral curse in *The House of the Seven Gables* (1851). The hapless Clifford, under the illusion of freedom while aboard a moving train, extravagantly hails the railroads as "positively the greatest blessing that the ages have wrought out for us." But Hawthorne himself was obviously less sanguine about the supposed blessings of "Modern Progress."

Earlier, in "The Celestial Railroad" (1843), where he had ironically professed to describe an easier way to heaven than the route followed in an
earlier day by Bunyan's toiling pilgrims, he had also provided cautionary
signs for his readers. The engineer, "own brother to the engine that he
rides upon," is Apollyon, the "old antagonist" of Bunyan's struggling
Christian, who now seems happily transformed by the spirit of progress
into a useful citizen; his Iron Horse, however, looks "much more like a sort
of mechanical demon, that would hurry us to the infernal regions, than a
laudable contrivance for smoothing our way to the Celestial City."

In later American writing of a more realistic cast the railroad figures
repeatedly as the normal means of long-distance transportation—if not
to heaven or hell, at least to wherever the trains are running—during the
hundred years between travel by stagecoach and our own century of travel
by automobile or airplane. Within less than a dozen years of Mark Twain's
trip to Nevada Territory by stage in 1861, passengers were crossing the
entire continent in "Pullman's hotels on wheels," as he noted in *Roughing
It* (1872). The well-appointed trains represented a new standard of luxury
for many Americans. "Ever been in a parlor-car before?" asks the groom
in Stephen Crane's "The Bride Comes to Yellow Sky" (1898), a story with
a Texas setting. "No," the bride replies. "I never was. It's fine, ain't it?"
"Great," he returns. "And then after a while we'll go forward to the diner,
and get a big lay-out. Finest meal in the world. Charge a dollar."

Now, alas, not only the dollar meal but also parlor cars, diners, and all
have for the most part vanished like the figures in Sandburg's "Limited":
their coaches and diners and sleepers have long since become scrap and rust
and their passengers of another era have indeed passed into ashes.[5]

Moving to the city in American fiction, one finds William Dean Howells
in *A Hazard of New Fortunes* (1890) celebrating "the superb spectacle" of
New York at night. "In the Central Depot" are "the great night trains
lying on the tracks dim under the rain of gas-lights," waiting there "like
fabled monsters of Arab story ready for the magician's touch, tractable,
reckless, willless—organized lifelessness full of a strange semblance of life."
Howells evidently "admired the impressive sight," sharing his characters'
"thrill of patriotic pride in the fact that the whole world perhaps could
not afford" anything quite like it. Such an attitude was a common one at
the time. By 1892, according to a double-edged passage in *The Education
of Henry Adams,* the American railway system seemed to have become the

"one active interest" of the country, an interest "to which all others were subservient, and which absorbed the energies of some sixty million people to the exclusion of every other force, real or imaginary." American society was "content with its creation, for the time, and with itself for creating it."

But not all Americans were unreservedly proud of the railroads and their place in national life. Of course the burgeoning companies and their customers were fair game for those more interested in making money than in serving the public, whether they were robber barons manipulating rail stocks on Wall Street or humbler villains like those depicted in that early movie *The Great Train Robbery* (1903). Thoreau had asked in *Walden* whether Americans rode on the railroads or the railroads on Americans; his question about masters and servants was posed again at the beginning of a new century in Frank Norris's novel *The Octopus* (1901). His book concerns the struggle of a group of California wheat farmers against the ruthlessly monopolistic Pacific and Southwestern Railroad—a transparent disguise for the grasping Southern Pacific of Stanford, Huntington, and Harriman.

Norris saw these opposing forces as respective embodiments of Nature, symbolized chiefly by the wheat, and of the Machine, the System—the railroad generally and the Iron Horse in particular. The contrast is sharply drawn in the very first chapter of *The Octopus,* where a herd of sheep, breaking through a wire fence, wanders onto the track, there to be run down by a speeding engine—an "iron monster . . . , merciless, inexorable," like the whole economic mechanism it both serves and represents. To the poet Presley, a surrogate for Norris himself who witnesses this "massacre of innocents," the locomotive is a "terror of steel and steam, with its single eye, Cyclopean," whistling "with the accents of menace and defiance," appearing to him as "the symbol of a vast power, huge, terrible, flinging the echo of its thunder over all the reaches of the valley, leaving blood and destruction on its path, the leviathan, with tentacles of steel clutching into the soil, the soulless Force, the iron-hearted Power, the monster, the Colossus, the Octopus."

There is a similar polarity, rhetorically understated by comparison, in one of the poems included in Robert Frost's volume of 1928, *West-Running Brook.* A lone man who hates the railroad would gladly wreck a passing engine if only he could. "Too late though, now," he cries. Then, picking up a turtle's living egg, he confronts "the gods in the machine":

"I am armed for war.
The next machine that has the power to pass
Will get this plasm in its goggle glass."[6]

More commonly, however, mention of the railroad in American writing of the 1920s and 1930s involves not confrontation but evocation.

Consider Nick Carraway in Scott Fitzgerald's *Great Gatsby* (1925), with his nostalgic "memories . . . of coming back West" at Christmastime on "the thrilling returning trains of my youth," the "murky yellow cars of the Chicago, Milwaukee & St. Paul railroad," passing "the dim lights of small Wisconsin stations" on its way to the Twin Cities. Think of Thomas Wolfe and his various fictional spokesmen, responding with all their senses to the sights, sounds, and movement of the railroad—even to "the acrid and powerfully exciting smell of engine smoke." In railroad stations across the country Wolfe's characters admire the waiting locomotives, which, "passive and alert as cats, purred and panted softly, with the couched menace of their tremendous stroke." This is from *Of Time and the River* (1935), which is characteristically filled with images of a vast, sprawling America rushing past in the night outside the windows of her darkened passenger trains,

> the great barn-shapes and solid shadows in the running sweep of the moon-whited countryside, the wailing whistle of the fast express . . . flares and steamings on the tracks, and the swing and bob and tottering dance of lanterns in the yards; . . . dings and knellings and the sudden glare of mighty engines over sleeping faces in the night; . . . the Transcontinental Limited . . . stroking eighty miles an hour across the continent and the small dark towns whip by like bullets. . . .

For Fitzgerald and Wolfe, with their recurrent feeling for the passage of time, the loss of youth and the dream, these remembered trains were symbolic less of modern progress than of an era already vanishing—vanishing with a speed that even they themselves could scarcely realize, though both lived long enough to be familiar with the newer modes of travel that in a relatively few years would doom most railroad passenger service in the United States. The "terrific pistoned wheels" of the steam locomotive that so entranced Wolfe gave way in the 1940s and 1950s to the prosaic trucks of the more efficient but far less romantic diesel. And those expressive steam whistles, worthy of Walt Whitman's admiration and responsive to the expert touch of a Casey Jones, were succeeded by merely blatant air horns—though at the time of conversion from steam to diesel power the Chicago and North Western assured the public that the horns on its shiny new engines were being tuned to sound as much like the old steam whistles as possible!

But an age has now passed, the Age of Steam, and the poetic spectacle of the older locomotives is gone from the rails—excepting, of course, a few retired Iron Horses, standing patiently along the main line as fixed monuments to other times, or museum dwellers occasionally brought out of their stables for excursion runs into yesterday. If you visit a railroad museum—there are many across the country—where the rolling stock is not altogether off limits, climb into the cupola of a freight train's caboose and look ahead, like the boy in William Faulkner's "The Bear" (1935/1942), at all that's left from the Age of Steam: "Then the little locomotive shrieked and began to move: a rapid churning of exhaust, a lethargic deliberate clashing of slack couplings travelling backward along the train, the exhaust changing to the deep slow clapping bites of power as the caboose too began to move. . . ." So it is with a little ten-wheeler Baldwin I know, built in 1906 and ultimately retired to pasture in North Freedom, Wisconsin, after years of faithful service in Faulkner's South.

Now we are back in the present, no longer in the Age of Steam but in the new Age of Flight—like it or not. Yes, the railroads are still very much in operation, though chiefly as freight-haulers. But who today is making poems about moving wheat or coal by unit trains, about piggyback loading, and about double-headed diesels? By and large, traveling Americans have cast their votes for speed, thus shifting allegiance from the railroad to a newer, faster "emblem of motion and power," a newer symbol of modernity than the old Iron Horse. In our hurried times, when human beings are journeying not only across the plains, or from small towns to the city, but around the moon, the popular imagination is not likely to fix itself on an earth-bound AMTRAK train. The older locomotive still surviving and active—and of course I mean the working steam engine, with its mechanism honestly visible, busily smoking, hissing, and whistling, not a buttoned-up diesel—can no longer typify "the modern" as it did for Whitman in 1876; the competition has undoubtedly taken over. For us the Iron Horse is less a symbol, even of the past, than just a relic—a literal museum-piece, standing at the end of the line and addressing us directly like Frost's "Oven Bird," asking "in all but words . . . what to make of a diminished thing."

9.

Emerson Then and Now

"The fame of a great man is not rigid and stony like his bust. It changes with time. It needs time to give it due perspective." So said Ralph Waldo Emerson in 1835, in the course of an early lecture, "Milton," adding that a man's fame "characterizes those who give it, as much as him who receives it." If this remark was true of Milton's reputation in the nineteenth century, and indeed it was, it is equally applicable to Emerson's own fame in the twentieth, with a genuine Emerson revival under way—a revival that reached a high point in 1982, the centennial anniversary of his death, and has continued even more vigorously since that time.

The Emerson revival is a comparatively recent development, as I have cause to know. Nearly thirty years ago, not long after I had joined an editorial team working on a projected scholarly edition of Emerson's *Journals and Miscellaneous Notebooks,* a concerned colleague from another discipline paid a special visit to my study to give me a friendly warning: since Emerson had nothing to say to present generations, it would be the ruin of my professional career if I became known as an "Emersonian." But I survived professionally, and by 1982 the new edition of the *Journals* stood complete in sixteen volumes. A scholar already known for his two books on Emerson, Joel Porte, has since published a volume of selections from the complete text called *Emerson in His Journals,* intended primarily for the general reader, and other Emersonians—or would-be Emersonians—have come out of the closet everywhere. More than two dozen books on Emerson have appeared since the 1950s, and I know of several more, including one of mine, that are either in progress or actually in press. Once again, Emerson is "in."

During Emerson's own day his fame developed only gradually, first in his native New England through the 1820s and 1830s, then in the mid-Atlantic states and across the ocean in England and Scotland during the 1840s, and finally in what was then "the West"—Ohio, Illinois, Missouri, Michigan, Wisconsin—during the 1850s. In these years he became known initially as a preacher, then as a lecturer, an essayist, and a poet. To many listeners and readers, however, he was a controversial figure. His address to the senior class at the Harvard Divinity School in 1838 outraged conservative Unitarians and led one of them, Andrews Norton—nicknamed "the Unitarian Pope"—to fulminate in his celebrated "Discourse on the Latest Form of Infidelity." In secular affairs, Emerson's long refusal to turn his hatred of slavery into political activism disappointed his more radical contemporaries in the Abolitionist movement, but when he approved John Brown's resort to violence in the 1850s he again shocked conservatives. Even so, he gradually became "the most steadily attractive lecturer in America," according to James Russell Lowell, and by the 1860s he was considered something of a national institution. Lowell, writing in 1868, recognized "how much the country's intellectual emancipation was due to the stimulus of his teaching and example," but he felt that younger members of Emerson's audiences were beginning to take him for granted.

It is ironic that Emerson's greatest fame—and, incidentally, his highest fees as a lecturer—came during his later years, when his most original thinking and writing were behind him and both his physical and his mental powers were failing. By the time of his death in 1882 his admirers had come to speak of him with the awe and reverence due a saint, and over the next twenty years, as the centennial of his birth in 1803 approached, Emerson's biographers and critics erected a "rigid and stony" statue of him—a statue whose "shape and pose," in the words of H. L. Kleinfield, "clashed with the figure of the man and the spirit of his beliefs." Kleinfield makes this observation in a fascinating essay in cultural history called "The Structure of Emerson's Death," in which he explores what newspapers and magazines were saying about Emerson as the nineteenth century gave way to the twentieth. It was just that "rigid and stony" image against which later generations were to react so strongly, beginning with the general revolt against one's parents and grandparents, literal or figurative, that characterized the years of World War I and the decade that followed it. That nineteenth-century writers like Emerson in this country and Matthew

Arnold in England had become symbols of all that the young of that period rejected is tellingly illustrated in a poem of 1915 by T. S. Eliot about "Cousin Nancy": her aunts look on in obvious puzzlement as she pursues everything that is "modern," while "Matthew and Waldo" keep their silent watch "upon the glazen shelves."

It was that very conception of Emerson as an inflexible "guardian of the faith" and champion of "unalterable law" that was in the mind of my colleague of the 1960s who warned me that for the twentieth century, Waldo Emerson was not only dead but forever incapable of resurrection. Yet it is not difficult to show how greatly the living figure of Emerson the man and the life-giving spirit of his writings contrast with this lifeless image. For a typical example, consider the opening paragraph of his first book, *Nature,* published in 1836, when he was thirty-three:

> Our age is retrospective. It builds the sepulchres of the fathers. It writes biographies, histories, and criticism. The foregoing generations beheld God and nature face to face; we, through their eyes. Why should not we also enjoy an original relation to the universe? Why should not we have a poetry and philosophy of insight and not of tradition, and a religion by revelation to us, and not the history of theirs? . . . [W]hy should we grope among the dry bones of the past, or put the living generation into masquerade out of its faded wardrobe? The sun shines today also. There is more wool and flax in the fields. There are new lands, new men, new thoughts. Let us demand our own works and laws and worship.

Words such as these made Emerson appear a dangerous radical to some of his contemporaries, just as certain men of *this* century who have worked innovatively in the Emersonian spirit—Frank Lloyd Wright, for an apt example—have seemed beyond the pale to followers of tradition rather than insight. "Beware when the great God lets loose a thinker on this planet," said Emerson in 1841. "Then all things are at risk." Staunch traditionalists do not *like* to think of all things as being "at risk"; indeed, some would prefer not to think at all! Yet Emerson himself characterized his "true scholar," his *American* Scholar, as *"Man Thinking"*—capital *M* and capital *T*— speaking *for* all mankind *to* all mankind. And what he liked to call "the scholar's courage" was a form of self-reliance, his cardinal principle. As early as 1833, when he was thirty, he affirmed that "A man contains all that is needful to his government within himself. He is made a law unto himself. All real good or evil that can befall him must be from himself. He only can do himself any good or any harm. . . . The purpose of life seems to be to acquaint a man with himself." Then comes the key sentence: "The highest revelation is that God is in every man."

For Waldo Emerson, as these remarkable words should make crystal clear, the vital center of his thinking, and especially of his concept of self-reliance, was his intuitive certainty of a divine presence within the private self. On this moral and religious basis he deplored imitation of any model, however fine, and refused conformity to all wholly external patterns, rituals, creeds, sects, parties, precedents, curricula, or institutions of any kind, including churches, colleges, and governments. The law he followed, though wholly internal, was rigorous: "If any one imagine that this law is lax," as he said in his essay "Self-Reliance," "let him keep its commandments one day." When a man can look within and "read God directly," as "The American Scholar" has it, the hour is too precious for secondhand readings. Holding to this conviction, and looking back with a measure of detachment on the Divinity School controversy of 1838, he could write two years later, "In all my lectures I have taught one doctrine, namely, the infinitude of the private man." His conception of "the private man," essentially religious, idealistic, and optimistic, was the basis of his faith in democracy, in "a nation of men" in which each individual is—potentially if not actually—"inspired by the Divine Soul which also inspires all men."

From Emerson's day to our own, many listeners and readers have ignored or misconstrued both the religious and the democratic implications of his thought. In 1860, for example, a Wisconsin newspaper, the *Kenosha Democrat,* labeled him as both "an infidel" and "a monarchist"; in the twentieth century, though Unitarians and Universalists have come to terms with him, there are still orthodox Trinitarians who regard him as heretical, as there are political egalitarians who think him elitist. Both then and now, some listeners and readers have found him obscure or impractical; even his Scottish friend Thomas Carlyle once called his writings "moonshine." On the other hand, by the principle of guilt by association, still others have made him out to be an apostle of American rugged individualism—Andrew Carnegie read Emerson, and so now does Woody Hayes—or of German fascism: Friedrich Nietzsche read Emerson, and, since Adolf Hitler read Nietzsche, Emerson somehow begat Hitler's version of the *Übermensch.*

In a baccalaureate address of 1981 the president of Yale University added his indictment on the basis of a single essay, "Power" (1860), charging Emerson with worshiping sheer naked energy and force: through his teaching, declared the late A. Bartlett Giamatti, Emerson "freed our politics and our politicians from any sense of restraint by extolling self-generated, unaffiliated power as the best foot to place in the small of the back in front of you."

To those with Yale associations who also know Emerson, these were fighting words, and I'm sure that President Giamatti heard from more than one alumnus who endeavored to set him straight about the real nature of Emersonian self-reliance. It is undeniably true, however, that if one cuts Emerson's individualism loose from its religious roots, as secular-minded readers and skeptical critics may very well do, it *can* be made to support a frightening concept of self-centeredness and self-advancement at the expense of others—essentially the same ghost that has haunted political theorists since the time of Plato, who wrote in the *Republic* that tyranny is the necessary sequel to individualism and the democratic state. But Emerson never advocated the divorce between self-reliance and God-reliance that his hostile critics seem to take for granted, and to charge *him* with responsibility for what other men have made of his teaching is surely to fire at the wrong target.

On the more positive side, what has long engaged Emersonians is less a body of doctrine than the spirit of the man himself. "We do not go to hear what Emerson says so much as to hear Emerson," wrote Lowell in the nineteenth century; during my years in the classroom I used to hear something very similar from students about *reading* Emerson. At first many of them were puzzled, expecting to find in his writings the kind of logical arguments and reasoned conclusions that are the staples of academic philosophy. But Emerson was not a philosopher, or a theologian, or even an academic. In his own self-image he was simply "the Scholar," and for him, as we know, the true scholar was never "a mere thinker" but a surrogate for all mankind: the Scholar is "*Man* Thinking." "In every work of genius," he wrote in the essay "Self-Reliance," "we recognize our own rejected thoughts," and in his own writings, it has been well said by Lyon Richardson, other thinkers have found "diaries of their own which they had not kept." If that statement applies to Emerson's published works it is even more true of his less-polished writing—his letters, his sermons and lectures, and above all, his journals and notebooks, which were not fully available in print until the new edition appeared.

In the lectures, as we have come to see since the manuscript texts have been published, Emerson included more personal anecdotes and even more humor than he permitted himself in his formal essays, where he maintained a greater distance between author and reader than there had been between speaker and lecture-goer. The journals bring Emerson even closer. "Life," he once wrote, "consists in what a man is thinking of all day," and much of Emerson's own thinking is recorded in the journals, the "Savings Bank" from which he drew the basic material of his sermons, lectures, and essays.

Early in this century, it should be said, the journals were published in part, first in a ten-volume edition prepared by Emerson's son and grandson that appeared between 1909 and 1914 and later in a single volume of selections in 1926, but in the fashion of their day the editors presented a genteel and decorous Emerson—always "*Mr.* Emerson," a carefully crafted image that seems singularly bloodless, especially to any modern scholar who has gone to the manuscripts themselves, as I have been fortunate enough to do, or worked with the new sixteen-volume Harvard edition, or even read through the shorter *Emerson in His Journals.* The current interest in Emerson is directly traceable to the rediscovery of the man behind the formal writings, "not rigid and stony like his bust," in Emerson's own phrasing, but a living, breathing, *thinking* human being. "Emerson's revised reputation," an Emersonian wrote prophetically thirty years ago, "will be founded upon a thoroughgoing critical revaluation of the Journals." Much work since then has indeed been *journal-centered,* and such study has in turn served to modify presentation of Emerson in the classroom and to the general public.

Of course there have always been readers of Emerson, from his day to ours, who knew all along that the man was alive in his writings. But for others, those who for the first time have gone behind the long-prevailing public image, what Emerson himself said of a man's changing reputation has certainly proved true: his fame not only "needs time to give it due perspective," but it "characterizes those who give it, as much as him who receives it."

10.

The Scholar Idealized

I have reached the middle age of man; yet I believe I am not less
glad or sanguine at the meeting of scholars, than when, a boy,
I first saw the graduates of my own College assembled at their
anniversary. Neither years nor books have yet failed to extirpate
a prejudice then rooted in me, that a scholar is the favorite of
Heaven and earth, the excellency of his country, the happiest
of men.

—Emerson, "Literary Ethics" (*CW* 1:99)

On 24 July 1838, speaking by invitation before the literary societies of Dartmouth College, Ralph Waldo Emerson delivered an
oration on the scholar's place in society that he later published
under the title "Literary Ethics." Should any of his student listeners be
thinking of themselves as called by God "to explore truth and beauty," the
orator admonished them in his peroration to "be bold, be firm, be true"
and dare to choose the life of a scholar. "The hour of that choice is the
crisis of your history," he declared; "see that you hold yourself fast by the
intellect" (*CW* 1:115).

In his public addresses Emerson often drew freely but guardedly on his
own experience; for him, "the capital secret" of a writer and speaker is "to
convert life into truth" (*CW* 1:86). When telling the Dartmouth students
that the hour of vocational choice is "the crisis of your history" he was surely
remembering his own decision, made shortly before he turned twenty-one,
to enter the Unitarian ministry—a decision he came to regret in time.
While still in his thirties he had resigned his first pastorate at Boston after

less than three years of service and begun a protracted search for a new calling. Between 1832 and 1838, the year of his appearance at Dartmouth, he was regularly speaking and writing, both as an occasional supply preacher and, with increasing success, as a secular lecturer and orator. Although he continued to regard the clergy as "always, more universally than any other class, the scholars of their day," as he said in 1837 (*CW* 1:59), he ultimately gave up preaching altogether in favor of lecturing and publishing, no longer using the title "Reverend." By 1837 he was thinking of himself simply as a scholar among scholars.

Central to Emerson's mature thought is a basic dichotomy between the actual and the ideal—or, in the Coleridgean terminology he used in the 1830s, between the mundane province of the Understanding and the ideal realm of the Reason. As early as December of 1834 he had applied this distinction to his idea of the scholar: "there is a real object in Nature . . . [,] the intellectual man," he wrote in his Journal A, "& though the scholar is not that object, he is its representative, & is, with more or less symptoms of distrust, honored for that which he ought to be" (*JMN* 4:370). The scholar as we see him in everyday life thus *represents* a perhaps unattainable ideal—a kind of Platonic idea of the Scholar as "the intellectual man"— that can be envisioned only with what Emerson liked to call "the eye of Reason" (*CW* 1:30). Because it is this ideal figure that is celebrated in "The American Scholar," one is not strictly accurate in saying that Emerson "defined himself as the 'American Scholar,'" as Robert E. Spiller once remarked,[1] since Emerson's self-definition pertains to an ideal he had come to conceive rather than an actuality he had in fact attained. In the language of "Circles" (1841), that ideal conception had become the helm which he as scholar sought to obey, "the idea after which all his facts are classified." But any idea is not only subject to "the moral fact of the Unattainable, the flying Perfect, around which the hands of man can never meet"; it is also open to expansion and change: "the principle that seemed to explain nature, will itself be included as one example of a bolder generalization. . . . Every man is not so much a workman in the world, as he is a suggestion of that he should be" (*CW* 2:180, 179, 181).

The concept of the ideal Scholar had gradually taken form in Emerson's private journal—his literary "Savings Bank" (*JMN* 4:250)—during the early 1830s, when the sometime minister who had preached a sermon entitled "Find Your Calling" was still wrestling with problems of vocation and identity. Though natural science, the lives of great men, and landmarks of English literature attracted him in turn when he began giving public lectures, the implications of these topics for moral and religious life were always in his mind. He thought of becoming a naturalist, a lay religious teacher, or perhaps a writer—a poet, in the sense of one who sees and loves "the harmonies that are in the soul & in matter" (*L* 1:435). All of these concerns are taken up in his image of himself as a scholar—ideally, as *the Scholar.*

In August of 1835, with the new formulation well under way, Emerson began making notes in his journal for a future "chapter on Literary Ethics or the Duty & Discipline of a Scholar" (*JMN* 5:84); his entries look forward to both "The American Scholar" in 1837 and "Literary Ethics" the next year. Many a listener and reader since Emerson spoke at Dartmouth in 1838 has taken note of his "frequent invocation of the 'scholar,'" as the junior Henry James did in reviewing Cabot's *Memoir* of Emerson in 1887. James found "a friendly vagueness and convenience" in Emerson's use of the term, which he regarded as "charming yet ever so slightly droll." James thought that by "scholar" Emerson meant "simply the cultivated man, the man who has had a liberal education," and it seemed incongruous to expect of such a person "all the heroic and uncomfortable things, the concentrations and relinquishments, that make up the noble life."[2] But the term had a much more complex meaning for Emerson than James surmised, as later critics have come to see—particularly when the full text of Emerson's journals became available for study. There the word is almost ubiquitous, though Emerson used it less often in his lectures and in his published works other than "The American Scholar" and "Literary Ethics."

A turning point in interpretation since James wrote came in 1939 with a penetrating essay, "Emerson's Problem of Vocation," by the late Henry Nash Smith. If Emerson "found no profession already formed for him" as he separated himself from the church, Smith declared, "he must create one for himself, even if only as an ideal." Moreover, this ideal "must not only be defensible before the world, but also represent adequately all the forces of tradition, temperament, and literary contagion that were at work" in Emerson himself. Of the various figures that he delineated as ideal self-images, and there were many, the most characteristic and certainly the best known, as Smith remarked, "is of course the Scholar." Indeed, "The Scholar is the hero of Emerson's unwritten *Prelude,* and belongs with all the Werthers and the Childe Harolds and the Teufelsdröckhs of the period."3

Smith's fine essay might well have grown into a full-length biography of Emerson had its author not turned his attention from New England to the American West and from Emerson to Mark Twain. Certainly all subsequent Emersonians have had to take account of his provocative analysis, whether or not we accept all of Smith's hypotheses in other sections of his essay. He was surely right in saying, for instance, that one can understand "the strongly apologetic basis of Emerson's conception of the Scholar" only by envisaging the Scholar's polar opposite, whatever his label—"the Actor," as Smith called him, or "the Man of the World," as Emerson himself referred to the antitype Napoleon in *Representative Men* (1850). But my own investigations have led me to think that the terms *actor* and *action* had anything but fixed connotations for Emerson, so that once again their every occurrence also "presents a fresh problem" for the reader (to borrow a phrase from Smith). Smith's objection that "The American Scholar" in particular addresses "the issue of Action *versus* Contemplation" only in "a long and confused discussion"4 demands reconsideration.

Since 1939 there have been illuminating studies of such talismanic Emersonian phrasing as "correspondence," "freedom and fate," "truth and nature," "race and history," "virtue," "compensation," and "the soul,"5 but neither *action* nor the magic word *scholar* itself has yet received the thorough examination they both deserve. None of Emerson's several biographers fully tests Smith's identification of the Scholar as the protagonist of Emerson's "unwritten *Prelude*," although the late Stephen Whicher's "Inner Life" of 1953 posited a change in Emerson's self-conception following his "second crisis" of 1838–1844 and so implicitly challenged Smith's assertion that "the ideal of the Scholar seems not to have undergone any significant evolution" in his thinking after 1842. But Smith's detailed examination of the canon stopped with "The Transcendentalist" (1841) without going on to trace the course of Emerson's thinking through the eventful decades of the 1840s and 1850s. Instead, he cited only two very late addresses, "The Man of Letters" (1863) and "The Scholar" (1876), which in his words "are little more than repetitions of Emerson's earlier utterances."6

Smith's groundbreaking essay appeared before the publication of Emerson's *Letters* and *Early Lectures* and the new editions of his *Journals and Miscellaneous Notebooks* and *Collected Works*. There is more to be learned about the evolving concept of the Scholar from these new editions, the full text of the journals in particular. But though some of the critics making use of these primary sources have challenged Whicher's interpretation of the later Emerson, as Leonard Neufeldt explicitly does in *The House of Emerson* (1982), Smith's contention that Emerson's "ideal of the Scholar" remained essentially unchanged after 1842 has yet to be systematically reexamined.

The purpose of my *Emerson on the Scholar* (1992) is to trace Emerson's self-image as the Scholar throughout his mature years, from its beginnings in the early 1830s until the very end of his life. Part One of that book, "Toward 'The American Scholar,'" shows how the term gradually took on special meaning for him during the early 1830s. Dissatisfaction with his role as a Unitarian minister led him first to resign his pulpit and then to identify in turn with various personae, such as the Naturalist, the Teacher, the Poet, and the Thinker, as he sought both a new vocation and a new identity. Between 1835 and 1837, the year "The American Scholar" was written, the long-familiar image of the Scholar emerged as the ideal figure of greatest significance. As "Man Thinking," the idealized Scholar of the oration ultimately subsumed *all* of these converging roles. Part Two, "The Scholar Engaged," deals with the period of challenge and testing that began with the storm over Emerson's Divinity School Address of 1838 and continued through more than two decades of personal and civic crises. His "angle of vision," as he called it, was consistently that of the Scholar, though he seldom invoked the term explicitly unless he was addressing an academic audience. To understand his thinking during these later years about the Scholar—and particularly about the Scholar's duty as a member of society—requires consideration of the whole context of his speaking and writing.

Long before purely academic scholars in this country began fulminating over the supposed dichotomy of "publish or perish," Emerson consistently affirmed that "the true scholar"—a favorite phrase—must be both a *see*-er and a *say*-er; for him there could be no real severance between the pursuit of learning and its dissemination. The scholar and the teacher, he believed, were essentially one. A much more troublesome problem for him, as Smith long ago pointed out, was the proper role of the scholar-teacher in the world of public affairs: should the see-er be a *do*-er as well as a *say*-er, a man of action as well as a man of thought?

Emerson in fact believed that the scholar has the duty and responsibility to "act upon the Public," as he said as early as 1834 (*JMN* 4:368). But did action mean participating directly in public affairs and taking a stand on every issue of the day? In particular, how deeply should Waldo Emerson involve himself in active opposition to slavery, an institution that he abhorred? From the years of his pastorate in Boston, when he opened his pulpit to the reform agitator Samuel May, this was an increasingly acute question for Emerson; on the eve of the Civil War he surprised even some of his closest friends and deeply offended his more conservative contemporaries by his public support of John Brown, both before and after the events of 1859 at Harpers Ferry. On the pressing issue of slavery, it seems clear, his thinking underwent a gradual evolution, and that evolution is reflected too in his conception of the public duty of scholars as representatives of Intellect. To follow what he came to say and do in the 1840s and after is not only to grasp the full development of Emerson's thought but also to encounter a perennial challenge: what part should any man or woman of ideas play in American society, then and now?

Throughout the writing of *Emerson on the Scholar* I kept in mind that "fundamental law of criticism" that Emerson himself liked to cite from George Fox: works under examination, like the Scriptures themselves, must be interpreted "by the same spirit that gave them forth" (*JMN* 4:31; cf. *JMN* 4:94; *EL* 1:170, 210–11; *CW* 1:23). "The key to every man is his thought," Emerson wrote (*CW* 2:180), and since "life" for him consisted "in what a man is thinking of all day," as he said in the 1840s (*JMN* 10:146; *W* 12:10), the primary focus here is on the course of his own thinking over the years, not on his literary sources. Though Emerson read widely, his goal as a writer and speaker was original creation. "Books are for the scholar's idle times," he declared in a memorable passage of "The American Scholar," believing as he did that when the scholar "can read God directly, the hour is too precious to be wasted in other men's transcripts of their readings" (*CW* 1:57). Seeking to interpret Emerson's thinking about the Scholar by the spirit that gave it forth, I have honored these characteristic pronouncements.

The Man and the Scholar Today

Throughout his career Emerson used the term *scholar* to include a variety of intellectual activities: those of clerics, orators, poets, philosophers, and writers generally—even traveling lecturers. "The true scholar," he held, will be perpetually a student, always learning, always thinking—not only for himself but also as the cause of thinking in others; he will be a sayer as well as a seer and thus a teacher as well as a student. In one sense Smith was surely correct in his conclusion of 1939 that Emerson's conception of the scholar "seems not to have undergone any significant evolution" during the 1840s and after: as late as the 1870s Emerson still thought of scholars as representing, more or less faithfully, the intellectual ideal. But by that period, in response to events of the day and to his low estimate of professional scholars among his contemporaries, his understanding of the scholar's ethics, or his "duty and discipline," and particularly of what he himself *ought* to be saying and doing as an American and a scholar, had undergone significant change.

It was during the 1840s, when the former clergyman's thinking became more secular, more critical and even skeptical, that Emerson began to pay greater attention to public affairs and to reappraise his early conviction that the scholar's position with respect to current issues should be solely that of "an observer, a dispassionate reporter, no partisan." Though continually pressed to join actively in organized reform movements, especially the Anti-Slavery Society, to which his wife and many of his Concord friends belonged, he had remained disengaged, committing himself only to reform in general, as a member of what he called the Movement party, rather than to particular causes, and trusting for eventual reform to what he saw as a universal tendency in nature toward "melioration." But beginning in 1844, when he called publicly for America to follow the example of Great Britain and emancipate its slaves, he began gradually to shift his position. Passage in 1850 of the Fugitive Slave Act and its subsequent enforcement in Massachusetts presented him with a scholar's dilemma: should he simply continue his efforts to free those "quite other slaves"—imprisoned spirits and imprisoned thoughts—that he was addressing through his lectures and essays, or should he work actively for Abolition?

Emerson's decision was that as a scholar, he had a moral obligation to do both, though he was scrupulous about separating his public addresses calling for action against slavery from his scheduled lectures and from his published writings. It was the imperatives of what he had long called "the moral sentiment" that finally caused him to abandon the scholar's "armed neutrality," to attack those who condoned the evil of slavery, and to castigate those individuals and educational institutions that had betrayed the scholarly ideal in an age of increasing materialism. True scholars, he said repeatedly, "represent the intellect, by which man is man"—and in that sense he regarded *every* individual as a potential scholar.

During his later and less creative years, while remaining active as a speaker and writer, Emerson drew heavily on the rich literary capital he had stored up in the 1830s and 1840s, but with some modifications. One pertinent example is a change of emphasis in his treatment of intellect and intellectuals: in 1844 he remarked, with reference to Napoleon, that "there is no crime to the intellect," which is "antinomian or hypernomian" (*CW* 3:45), but in the 1850s and 1860s, particularly in addressing college audiences on "the eternal topic the praise of intellect," he came more and more to emphasize his belief in "the unity of thought and morals," the oneness of intellect and the moral sentiment.

The early development of Emerson's conception of the intellectual man, epitomized in his guiding image of the Scholar, and the subsequent testing of that image in later years of crisis, for himself and for his country, were my primary concerns during the writing of *Emerson on the Scholar.* "As a good chimney burns its smoke," he wrote in *Representative Men,* so a thinker like Plato "converts the value of all his fortunes into his intellectual performances" (*CW* 4:25). This conversion of experience into thought and thought into creative expression is manifest in Emerson's thinking and writing as an American Scholar.

11.

"The Flower of Fame"

A Centennial Tribute to Herman Melville

On 29 September 1891 a New York newspaper carried a brief notice headed "Death of a Once Popular Author":

> There died yesterday at his quiet home in this city a man who, although he had done almost no literary work during the past sixteen years, was once one of the most popular writers in the United States.
>
> Herman Melville probably reached the height of his fame about 1852, his first novel having been published about 1847. . . . Of late years Mr. Melville . . . has fallen into a literary decline, as the result of which his books are now little known.
>
> Probably, . . . even his own generation has long thought him dead, so quiet have been the later years of his life.[1]

Another New York paper, also in taking note of Melville's death, observed that in earlier years he had "won considerable fame" by the publication of *Typee.* That first book "was his best work," this paper declared, "although he has since written a number of other stories, which were published more for private than public circulation."[2] Unmentioned among those "other stories" was *Moby-Dick,* now Melville's best-known work, which first appeared in November 1851 but had to wait during the greater part of a century for the recognition he had hoped it would gain. Such were the blooming, the decay, and the much-delayed second growth of what Melville himself once called "The belated funeral flower of fame." His words are from the concluding line of a little-known poem to which he gave the interrogative title "Thy Aim, Thy Aim?" There he employs the flower imagery that he

characteristically used when referring to his own development and, during
his later years, to his faded repute as an author:

> if, living, you kindle a flame,
> Your guerdon will be but a flower,
> Only a flower,
> The flower of repute,
> flower cut down in an hour. (*Poems*, 378)

What I wish to consider here is twofold: Melville's idea of transient
fame and the striking changes that have taken place in his popular and
critical reputation, first during his lifetime, as a once celebrated but then
forgotten writer, and then during the hundred years since his death, when
"the author of *Typee*" returned to prominence as the author of *Moby-Dick*.
The remarkable shift in outlook and values that came with World War
I helps to explain the beginning of the modern Melville Revival, part
of a new awareness among Americans of the strength and variety of our
national literature. By the time of World War II these developments had
made themselves felt on college and university campuses, and along with
Moby-Dick, students were reading such other neglected masterworks of the
1850s as Henry Thoreau's *Walden* and Walt Whitman's "Song of Myself."
In 1956 and again in 1972 the Modern Language Association recognized
Melville, Thoreau, and Whitman as major nineteenth-century writers by
including them in an MLA publication entitled *Eight American Authors: A
Review of Research and Criticism*. But tastes continue to change, and today
the predominance of white males in the MLA's literary canon is under
challenge in some quarters. As we approach the twenty-first century I must
observe that new generations of readers, critics, and classroom teachers are
yet to determine Herman Melville's eventual standing in America.

i. "the author of *Typee*"

As we now know, Herman Melville "reached the height of his fame"
in his own century with the appearance of his fifth book, *White-Jacket,
or The World in a Man-of-War*, in 1850. Thus the high point did not
come "about 1852," as the first newspaper quoted above would have it,

for *Moby-Dick,* published in 1851, was by no measure as well received as *White-Jacket* had been a year before. A former sailor turned writer, Melville had emerged from obscurity in 1846 with *Typee,* the work with which his name would be perennially linked throughout his lifetime; when *Typee* became an immediate success, its young author began to think of himself as a kind of Byron who "woke one morning and found himself famous" (*Correspondence,* 59). *Omoo* (1847), the immediate sequel to *Typee,* the subsequent *Redburn: His First Voyage,* and then *White-Jacket* all enhanced his reputation among reviewers and the reading public alike. When he went to London to arrange for the English publication of *White-Jacket,* he wryly remarked in his journal that he was returning to English soil "after the lapse of ten years—*then* a sailor, *now* H.M. author of 'Peedee' 'Hullabaloo' & 'Pog-Dog' " (*Journals,* 12).

The books on which Melville's growing reputation rested in these years were not "novels," as later usage would have it, but what he himself called "narratives of voyages": works based loosely on his own experience but substantially enhanced by levies on his wide reading and made vivid by his imaginative and rhetorical gifts. But there was one conspicuous exception: *Mardi* (1849), an ambitious experiment in out-and-out fiction that he labored over, during the period between *Omoo* and *Redburn,* for some two years. When *Mardi* pleased neither the critics nor the public, Melville remarked that severe critical notices are "essential to the building up of any permanent reputation—if such should ever prove to be mine." But such a reputation, he felt, could not be based on works meant only "to entertain," and though he had something far greater in mind, popular books were what critics and the public had come to expect from him (*Correspondence,* 130, 131).

In an attempt to offset the poor reception of *Mardi* and put money in his depleted purse, Melville quickly wrote both *Redburn* and *White-Jacket* during the summer of 1849, but as he told his father-in-law at the time, "no reputation that is gratifying to me, can possibly be achieved by either of these books. They are two *jobs,* which I have done for money. . . . So far as I am individually concerned, & independent of my pocket, it is my earnest desire to write those sort of books which are said to 'fail' " (*Correspondence,* 138–39). Though he knew well enough that with a growing family to support he could not afford another failure like *Mardi,* he was unwilling to continue writing in the *Typee*-like vein of *Redburn* and *White-Jacket,* as the critics were urging him to do, even though both of these works were better than he cared to grant. Like the Mardian poet Lombardo, a surrogate for himself, he came to his writing impelled by "a full heart:—brimfull, bubbling, sparkling, and running over" as though it were a flagon of wine (*Mardi*, 592), but there was also the compelling need for that same writing to bring in an adequate income. This was his dilemma. As he later told Nathaniel Hawthorne in a moment of discouragement while struggling to finish *Moby-Dick*, "Dollars damn me. . . . What I feel most moved to write, that is banned,—it will not pay. Yet, altogether, write the *other* way I cannot. So the product is a final hash, and all my books are botches" (*Correspondence*, 191).

ii. The Author of *Moby-Dick*

The year 1850 was a memorable one for Melville. On his return from Europe, surprised by the unexpectedly favorable reception of both *Redburn* and *White-Jacket*, he began to write his sixth book, the work that became *Moby-Dick*. In August he first met Hawthorne, and while both authors were residing in the Berkshire region of western Massachusetts they enjoyed a close relationship. As he wrote of Hawthorne's *Mosses from an Old Manse* in a glowing review published immediately after their initial meeting, the example of Hawthorne's writings persuaded him that American authors of the nineteenth century could go "as far as Shakespeare into the universe" (*Piazza Tales*, 245). He was surely thinking of himself as well as Hawthorne when he declared that if given due recognition, our native writers might be prompted to "the full flower of some still greater achievement" than anything they had yet written (*Piazza Tales*, 249).

There is further evidence of Melville's high ambition in his correspondence during his first few months in the Berkshires, where he had moved from New York in September after buying the property near Pittsfield that he called "Arrowhead." In a letter to a New York friend he facetiously asked for "about fifty fast-writing youths" to serve him as copyists, "because since I have been here I have planned about that number of future works & cant find enough time to think about them separately" (*Correspondence*, 174).[3] But during the following winter and spring, as he drove himself to complete the book then taking form under his hand, he began to fear that he was wearing himself out, and that *Moby-Dick* would turn out not as the masterwork he had envisioned but as only another failed *Mardi*.

In one of Melville's remarkable letters to Hawthorne he wrote retrospectively that his inner development had been "all within a few years past"—since he had left the sea and begun his new career as a writer. Though Ishmael in *Moby-Dick* celebrates "a whale-ship" as "my Yale College and my Harvard" (*Moby-Dick*, 112), Melville himself believed that during his own childhood and youth, his years at sea included, he had experienced "no development at all"; only from his twenty-fifth year, he told Hawthorne, did he date his life. "Three weeks have scarcely passed, at any time between then and now," he declared in 1851, "that I have not unfolded within myself." The continuous inner growth that he thus recognized had indeed transformed him from "the author of Typee" into the author of *Moby-Dick*. Through omnivorous reading, through the growing habit of reflection that he called "pondering," and through the actual practice of his craft he had developed into a wide-ranging thinker and an increasingly proficient writer. "But I feel that I am now come to the inmost leaf of the bulb," he added, "and that shortly the flower must fall to the mould" (*Correspondence*, 193).

In this same revealing letter Melville also remarked that within the year just past he had "come to regard this matter of Fame as the most transparent of all vanities." "All Fame is patronage," he told Hawthorne. "Let me be infamous: there is no patronage in *that*" (*Correspondence*, 193). What he very likely had in mind was the verdict of his more patronizing critics that by publishing *Redburn* and *White-Jacket* after the failed experiment of *Mardi* "the author of Typee" had resumed his rightful place as a pleasing and popular writer for the general public. But Melville had come to loathe his identification with *Typee* as his professional ambition expanded. By the time of *Moby-Dick* he looked back on his first book as a work destined to be given to children "with their gingerbread." "What 'reputation'" it had brought him he now thought of as "horrible. Think of it! To go down to posterity is bad enough, any way; but to go down as a 'man who lived among the cannibals'!" (*Correspondence*, 193).

When Melville had at last finished what he called "my ditcher's work" on the remaining chapters of *Moby-Dick*, he was immensely gratified by a "joy-giving and exultation-breeding letter" from Hawthorne. In his impassioned reply he wrote that though no man who is wise should "expect appreciative recognition from his fellows," he now felt "a sense of unspeakable security" because of his friend's "having understood" *Moby-Dick*. "You did not care a penny for the book," he went on to say. "But, now and then as you read, you understood the pervading thought that impelled the book—and that you praised. Was it not so?" (*Correspondence,* 212–13).

It was well for Melville that he had Hawthorne's private approval of his work, for the first reviewers of *Moby-Dick* on both sides of the Atlantic returned what were at best mixed verdicts. In general, they responded favorably to his knowledgeable treatment of whales and whaling, for both the United States and Great Britain had an established maritime tradition and the whale fishery was still a matter of current interest, romantic as well as commercial. "Herman Melville knows more about whales than any man from Jonah downwards," said one British reviewer who called this latest work his "greatest." But "Extravagance is the bane of the book," this critic continued, "and the stumbling block of the author. He allows his fancy not only to run riot, but absolutely to run amuck."[4] Other British commentators, while recognizing *Moby-Dick* as a work of imaginative literature, deplored Melville's seeming indifference to the established conventions of fiction; one London reviewer charged that here "all the regular rules of narrative or story are spurned and set at defiance."[5] Specifically, they complained that Ishmael's first-person point of view is not maintained throughout the book and that—since the Epilogue was absent in the first English edition though present in the American—readers are not given an explanation of how he survived to tell his story.

Although later British reviews were much more favorable, they did not reach the United States in time to affect American opinion of the book. Many reviewers here, as Hershel Parker has remarked, had already "made up their minds about Melville: they enjoyed him, despite some reservations, but they certainly did not expect him to write great works of literature."[6] Conservative critics of *Typee* and *Omoo* who had previously deplored his animadversions against the shortcomings of some Polynesian missionaries now leveled charges of irreverence, indelicacy, and even indecency against *Moby-Dick:* one New York paper, for example, protested that Melville "is guilty of sneering at the truths of revealed religion" and even makes Ishmael "unite with a Polynesian"—Queequeg—"in worshipping and offering incense to an idol."[7] One of the most significant American reviews—an appraisal that hurt Melville both professionally and personally—was a long two-part notice in the *Literary World,* a weekly paper comparable in influence to today's *New York Times Book Review* and *New York Review of Books.* The man who presumably wrote the review was his friend Evert Duyckinck, who had first introduced him into New York literary circles, had followed and actively promoted his successive writings as they appeared, and had kept in touch with him as *Moby-Dick* was in progress, but what Duyckinck said of the book in print caused a serious rupture in their relationship.

The *Literary World* liked Melville's "brilliantly illustrated" account of the great Sperm Whale, identifying Moby Dick as his "hero." Captain Ahab, that "Faust of the quarter-deck," is "a striking conception," the reviewer granted, but his characterization is "too long drawn out," with not enough left to the reader's imagination. Moreover, the story of Ahab's career constituted something less than a tragedy for Duyckinck, who called it rather a "romance" or "a bit of German melodrama." But it was Ishmael's role, "appropriating perhaps a fourth" of the entire book, that drew the reviewer's most severe strictures. Ishmael's "vein of moralizing, half essay, half rhapsody," mingles "quaint conceit and extravagant daring speculation" with "much refinement and subtlety, and no little poetical feeling," he acknowledged, but Ishmael's—or Melville's—"piratical running down of creeds and opinions" he found "out of place and uncomfortable." The Duyckincks were devout churchmen, and as their review went on to say, "We do not like to see . . . the most sacred associations of life" thus "violated and defaced" in a work of fiction.[8]

Ishmael's departures from religious orthodoxy, his scarcely concealed skepticism, and Ahab's outright blasphemy—if readers went far enough into the story to encounter it—must all have repelled other contemporary readers of a conservative bent. Outwardly, at least, the mid–nineteenth century in America was a period of conventional belief in God and optimistic faith in man's inevitable progress toward perfection. But Melville, as Hawthorne once wrote of him, could "neither believe, nor be comfortable in his unbelief,"[9] and he had seen too much of the world to accept the idea of "steady unretracing progress" (*Moby-Dick,* 492),[10] whether by individuals or by mankind as a whole.

In one of his blacker moods the author of *Moby-Dick* had come to ask himself, "What's the use of elaborating what, in its very essence, is so short-lived as a modern book?" (*Correspondence,* 192). His countrymen did little to encourage American writers, Melville told his London publisher, charging that "the overwhelming majority" are unconcerned with a national literature and that their leaders—"sturdy backwoodsmen"—"care not a fig for any authors except those who write those most saleable of all books nowadays . . . the newspapers, & magazines" (*Correspondence, 198*). In the absence of international copyright, as he well knew, piratical book publishers in the United States were reprinting the latest works of Dickens, Thackeray, and other leading English writers without paying royalties—to the obvious disadvantage of American authors. Moreover, as Ann Douglas has contended in *The Feminization of American Culture,* "the prime consumers" of that culture in the mid–nineteenth century were women. They accordingly exerted a powerful influence on those popular writers responsive to their tastes, "who were being read while Melville and Thoreau were ignored."[11] (Whitman's poetry, one might add, was more than ignored, it was utterly shunned; Emily Dickinson was told that Whitman himself was "disgraceful."[12]) The best-sellers of the day were writings for a largely female audience by what Hawthorne—in an outburst that has since become famous—called "a d——d mob of scribbling women."[13]

Melville, who was well aware that most American readers of the time were female and who knew what the women of his own family were reading, professed to be "really amazed" that Hawthorne's wife liked *Moby-Dick.* She was "the only *woman*" who did, he told her, noting that "as a general thing, women have small taste for the sea" (*Correspondence,* 218–19). By March of 1853, sixteen months after the New York edition of *Moby-Dick* had appeared, twenty-three hundred copies in all had been sold;[14] in that same year alone, sales of *Fern Leaves from Fanny's Portfolio,* by the phenomenally popular Fanny Fern, reached seventy thousand. The real best-seller of the 1850s, of course, was Harriet Beecher Stowe's *Uncle Tom's Cabin.* First serialized in 1851 and 1852, her book had sold over three hundred thousand copies by 1853—the equivalent of more than three million copies in twentieth-century America.[15] Such was the competition that Hawthorne and Melville had to face from contemporary authors.

iii. After *Moby-Dick*

Always in need of money, Melville began his seventh book even before *Moby-Dick* was published. This was *Pierre, or the Ambiguities,* his first land-based work of fiction and a book that he may have intended to appeal especially to a feminine audience; he described it to his London publisher as "treating of utterly new scenes & characters" and as a work "very much more calculated for popularity than anything you have yet published of mine" (*Correspondence,* 226). But Richard Bentley, who had already lost money on Melville's books, refused to accept *Pierre* without extensive alterations that Melville in turn declined to permit. Meanwhile, knowing of the early British reviews of *Moby-Dick* and angered by what American critics were saying, Melville responded by writing into *Pierre* a scathing indictment of the current literary establishment, the Duyckincks included. When the new book was published in New York the verdict was unanimously negative. Critics disliked its extravagant language and deplored its hints at possible sexual irregularities. "HERMAN MELVILLE CRAZY," ran the heading of one hostile review,[16] and even Melville's relatives, alert to his drafts on family history and his transparent allusions to his own experience as a writer, were privately troubled, then and later, by doubts of his sanity.[17]

"For most of the American literary world," Hershel Parker has remarked, "the debacle of *Pierre* obliterated *Moby-Dick.*"[18] When later commentators lamented the decline in Melville's career after the success of *White-Jacket,* if they mentioned these two books at all it was only to link them with the earlier *Mardi* as further departures from his supposedly true vein. Well-meaning but patronizing critics admonished him to give over what one of them called his "metaphysical and morbid meditations"[19] and return once again to the kind of straightforward writing that had so pleased the public in *Typee* and *Omoo.* By the spring of 1853, a time when his family became anxious about "the strain on his health,"[20] he had completed another book-length manuscript entitled *The Isle of the Cross*—presumably the story of a betrayed wife that he had previously discussed with Hawthorne—but was "prevented from printing" (*Correspondence,* 250);[21] his American publisher, Harper & Brothers, apparently suggested instead that he write anonymously for the house magazine. During the next three years, though beset by increasing debts and by debilitating attacks of rheumatism and sciatica, he managed to turn out fifteen contributions that appeared in *Harper's New Monthly Magazine* and its younger rival *Putnam's Monthly,* plus a book-length serial for *Putnam's* (*Israel Potter*) that was later published separately. Two other books followed: *The Piazza Tales,* a selection of five of the magazine pieces plus a new title sketch, and *The Confidence-Man:*

His Masquerade. Their publisher fell victim to hard times, however, before Melville could gain financially from either work, and *The Confidence-Man* marked the end of his career as a professional writer of fiction.

Meanwhile, Melville's relatives, hoping to free him from the drudgery of further desk work, had been unsuccessfully seeking to secure an appointment for him as American consul in some foreign port. In 1856 they finally arranged a trip to the Mediterranean that began in October and lasted until the following spring; though it provided material for a season of lecturing and a later narrative poem, there was no permanent benefit to his health, which was further affected by a road accident in 1862. After three seasons on the lecture platform, for which he was not ideally suited, and a voyage around Cape Horn in 1860 as a passenger on a clipper ship, Melville moved his family from Pittsfield to New York, where he spent nearly two decades as an obscure Inspector of Customs. During his remaining years, though he brought out four volumes of verse, his name was virtually forgotten by his countrymen; when it was remembered at all by contemporary literary historians he was likely to be identified as "the author of *Typee*," not as the creator of Ishmael, Ahab, and the White Whale.

Arthur Stedman, a young writer and editor who came to know Melville during his last years and served as literary executor after his older friend's death in 1891, believed that "had Melville been willing to join freely in the literary movements of New York, his name would have remained before the public and a larger sale of his works would have been insured."22 Other writers of the day had benefited in this way, but what Melville thought of crassly promoting one's own literary reputation is suggested by his remark about fame in a letter of December 1885 to one of his English correspondents: "the further our civilization advances upon its present lines so much the cheaper sort of thing does 'fame' become, especially of the literary sort" (*Correspondence,* 492). As Stedman observed, Melville seemed willing to "trust the verdict of the future" concerning his writings.23

Even so, one detects on Melville's part a shift in attitude during his late years from the comment he had once made to Hawthorne: "All Fame is patronage. Let me be infamous." Shortly before his death in 1891 he came across and checked a remark by Tacitus that he may well have applied to himself: "The lust of fame is the last that a wise man shakes forth." And the familiar lines from Milton's *Lycidas* must have run through his mind— "Fame is the spur that the clear spirit doth raise / (That last infirmity of noble mind)"—as he wrote the Nelson chapters of *Billy Budd, Sailor,* and essayed his portrait of Captain Vere, who "never attained the fulness of fame," though, "spite its philosophic austerity," his spirit "may yet have indulged in the most secret of all passions, ambition" (*Billy Budd,* 129). And as even "the belated funeral flower" was denied to Vere, so it seemed beyond the reach of another austere philosopher who in years gone by had awakened to find himself a celebrity: "the author of *Typee.*"

As Stedman remarked after his friend's death, Melville "would have been more than mortal if he had been indifferent to his loss of popularity. . . . That he had faith in the eventual reinstatement of his reputation cannot be doubted."[24] During his last years he for the first time allowed his portrait to be published, in an anthology and in various reference works—something he had previously forbidden. But in the language of his late verse, most of it known only within his immediate family, true fame cannot be induced through any mere artifice; it must grow organically. Like other natural flowerings, moreover, it may "for decades" be delayed, "owing," as he put it, "to something retarding in the environment or soil."[25]

iv. The Melville Revival

Why did Melville lose the popularity he had gained during the years from 1846 to 1850, and what would be required to realize his hope for a second flowering of his fame in a more hospitable environment? A passage from Schopenhauer that he read and marked shortly before his death may suggest how he himself might have responded to such questions:

> the more a man belongs to posterity, in other words, to humanity in general, the more of an alien he is to his contemporaries; since his work is not meant for them as such, but only for them in so far as they form part of humanity at large. . . . [W]hat he does, fails of recognition because it is strange. People are more likely to appreciate the man who serves the circumstances of his own brief hour, or the temper of the moment,—belonging to it, and living and dying with it.[26]

These words must have struck Melville as an apt comment on his own relations with his place and time in America. In Britain, by contrast, he knew from correspondents that his works had long been favorites among a select group of readers, including men and women who also admired Thoreau and Whitman.

After Melville's death and with the approval of his widow, Stedman brought out new American editions of *Typee, Omoo, White-Jacket,* and *Moby-Dick* in the hope of reviving his name and fame at a time of renewed interest in the South Seas. The books received favorable notice, but the publisher was soon forced into bankruptcy. Stedman's biographical sketch of Melville in the first of these volumes was the chief source of information about him during the next several decades, when various American publishers used these same plates for occasional reprintings. More and more articles about his life and work gradually began to appear in both the United States and England, especially in the centennial year of Melville's birth, 1919.[27] In 1922–1923 a British publisher, Constable and Company, brought out a new twelve-volume edition of Melville's prose works. An American professor, Raymond Weaver, wrote the first book-length biography, *Herman Melville: Mariner and Mystic,* published in 1921, and prepared four additional volumes of prose and verse for the new Constable edition, including the first printing in 1924 of those manuscripts Melville had left unpublished; among them was the late novella now known as *Billy Budd, Sailor.* The second flowering was at last beginning.

"Whenever a dead author is 'revived,'" wrote an American observer of the 1920s, when Melville was clearly coming into his own, "we must bear in mind that nothing of him has been changed. It is we, his readers, who are changed, and for whom he has gained other values."[28] World war had made a difference, and for many readers—especially young readers—the less conventional nineteenth-century authors like Thoreau, Whitman, and Melville were indeed gaining other values. Hawthorne had long ago praised what he called Melville's "freedom of view";[29] Weaver's biography depicted him as a rebel's rebel against both human society and the cosmos itself, and rebellious young moderns were extolling those very aspects of his writing that had so offended his contemporaries. With the young, *Moby-Dick* rather than *Typee* was the great favorite. Melville had assumed that books about the sea appealed only to masculine readers; in 1920 a woman novelist and poet, Viola Meynell, declared that to read and absorb *Moby-Dick* is "the crown of one's reading life."[30]

During the seventy years between 1851 and the appearance of Weaver's biography, only six editions of *Moby-Dick* had been published in America

and England; by 1930 there were eighteen, and by 1951, the year of
the book's centennial, twenty-eight; by 1976 that last figure had doubled
to fifty-six, and more editions have since appeared.[31] Publishers, editors,
adapters, and even Hollywood producers hurried to see what profitable oil
could be extracted by cutting into Melville's book—or even by cutting *out* of
it, as one can gather from the numerous shortened versions for children and
even for adults that have proliferated over the years.[32] Deleted from most
of the abridgments are what one editor referred to as Melville's "philosophy,
mysticism, and technical natural history";[33] in view of nineteenth-century
objections to his "metaphysical and morbid meditations," the book might
well have fared better in his own day if it had been abridged then along
similar lines, as at least one or two reviewers of the 1850s suggested.[34] But
"You must have plenty of sea-room to tell the Truth in," Melville believed,[35]
and any abridged version is only a diminished *Moby-Dick*.

Even more tinkering has attended the several attempts to translate *Moby-
Dick* into the language of film. There have been three motion-picture
versions to date: in 1925 and 1930, with John Barrymore as Ahab, and
in 1955, with Gregory Peck. That of 1925, rechristened *The Sea Beast,* is
especially notable as an effort to improve the story not by subtraction, as
in the various abridged printings, but by a predictable addition. "What
we are going to do for a love interest I don't quite know," Barrymore
wrote as filming began, adding prophetically that "Hollywood will find
a way"[36]—and indeed Hollywood did, concocting a triangle that pitted
Ahab against a newly invented brother as they contested for the love of
a beautiful woman![37] The revival also prompted a film called *Enchanted
Island,* suggested by *Typee,* that drew little attention. More prominent were
several versions of *Billy Budd:* a play, an opera with libretto by E. M.
Forster and score by Benjamin Britten, and a film with Peter Ustinov as
a portly Captain Vere. As these items suggest, popular interest in Melville
has extended to more of his writings than *Moby-Dick* alone.

Meanwhile, back in academia, the interpreters, critics, and scholars were
following their own divergent paths, encouraged by the awakening interest
in American literature generally. More and more prospective teachers of
literature were attracted to American authors, and by the mid-1940s, when
young veterans like myself were returning from the wars to resume their
careers, the list of scholarly and critical works on Melville in particular began
to grow exponentially.[38] A Harvard professor quipped in the 1950s that "the

investigation of *Moby-Dick* might almost be said to have taken the place of whaling among the industries of New England."[39] Such developments, as I well remember, threatened to set off another Battle of the Books: on the one side were champions of American and contemporary literature and criticism; on the other, traditionalists defending the established canon who deplored what one of them called our "uncritical acceptance of Faulkner or Melville as great authors."[40] But the new movement was not to be halted, either on campus or off, as more and more readers and students found that such writers were speaking to them and for them.

v. In Retrospect and in Prospect

When I myself came upon Melville in the late 1930s, as a young graduate student and would-be Miltonist electing his very first course in American literature, it was Melville's "bold and nervous lofty language"—to borrow a phrase from *Moby-Dick* (73)—that especially attracted me. And as I read through his successive works, from *Typee* to *Billy Budd,* and began to learn more about their author, I came to appreciate the remarkable range and depth of his thinking and writing and to advance slowly, under his prompting, into "the world of mind," as he called it in *Mardi* (557), that he had begun to explore in that book. Today, after more than fifty years of studying and teaching, not as a Miltonist but as a confirmed Americanist and professing Mel*villain,* I find the man and his works as engaging and challenging as ever.

As I look back, I can now distinguish three stages in my approach to Melville, using names originated by Alfred North Whitehead in *The Aims of Education:* "the stage of romance, the stage of precision, and the stage of generalisation." Having proceeded through the first two of these educational stages, I shall conclude this account with a few generalizations, briefly noting two corresponding stages in the belated second flowering of Melville's fame.

Writing in 1948, the respected American critic Malcolm Cowley ventured to suggest that "perhaps the principal creative work of the last three decades in this country . . . has been the critical rediscovery and reinterpretation of Melville's *Moby-Dick.*"[41] This is a comment still worth pondering—especially in view of the fact that *Moby-Dick,* like the writings of Thoreau, Whitman, and even Poe, had long since received more attention and celebration abroad than at home. Cowley was referring to what I regard as the first and early second stages of the Melville Revival. During the first stage—the stage of romance—enthusiastic commentators and pioneering biographers, lacking the hard evidence that has since been uncovered, accepted the family tradition Arthur Stedman had previously honored, simply assuming that Melville's "narratives of voyages" were straightforward accounts of his own experience. Then, in 1939, Charles R. Anderson published a groundbreaking book, *Melville in the South Seas,* that demonstrated how very deeply Melville's writing was indebted to his omnivorous reading. Anderson inaugurated a new stage of precision in Melville studies. Cohorts of young scholars were soon following his lead, not only in uncovering more of Melville's sources but also in minutely tracing his personal life and professional career, establishing accurate texts of his various writings, and intensely studying individual works—not only *Billy Budd, Sailor,* and the long-neglected short stories and later verse, but also the long-scorned *Mardi* and *Pierre.* This stage continues even now, for there is still "a Melville who awaits discovery,"[42] and truly adequate generalizing about him is therefore yet to come.

Meanwhile, just as my own generation sought a place in the canon for American and contemporary literature and theory, so some younger scholars and teachers of today—feminists, multiculturalists, and various theorists—are seeking to make still further revisions.[43] In order to accommodate new material, some Americanists would omit *Moby-Dick* in favor of a shorter but less representative work by Melville—perhaps *Billy Budd* or one or two of the magazine pieces, though not *Typee.* Others may be tempted to drop Melville altogether, though he survives on at least one campus, along with Hawthorne and Faulkner, in a very up-to-date course entitled "White Male Authors."[44] Such narrow categorizing would surely surprise Melville himself—along with such perceptive feminine readers as Sophia Hawthorne and Viola Meynell!

While the literary canon will never be settled for all eternity, I cannot believe that Melville, who dreaded going down to posterity only as "a 'man who lived among the cannibals,'" will in another hundred years be regarded once again only as "the author of *Typee*"—or even as the author of *Moby-Dick* alone, great as it surely is, for his achievements as a writer deserve to be valued in their totality. Moreover, discerning readers of other nations and other languages than ours—readers who in Schopenhauer's words "form part of humanity at large"—have come to regard Melville not as a merely parochial figure in the changing canon of a single national literature, but as an author of world importance, one written about not only in English but also in French, German, Italian, Portuguese, Swedish, Russian, Japanese, and perhaps even more languages spoken abroad. And so, belatedly, the flower of fame has bloomed once again in our century—this time for one who belongs not just to us as Americans, but rather "to humanity in general."

Part Three
1993–1995

12.

The Presence of Walt Whitman

> I and mine do not convince by arguments, similes, rhymes, We
> convince by our presence.
> —Whitman, "Song of the Open Road," lines 138–39

The time is 1882, during the Easter season. The place is Germantown, Pennsylvania, a suburb of Philadelphia. The speaker is the
American essayist Logan Pearsall Smith, writing retrospectively in
the 1930s of "important news" he had heard when he was only seventeen
and a student at Haverford College. He and his sister Mary—the future
wife of Bernard Berenson—were both home for the holidays, in her case
from Smith College.

> There was a poet, she informed me and the rest of our family, a great
> American poet and prophet,—though most Americans were not at
> all aware of his greatness,—now living in poverty and neglect . . . not
> far from our neighborhood, and it was her purpose . . . to go without
> delay and offer him a due tribute of praise and admiration.[1]

When Mary's "perturbed relatives" asked how she had heard of this poet,
she replied that "a lady lecturer" from Boston had come to her college and
praised the poet's works. She herself had immediately ordered a copy, which
"revealed to her a message of tremendous import" that she intended now
to discuss with the poet himself.

> Consternation fell upon us all, and my father at once forbade it. He
> vaguely knew the name of the poet, which was by no means a name

129

of good repute in Philadelphia; the district in which he lived was a district not visited by people who respected their own position; no daughter of his . . . should, while she lived under his roof, be allowed to undertake so unseemly a step.

By this point in the story you will have surmised not only that the poet's name was Walt Whitman but that the father himself, "being in his heart well aware of the powerlessness of American parents in their dealings with their daughters," would ultimately agree to escort Mary Smith and her brother on a visit to Whitman. And so all three set out in Father Smith's carriage, by way of the ferry across the Delaware River to New Jersey, for the poet's "little two-story wooden house in Camden." Their unexpected appearance didn't seem to startle Whitman in the least. He invited them upstairs to his den, where the young people engaged in "lively talk" with the poet and their father surprised them, not only by joining in "this friendly conversation" but by impulsively inviting "the object of his great disapprobation to drive back . . . to Germantown and spend the night."

Whitman at first demurred, as Smith remembered, but when he looked out the window and saw the fine carriage he changed his mind, and following his arrival in Germantown he "remained with us for a month." After this first visit with the Smiths he often returned, becoming "a familiar and friendly inmate of the house." But the reputation he had acquired by "that daring and not decent publication" *Leaves of Grass* "was a dubious one in America at that time." It had reached the Smiths' "Quaker suburb, and our neighbors and relations avoided our house, and forbade their children to visit it, when it was known that Walt Whitman was staying with us."

I have quoted this much from Smith for two reasons, the first being to remind you of Whitman's "dubious reputation" in America as late as the 1880s, and the second to suggest what the presence of Walt Whitman meant to those who actually came to know him. Whitman, then in his sixties, had aged early, and as Smith remembered, it was "the calm serenity of age . . . which diffused about him that atmosphere of peace and leisure which made his companionship so genial, and our endless conversations with him so great a pleasure." But if Whitman was still unacceptable to many Americans who knew him only by reputation, he had found distinguished readers abroad, as Smith tells us in describing the poet's upstairs room in Camden. The floor "was covered to the depth of a foot or so with a sea of papers, and now and then [Whitman] would stir this pool with his stick and fish up a letter from an English admirer—Tennyson perhaps, or Symonds, or Edward Dowden."

It would be tempting to continue quoting from Smith's delightful chapter on Whitman in his book of reminiscences called *Unforgotten Years*, which I commend to you in its entirety. It is one of those "agreeable, grateful, and companionable" volumes that "we pick up by chance here and there," as Melville put it in *White-Jacket*. (I came across my own copy back in 1955, waiting for me on a used-book shelf, priced at a dime.) Instead, I shall pursue my theme, the presence of Walt Whitman, by turning now to *Leaves of Grass* itself. In examining the selections that follow I want to stress the unique relationship that Whitman sought to establish between himself and his readers—readers then and now. Addressing them through the persona, the "I," who speaks in his printed verses, he hails them again and again in a characteristic phrase: "you, whoever you are."

i

First of all, here are some lines from a poem that Whitman included in the third edition of *Leaves of Grass* in 1860—a most unusual poem, as I think you'll agree. In addition to the "I—you" pattern, note the phrase "holding me now" in the very first line, one of the many instances in which Whitman denotes continuing action taking place in present time by using present participles—words ending in "-ing":

1. Whoever you are *holding me now* in hand,
   Without one thing all will be useless,
   I give you fair warning, before you attempt me further,
   I am not what you supposed, but far different.

2. Who is he that would become my follower?
   Who would sign himself a candidate for my affections?
   Are you he?

3. The way is suspicious—the result slow, uncertain, may-be
    destructive. . . .
   The whole past theory of your life and all conformity to the lives
    around you, would have to be abandoned;
   Therefore release me now, before *troubling yourself* any further—
   Let go your hand from my shoulders,
   Put me down, and depart on your way.[2]

Though there's more to the poem than this extract, you can see already
that a lot is going on here, as the verb forms are telling you—I too must
use present participles. Here the speaker—the "I"—is talking out of the
pages of *Leaves of Grass* to the reader, who is literally *holding* the book
in his hand, and in other verse by Whitman the speaker is once again
looking "upward out of this page, *studying you*, dear friend, *whoever you are*"
(emphasis added).[3] In a late poem entitled "So Long!" he even mentions the
possibility of his *springing* "from the pages into your arms." "So Long!" also
declares in so many words that *Leaves of Grass* itself "is no book," for "Who
touches *this* touches *a man*" (emphasis added).[4] To return to the poem of
1860 that we have been examining, the speaker offers this alternative to
the parting he has previously suggested:

5. Or if you will, *thrusting me* beneath your clothing,
   Where I may feel the throbs of your heart, or rest upon your hip,
   Carry me when you go forth over land or sea;
   For thus merely *touching you*, is enough—is best,
   And *thus touching you* would I silently sleep and be carried eternally.

In *touching* "these leaves"—the pages of *Leaves of Grass* and also the book
itself—you are somehow touching the "I" who is speaking, and conversely,
should you thrust the book "beneath your clothing" and carry it with
you, the "I" will be "thus touching you" in return. All the lines I have
quoted from this poem are characteristically Whitmanesque, being clearly
intended to establish a direct personal relationship with "you, whoever you
are": you who may be holding the speaker's book or placing your hand
on his shoulder, who may be reading his words or hearing them spoken
or perhaps simply remembering them. We are presumably to identify the
speaker with Whitman himself, and the result is that *Leaves of Grass,* as
Carl Sandburg once said, is "the most intensely personal book in American
literature."[5]

ii

My theme and title, "The Presence of Walt Whitman," come from a little book published more than thirty years ago: a collection of papers on Whitman written for and discussed by a group of English teachers meeting at Columbia University in 1960 and 1961. As its editor observed, the volume testifies to the poet's "remarkable and continuing *presence* . . . , despite persistent efforts . . . over many years to belittle or simply to neglect him."[6] Now that twentieth-century readers and critics have at last responded with due appreciation to the man and his work, there remains a mystery about him that has yet to be satisfactorily explained: just *how* did this sometime carpenter, journeyman printer, and newspaper reporter and editor with little formal education manage to transform himself into the poet who at age thirty-six produced in 1855 the first edition of *Leaves of Grass*?

Whitman himself has left us what might be called, in his own phrase, "faint clues and indirections" concerning the nature of that transformation. In a poem appearing without title in the 1855 edition he has this to tell us about the development of a child very much like himself as he grew into maturity and became the writer whose poem we are reading. Much of the poem, now known as "There Was a Child Went Forth," is a succession of brief images—what Whitman himself liked to call "pictures"—of what this child saw, heard, smelled, touched, and felt, images that came to be parts of his very being:

> There was a child went forth every day,
> And the first object he looked upon and received with wonder
>   or pity or love or dread, that object he became,
> And that object became part of him for the day or a
>   certain part of the day . . . or for many years or
>   stretching cycles of years. . . .[7]

Thus the child becomes aware of growing things: lilacs, grass, and flowers; animals of various kinds; human beings of both sexes—all realistically observed and absorbed into himself:

> the old drunkard staggering home from the outhouse
> of the tavern whence he had lately risen,

> And the schoolmistress that passed on her way to the
>   school . . . and the friendly boys that passed . . . and the
>   tidy and freshcheeked girls . . . and the barefoot
>   negro boy and girl,
> And all the changes of city and country wherever he went.

Appearing next are the boy's parents, not unlike Whitman's own as they have been reported to us: the mother "with mild words"; the father, "strong, selfsufficient, manly, mean, angered, unjust." Other men and women also appear, "crowding fast in the streets" nearby, and then comes a whole series of varied images as the poem opens out toward a still larger world beyond. Here Whitman uses his favored participial verb forms to arrest continuing actions, as in a photographic snapshot:

> The village on the highland seen from afar at sunset
>   . . . the river between,
> Shadows . . . aureola and mist . . . light falling on roofs
>   and gables of white or brown, three miles off,
> The schooner nearby, sleepily dropping down the tide
>   . . . the little boat slack towed astern,
> The hurrying tumbling waves and quick broken crests and
>   slapping;
> The strata of colored clouds . . . the long bar of maroon tint
>   away solitary by itself . . . the spread of purity it
>   lies motionless in,
> The horizon's edge, the flying sea crow, the fragrance of
>   salt marsh and shore mud;

—and here the poem opens out once again, not spatially but in time, as the verbs shift from past tense to present and future:

> These became part of that child who went forth every day,
>   and who now goes and will always go forth every day,

And these same entities, Whitman adds in the final present-tense line of the poem, also become part of "him or her that peruses them now"—which is to say *you*, my reader, "whoever you are."

iii

Elsewhere in the first edition of *Leaves of Grass,* notably in the all-encompassing poem that Whitman later called "Song of Myself,"[8] we again find familiar patterns and devices. The entire poem can be read as another running dialogue between speaker and reader. "I celebrate myself," it begins, "And what I assume you shall assume, / For every atom belonging to me as good belongs to you." Some 1,300 lines later it ends—without period in the 1855 printing—with a glance at the book's title and a farewell to the "you" he has been addressing:

> I bequeath myself to the dirt to grow from the grass
>   I love,
> If you want me again look for me under your boot soles.
>
> You will hardly know who I am or what I mean,
> But I shall be good health to you nevertheless,
> And filter and fibre your blood.
>
> *Failing* to find me at first keep encouraged,
> *Missing me* one place search another,
> I stop some where *waiting for you*
>   (lines 1329–36; emphasis added)

Like the third-person speaker of "There Was a Child Went Forth," the "I" who speaks in "Song of Myself" is acutely aware of the world about him. As early as the fifth line of the poem we find him "observing a spear of summer grass"; later he tries to answer a child who has asked him, "What is the grass?"

> I guess it must be the flag of my disposition, out of
>   hopeful green stuff woven.
>
> Or I guess it is the handkerchief of the Lord,
> A scented gift and remembrancer designedly dropped,
> Bearing the owner's name someway in the corners, that
>   we may see and remark, and say Whose?
>
> Or I guess the grass is itself a child . . . the produced
>   babe of the vegetation.

> Or I guess it is a uniform hieroglyphic,
> And it means, Sprouting alike in broad zones and narrow
> zones,
> Growing among black folks as among white,
> Kannuck, Tuckahoe, Congressman, Cuff, I give them the
> same, I receive them the same,
> And now it seems to me the beautiful uncut hair of
> graves.
>
> (lines 90–101)

"A leaf of grass," he says later, "is no less than the journey work of the stars," and "a mouse is miracle enough to stagger sextillions of infidels" (lines 662, 668). All living things, himself included, are encompassing manifestations of an evolving world:

> I find I incorporate gneiss and coal and long-threaded
> moss and fruits and grains and esculent roots,
> And am stucco'd with quadrupeds and birds all over,
> And have distanced what is behind me for good reasons,
> And call any thing close again when I desire it.
>
> (lines 670–73)

What most occupies his attention, however, is the world of men and women. "In all people I see myself, none more and not one a barleycorn less," he tells us, "And the good or bad I say of myself I say of them" (lines 401–2). In long passages sometimes referred to as Whitman's "catalogues" he introduces individuals of all kinds and conditions, briefly characterizing each one through images of sight, sound, and smell, motion and touch, much like those in "There Was a Child Went Forth." Here is a sample, notable for its successive verbs of action and its effective use of contrasting sights and sounds:

> The pure contralto sings in the organ loft,
> The carpenter dresses his plank . . . the tongue of his
> foreplane whistles its wild ascending lisp,
> The married and unmarried children ride home to their
> thanksgiving dinner,

The pilot seizes the king-pin, he heaves down with a
    strong arm,
The mate stands braced in the whaleboat, lance and
    harpoon are ready,
The duck-shooter walks by silent and cautious stretches,
The deacons are ordained with crossed hands at the altar,
The spinning-girl retreats and advances to the hum of
    the big wheel. . . .

(lines 257–64)

"These one and all tend inward to me," the speaker tells us in concluding this particular catalogue, "and I tend outward to them" (line 324). His empathy with other persons extends in some passages to complete identification. "I *become* any presence or truth of humanity," he declares (line 941; emphasis added), and the process of his becoming one with another human being is manifest most often in brief narrative passages where suffering or injury is involved: thus, "I am the man. . . . I suffered. . . . I was there" (line 827); "I am the hounded slave" (line 834); "I am the mashed fireman with breastbone broken. . . . tumbling walls buried me in their debris" (line 843).

Who, then, *is* this "I" who is continually addressing the reader throughout the many lines of "Song of Myself"? The poet, Emerson had written, should be *representative*, speaking of, for, and to all men and women, past, present, and to come, and Whitman agreed. As he says, speaking through the "I" of this poem,

These are the thoughts of all men in all ages and lands,
    they are not original with me,
If they are not yours as much as mine they are nothing
    or next to nothing. . . .

(lines 353–54)

"I give the sign of democracy," he tells us, and "I will accept nothing which all cannot have their counterpart of on the same terms" (lines 507–8). The late critic Malcolm Cowley, who considered this poem to be "Whitman's greatest work," held that it was a mistake for the poet to call it "Song of Myself" in later editions. According to Cowley, "Whitman had originally been writing about a not-myself, a representative figure who . . . had realized the possibilities latent in every man and woman." Thus the "I" for Cowley is not simply "Walt Whitman, an American, one of the roughs" (line 499), but rather an "idealized or dramatized self"—"the proletarian bard who was supposed to have done the writing."9

In both "There Was a Child Went Forth" and "Song of Myself" we have seen Whitman's tendency to "become" all that he looked upon, and in turn to have all objects and persons "become part of him." It is Whitman's "passionate sense of identification," according to the poet John Berryman, writing with reference to the longer poem, that "supplies the method by which the 'I' . . . is gradually expanded, characterized, and filled with meaning: not until near the end of the poem is the 'I' complete." Moreover, Berryman agrees with Cowley that when the "I" is speaking the voice isn't simply that of Walt Whitman the man. "A poet's first person personal pronoun is nearly always ambiguous," Berryman remarked out of his own experience,10 and the "I" of the poem tells us explicitly that through him we are hearing "many long dumb voices," "forbidden voices," "voices veiled, and I remove the veil, / Voices indecent by me clarified and transfigured" (lines 509–20).

Note that the "I" calls himself "the poet of the body" as well as "of the soul," "the poet of the woman the same as the man" (lines 422–23, 426). Speaking to men and women alike, he urges us not to be afraid of our own bodies or of what he delicately calls the "merge" of the sexes: "Undrape. . . . you are not guilty to me, nor stale nor discarded, / I see through the broadcloth and gingham whether or no . . ." (lines 136–37). It is passages like this—there are many more in Whitman—that so shocked contemporaries of the poet who were not used to such discourse; today, on the other hand, some readers overemphasize Whitman's frank treatment of sex at the expense of his equally open spirituality.11 "I hear and behold God in every object," declares the "I" near the conclusion of "Song of Myself":

> I see something of God each hour of the twenty-four,
>   and each moment then,
> In the faces of men and women I see God, and in my own
>   face in the glass,
> I find letters from God dropped in the street, and every
>   one is signed by God's name,

And I leave them where they are, for I know that others
    will punctually come forever and ever.

(lines 1274–80)

In looking at "Song of Myself" and quoting some representative passages I have touched on only a few aspects of this all-embracing poem; there are countless others for you the reader to discover and enjoy. "I am large," as the voice of its speaker declares, "I contain multitudes" (line 1316). Sometimes I think of Whitman the man as soaking up experience like a great sponge, hugging it to himself and making it a part of him, then as a poet squeezing it out into his verses, there to become a part of the reader as well. What he put into "Song of Myself," as poet Randall Jarrell wrote in an essay with a wonderful title, "Walt Whitman: He Had His Nerve," is "almost everything in the world, so that one responds to him, willingly or unwillingly, almost as one does to the world."[12]

iv

For a particularly striking example of the presence of Walt Whitman I turn now to another powerful early composition, printed initially in the second edition of *Leaves of Grass* in 1856 as "Sun-Down Poem," rechristened "Crossing Brooklyn Ferry" in the third edition of 1860, and carefully and effectively revised in subsequent printings.[13] The speaker of "Crossing Brooklyn Ferry," as I shall call the poem for convenience, is once again an "I"—this time seeming much closer to Whitman the man than the representative "I" of "Song of Myself." At the very beginning he is looking at water and sky, but his attention soon turns, as it always does with Whitman's speakers, to the human scene:

Flood-tide below me! I see you face to face!
Clouds of the west—sun there half an hour high—I see
    you also face to face.

Crowds of men and women attired in the usual costumes,
    how curious you are to me!
On the ferryboats the hundreds and hundreds that cross,

returning home, are more curious to me than you
suppose,
And you that shall cross from shore to shore years hence
are more to me, and more in my meditations, than you
might suppose.

(lines 1–5)

This opening section not only establishes the scene but sets up familiar
Whitmanesque patterns: the shifting of tense from present to future and
the use of direct address—"I" speaking to "you"—that we have seen before.
The most significant image of the poem is that of *crossing*, introduced here
and developed in sections 2, 3, and 4. Those men and women the speaker
is observing are "crossing Brooklyn Ferry" for the second time each day,
now "returning home" at sundown just as those *other* men and women
whose existence he is looking forward to "shall cross . . . years hence."
Whitman's characteristic present participles—"crossing" and "returning"—
denote action going on in the poem's present time; the "others" who
"shall cross" in the poem's future time will experience the same sights and
sounds:

Others will enter the gates of the ferry and cross from
shore to shore,
Others will watch the run of the flood-tide,
Others will see the shipping of Manhattan north and west,
and the heights of Brooklyn to the south and east,
Others will see the islands large and small,
Fifty years hence, others will see them as they cross,
the sun half an hour high,
A hundred years hence, or ever so many hundred years
hence, others will see them,
Will enjoy the sunset, the pouring-in of the flood-tide,
the falling back to the sea of the ebb-tide.

(lines 13–19)

Such shared experience transcends the separations brought about by
time, place, and individual differences. Common images constitute "the
ties" (line 11), not only between generations but between individuals as
well:

It avails not, time nor place—distance avails not,
I am with you, you men and women of a generation, or
    ever so many generations hence,
Just as you feel when you look on the river and sky,
    so I felt,
Just as any of you is one of a living crowd, I was
    one of a crowd,
Just as you are refresh'd by the gladness of the river
    and the bright flow, I was refresh'd. . . .

                                (lines 20–24)

The poet then goes on in section 3 to catalogue in impressive detail (lines 27–48) all that he saw in the water, in the sky, and on the shore as he crossed aboard the ferry in *his* time; so too will you the reader see these same objects in *your* time. He establishes his point in section 4:

These and all else were to me the same as they are to you.
I loved well these cities, loved well the stately and
    rapid river,
The men and women I saw were all near to me,
Others the same—others who look back on me because I
    look'd forward to them,
(The time will come, though I stop here today and tonight.)

                                (lines 49–53)

Sections 5 and 6 introduce new points of similarity between speaker and reader. In "There Was a Child Went Forth" Whitman had traced the normal course of a small boy's development, its stages marked by his growing awareness of his outward surroundings. All of us follow a similar pattern of *becoming* as we receive and develop our individual identities—first through our basic physical attributes, our bodies:

I too had been struck from the float forever held in
    solution,
I too had receiv'd identity by my body,
That I was I knew was of my body, and what I should
    be I knew I should be of my body.

                                (lines 62–64)

The earlier poem had touched on the child's "doubts of daytime and the doubts of nighttime" (lines 27–30); here the speaker mentions "the curious abrupt questions" that "stir within me" (line 59), adding in section 6 that such experience is universal:

> It is not upon you alone the dark patches fall,
> The dark threw its patches down upon me also,
> The best I had done seem'd to me blank and suspicious,
> My great thoughts as I supposed them, were they not
>   in reality meagre?
> Nor is it you alone who knows what it is to be evil,
> I am he who knew what it was to be evil. . . .
>
> (lines 65–70)

In the experience of living each of us plays that part which is what we make it—and which in turn determines whatever we will therefore become:

> [I] lived the same life with the rest, the same old
>   laughing, gnawing, sleeping,
> Play'd the part that still looks back on the actor or
>   actress,
> The same old role, the role that is what we make it,
>   as great as we like,
> Or as small as we like, or both great and small.
>
> (lines 82–85)

Section 7 draws writer and reader—the "I" and the "you"—even closer together, evoking the poet's presence here and now:

> Closer yet I approach you,
> What thought you have of me now, I had as much of you—
> I laid in my stores in advance,
> I consider'd long and seriously of you before you were born.
>
> Who was to know what should come home to me?
> Who knows but I am enjoying this?
> Who knows, for all the distance, but I am as good as
>   looking at you now, for all you cannot see me?
>
> (lines 86–91)

Section 8 returns to the initial setting of the poem, recalling once again, in a further series of questions, the shared images catalogued in section 3 that link the "I" and the "you":

> Ah, what can ever be more stately and admirable to
> me than mast-hemm'd Manhattan?
> River and sunset and scallop-edg'd waves of flood-tide?
> The sea-gulls oscillating their bodies, the hay-boat
> in the twilight, and the belated lighter?
> What gods can exceed these that clasp me by the hand,
> and with voices I love call me promptly and loudly
> by my nighest name as I approach?
> What is more subtle than this which ties me to the
> woman or man that looks in my face?
> Which fuses me into you now, and pours my meaning
> into you?
>
> We understand then do we not?
> What I promis'd without mentioning it, have you not
> accepted?
> What the study could not teach—what the preaching
> could not accomplish, is accomplish'd, is it
> not?
>
> (lines 92–100)

Section 9 opens with a recapitulation in which key images and phrases of the preceding sections are brought together in a new ordering, linked by a series of imperative verbs derived from earlier passages:

> Flow . . . flow . . . Frolic . . . drench . . . Cross . . .
> Stand up . . . stand up . . . Throb . . . throw out . . .
> Suspend . . . Gaze . . . Sound out . . . call . . . Live
> . . . play . . . Play. . . .

Then, turning to the reader, the "I" who is speaking asks, "Consider, you who peruse me, whether I may not in unknown ways be looking upon you" (line 112). Finally, addressing not only the reader but those objects, those images, that are now part of the speaker—another boy-become-man who

went forth every day and still goes forth every day—the poem concludes
with this memorable invocation:

> Appearances, now or henceforth, indicate what you are,
> You necessary film, continue to envelop the soul,
> About my body for me, and your body for you, be hung
> our divinest aromas,
> Thrive, cities—bring your freight, bring your shows,
> ample and sufficient rivers,
> Expand, being than which none else is perhaps more
> spiritual,
> Keep your places, objects than which none else is more
> lasting.
>
> You have waited, you always wait, you dumb, beautiful
> ministers,
> We receive you with free sense at last, and are insatiate
> henceforward,
> Not you any more shall be able to foil us, or withhold
> yourselves from us,
> We use you, and do not cast you aside—we plant you
> permanently within us,
> We fathom you not—we love you—there is perfection in
> you also,
> You furnish your parts toward eternity,
> Great or small, you furnish your parts toward the soul.
>
> (lines 120–32)

"Crossing Brooklyn Ferry" impressively demonstrates not only Whitman's mastery of language but his conception of overall structure and form.
His artful use of repeated key words and images throughout the poem, with
their effective recapitulation in the concluding section, has reminded many
readers of the practice of a skilled composer of music. (Whitman, by the
way, was a devotee of Italian opera, popular in New York during the 1850s,
and adapted some of its forms in his writing.) But nothing in the poem
seems contrived or artificial, since its imagery is based on direct observation
and since the poet's ensuing "meditations," as he calls them, grow directly
out of what he has seen and described. The theme of "crossing" and the
twice-daily passage of the ferry from shore to shore may well remind readers

of larger archetypal motifs, but the implication for human life is never made explicit in the verse itself. Instead, Whitman introduces his preferred topic of the interrelatedness of individuals and generations.

Along with "There Was a Child Went Forth," "Crossing Brooklyn Ferry" shows Whitman's preoccupation with personal identity and the process that psychologists call *individuation.* The body itself he thinks of as a "necessary film" that envelops the soul. Through it we "receive identity"; otherwise, we couldn't be distinguished from what he terms "the float forever held in solution"—apparently meaning for him a universal spiritual grounding akin to what Emerson in "The American Scholar" had called "the Divine Soul which . . . inspires all men." What we experience— and what we *choose* to experience—will necessarily determine what and who we ultimately become. The child of the earlier poem "became" the objects he looked upon, and they in turn became part of him; in "Brooklyn Ferry" those physical objects of the world beyond the self are hailed as "dumb, beautiful ministers"—ministers to our individual selves—that we "plant . . . permanently within us" that they may furnish parts toward our very beings.

Throughout "Crossing Brooklyn Ferry" you the reader are repeatedly reminded of the hovering presence of the "I" who is speaking, being asked in direct address to "Consider . . . whether I may not in unknown ways be looking upon you" as you read. There is no other poem in which the "I" seems as closely identified with Walt Whitman himself, though there are passages in his later work that are more explicitly revelatory: I think particularly of "Out of the Cradle Endlessly Rocking," which tells us— obliquely—how Whitman became a poet; the "Calamus" poems, which he termed "the frailest leaves of me";[14] and "As I Ebb'd with the Ocean of Life," another moving expression of his recurrent self-doubt. The fine earlier verses we have been examining—"There Was a Child Went Forth," "Song of Myself," and "Crossing Brooklyn Ferry"—besides standing magnificently by themselves, also anticipate the sense of empathy and compassion that infuses Whitman's deeply felt poetry of the Civil War years, much of it based on his experience as a voluntary aide in military hospitals. One piece, "The Wound-Dresser," perfectly exemplifies that memorable line from "Song of Myself": "I am the man. . . . I suffered. . . . *I was there,*" illustrating once more, in still another setting, the poet's ubiquitous presence.

But that is another story—and a long one.

13.

The "I" of *Walden*

I should not talk so much about myself if there were any body
else whom I knew as well.
—Thoreau, *Walden*, 3

I f you had happened to live in Concord, Massachusetts, during the
middle of the nineteenth century, you would have known the Thoreau
family, resident there since 1823. The father, John, operated a pencil-
making business; the mother, Cynthia, took in boarders to make ends meet.
There was money enough to send only one of their four children to college:
Henry (baptized David Henry but known as Henry David), the second son,
who graduated from Harvard in 1837. In October of that year he had begun
keeping a journal, prompted by a question from his fellow-townsman Ralph
Waldo Emerson: " 'What are you doing now?' he asked, 'Do you keep a
journal?'—So I make my first entry today"; immediately following are two
brief paragraphs characteristically headed "Solitude" (*Journal*, 1:5).

Until 1861, the year before his death, Thoreau faithfully continued to
make his journal entries, ultimately filling forty-seven manuscript volumes
with over two million words. "For a long time I was reporter to a journal,
of no very wide circulation," he remarked wryly in *Walden*, "whose editor
has never yet seen fit to print the bulk of my contributions, and, as is too
common with writers, I got only my labor for my pains" (18). For Thoreau
as for countless New Englanders before him, the journal was a record of
self-examination, a continuing appraisal of the state of one's inner being.
It also became something more: as Emerson had taught him, the journal
could serve as a "Savings Bank" for depositing his responses to the world

about him—the world of books included; then, as a would-be author, he could draw upon its resources for lectures and essays and ultimately for books of his own.[1]

But young Henry was slow in finding his way, as a man and as a writer. After leaving Harvard he had occupied himself variously as an occasional teacher, a handyman living with the Emersons, briefly as tutor to the sons of Emerson's brother William on Staten Island, as a worker in his father's pencil factory, and still later as a surveyor. He experienced an early disappointment in love and a shocking loss when his beloved brother John suffered an agonizing death from lockjaw in 1842. All of this was of course well known in a town as small as Concord. But Henry did not endear himself to his neighbors when, in the spring of 1844, he and a friend negligently set a fire that burned more than three hundred acres of woodland. The episode was long remembered by Concordians. Thoreau himself, who took pride in his skills as an outdoorsman, must have felt ashamed and guilty, but his references to the fire in his journal sought to minimize his offense.[2]

Thoreau caused further talk in Concord during the following year, 1845. On land owned by Emerson that lay along the shores of Walden Pond, Henry began cutting down pine trees, constructed a cabin for himself, and moved into it on Independence Day, remaining there for more than two years but by no means secluding himself as a hermit. While still living in the woods he gave occasional lectures before the Concord Lyceum, and lecturing provided a convenient opportunity for satisfying his townsmen's curiosity about his activities at the pond. Here are sentences from the opening paragraphs of a lecture that he gave in March of 1846: "I should not presume to talk so much about myself and my affairs as I shall in this lecture if very particular and personal inquiries had not been made concerning my mode of life. . . . In most lectures or stories the I, or first person is omitted; in this it will be inserted, that is the main difference" (FV 105–6).[3]

In these words of 1846 will be recognized the germ of the opening paragraphs of *Walden* (originally subtitled *Life in the Woods*), which would not be published until eight years later. But there is no reference in the lecture either to *Walden* or to the other book on which Thoreau was actively working during his stay at the pond: *A Week on the Concord and Merrimack Rivers,* published in 1849, which he thought of as a memorial to his late brother. We know now that one of his primary objectives in leaving the family home in Concord village and building his cabin was to establish a quiet place for the work of authorship. By the time he finally left the pond, in September of 1847, he probably had in hand not only a draft of *A Week* but material for a number of articles as well. He had also expanded the manuscript of his recent lectures into the initial version of *Walden*—about half as long as the book that he ultimately published in 1854.

i

In 1846, when Henry Thoreau first attempted to answer his neighbors' questions about his life at the pond, he was facing a curious and potentially hostile audience of Concord lecture-goers who well remembered his part in the fire of two years before. His ostensible response was to offer a straightforward first-person narrative telling how he cleared the land, assembled materials, built his cabin, and began raising his own food. He duly reported "the exact cost" of his dwelling with respect to materials "but not counting the work"—all of which, he said, "was done by myself"; the total was "$28.12 1/2." To this outlay he added other expenses for food, clothing, and incidental supplies, subtracted the money gained by selling farm produce and performing day labor, and arrived at a net gain of "$19.71 3/4."[4] Such precise accounting was obviously intended to impress hardheaded merchants and farmers and to counteract Concord's reservations about young Henry and his unconventional life.

At the same time, however, the lecturer had another theme to advance. Turning directly to his audience, he had this to say:

> Some of you who hear me we all know are poor, find it hard to live, are sometimes, as it were, gasping for breath. I have no doubt that some of you who are here tonight are unable to pay for all the dinners you have actually eaten, or for the coats and shoes which are fast wearing or already worn out, and have come here to spend borrowed time, robbing your creditors of an hour. (FV 107)

Believing as he did that "most men" are "so occupied with the factitious cares and coarse labors of life that its finer fruits cannot be plucked by them," he charged that they have "no time to be anything but a machine."

To all his listeners, whether poor or well-to-do, the lecturer then offered another kind of reckoning. Playing off the profit-and-loss accounting so familiar to men of business, he applied the "appropriately inappropriate" language of commerce to a less tangible scale of value than that of dollars and cents.[5] Convinced that the true cost of a thing is "the amount of *life* it requires to be exchanged for it—immediately or in the long run" (FV 120; emphasis added), he acknowledged that if he should attempt "to tell how I have desired to *spend my life* in years past" he would "probably only startle you who are somewhat acquainted with its actual history." After teasingly describing some of his past "enterprises"—"self appointed inspector of snow storms & rain storms," for example, and "Surveyor if not of highways then of forest paths, and all across lot routes"—he then considered his more recent decision to "go into business" at Walden Pond. "Strict business habits I have always endeavored to acquire," he insisted. "They are indispensable to every man. If your trade is with the Celestial empire, then some small counting house on the coast, some Salem harbor, will be fixture enough" (FV 112–14; emphasis added).

When the lecturer spoke of his endeavor "to acquire strict business habits" he had something other than mere "busyness" in mind, though his more literal-minded listeners may not have realized it: his project of opening trade with "the Celestial empire" (FV 114–15) meant something far less tangible than the profitable New England enterprise of commerce with China. For him, one's true business should be *life itself,* and what he was really asking his neighbors to consider was how they were *spending* their lives—and for what. With his punning reference to trade "with the Celestial empire," which he developed playfully in an extended paragraph, the lecturer was announcing themes that Thoreau continued to pursue as he expanded and enriched his manuscript. Of these themes, that of *life* and how to spend it is all-important; indeed, I like to think of *Walden,* the ultimate product of its author's private "business," as figuratively conjugating the verb *to live* in all its moods and tenses—an exercise that began with the lecture.

ii

After leaving the pond, Thoreau continued to prepare his recent writings for the press, but poor sales of *A Week* following its appearance in 1849 prevented him from placing a second book with a publisher for some time to come. He remained a faithful contributor to the journal, however, and during the early 1850s he was again at work on the manuscript of *Walden*. J. Lyndon Shanley, in his pioneering study of the origin and growth of the book, has distinguished seven stages in its composition between 1846 and 1854, noting that it benefited immeasurably in content and form from the enforced delay, which gave Thoreau both the time and the needed perspective to complete *Walden* as we now have it. At the outset, as Shanley observed,

> he did not have a clear view of what *Walden* was finally to be, nor did he have a plan for developing the account of his life in the woods which we can follow as he carried it out. What he had, as he began, was a memory of his experience and a sense of its significance which were not satisfied by the *Walden* of 1849. He achieved the imaginative recreation, upon which the final, satisfying account of his experience depended, only gradually and through long care to recollect his experience as richly as possible.[6]

What Shanley called "the *Walden* of 1849," which incorporated and expanded material of the 1846 lecture, comprised roughly 70 percent of the first half of the complete book, but it represents the component parts very unevenly.[7] This material Thoreau augmented and later divided into chapters: "Economy" and "Where I Lived and What I Lived For," which stand at the beginning, followed by six chapters grouped in complementary pairs: "Reading" and "Sounds"; next, "Solitude" and "Visitors"; then "The Beanfield" and "The Village." Each chapter prepares in some way for the chapter that follows. Like Emerson, Thoreau believed that "No sentence will hold the whole truth,"[8] and that even entire chapters might thus be paired in order to present complementary or even contradictory aspects of one's thinking.

Such is the case with "Solitude" and "Visitors," to take one apposite example. "I love to be alone," runs a passage in the chapter on "Solitude." "I never found the companion that was as companionable as solitude" (135); the very next chapter, "Visitors," begins, "I think that I love society as much as most, and am ready enough to fasten myself like a bloodsucker for the time to any full-blooded man that comes my way." (The implication, of course, is that "full-blooded" men are few.) "I am naturally no hermit, but might possibly sit out the sturdiest frequenter of the barroom"—with a significant qualification: "*if* my business called me thither" (140; emphasis added).[9] As every reader knows, what Thoreau considered his "business" was altogether different from the mere "busyness" that so occupied his neighbors.

In "Solitude" Thoreau also wrote of "a certain doubleness by which I can stand as remote from myself as from another. However intense my experience, I am conscious of the presence and criticism of a part of me, which, as it were, is not a part of me, but spectator, sharing no experience, but taking note of it, and that is no more I than it is you" (135). Sherman Paul, commenting on the "drama of selves" in this passage, has written that here Thoreau was seeking to distinguish "the empirical self" and "the eternal self, the passive center" of his being.[10] But the cryptic authorial statement may be more specifically applicable to that "part of" Henry Thoreau who as "spectator" took note of experience and, as "reporter to a journal," made a written record of it—a record that he could then draw upon in his public utterances.

As for *Walden,* Thoreau introduced a significant revision of his opening paragraphs as they had originally stood. He had begun his lecture in 1846 by saying that he would be talking in the first person in order to answer "very particular and personal inquiries" about his mode of life; in the published book, however, his narrative begins: "I should not talk so much about myself if there were any body else whom I knew as well" (3). The "I" who is speaking in the book frequently includes observations on his neighbors that Henry Thoreau would scarcely have offered in directly facing an audience at the Concord Lyceum, sharp as he had been in his lecture of 1846. An example is this scathing remark in "Economy": "The greater part of what my neighbors call good I believe in my soul to be bad, and if I repent of any thing, it is likely to be my good behavior. What demon possessed me that I behaved so well?" (10). And in "Where I Lived and What I Lived For" is an added comment on the speaker and his book that also appears as a motto on the 1854 title page of *Walden:* "I do not propose to write an ode to dejection, but to brag as lustily as chanticleer in the morning, standing on his roost, if only to wake my neighbors up" (84).[11]

The alert reader may see in all such self-assertive passages what Thoreau's mid–twentieth-century critics began to point out: that the narrative "I" of the book is what Joseph Moldenhauer called "a deliberately created verbal personality," a "dramatized Thoreau" that "should not be confused in critical analysis with the surveyor and pencil-maker of Concord: the *persona* stands in the same relation to the man as *Walden* [the book] stands to the literal fact of the Walden adventure."[12] Richard Lebeaux agrees: he identifies this created image as "a persona who was more independent and purer than the real man who had lived by the pond."[13] And, we might well add, this persona is even more guarded than the man who subsequently wrote of himself in the journal.

As for *Walden*, E. B. White once shrewdly remarked that the reader "is excluded from the private life of the author, who supplies almost no gossip about himself" while discoursing at length "about his neighbors, and about the universe."[14] Instead, he preferred to speak indirectly, through imagery and parable and through the general movement of the book. And to narrate his story, Thoreau created a dramatized figure, standing at an increasing remove from his own original experience at the pond. Speaking through this figure, the "I" of *Walden*, he tells us only what he would have us know and do.

iii

"Books," we are told in a third-person passage of "Reading," "must be read as deliberately and reservedly as they were written" (100–101). The word *deliberately* and its cognates appear frequently in *Walden*. Thoreau, with his training in the classics, knew Latin roots: "to deliberate" means literally "to weigh," from Latin *libra*, a scale, and "to reserve" is to keep back for some special use, from Latin *reservare*, to serve again. So he wrote *Walden*, drawing selectively on what he had stored away in the journal; so must we read the book, weighing his words and keeping them in reserve for our own special use. *Deliberately* occurs in a paragraph of "Where I Lived and What I Lived For" that Thoreau had drafted as early as the 1849 manuscript (FV 141);[15] it is another discourse on life and living:

> I went to the woods because I wished to live deliberately, to front only the essential facts of life, and see if I could not learn what it had to teach, and not, when I came to die, discover that I had not lived. I did not wish to live what was not life, living is so dear; nor did I

wish to practice resignation, unless it was quite necessary. I wanted to live deep and suck out all the marrow of life, to live so sturdily and Spartan-like as to put to rout all that was not life, to cut a broad swath and shave close, to drive life into a corner, and reduce it to its lowest terms, and, if it proved to be mean, why then to get the whole and genuine meanness of it, and publish its meanness to the world; or if it were sublime, to know it by experience, and be able to give a true account of it in my next excursion. (90–91)

This is not only "the best-known passage in the book," as F. O. Matthiessen remarked; it is also "the core of [Thoreau's] declaration of purpose."[16] His austere conception of life and living becomes more and more prominent in those chapters comprising the second half of *Walden,* written during the early 1850s when he settled upon an organizing principle that would unify the entire book: it is the recurrent cycle of the seasons that gives the completed narrative its basic structure.[17] "Not only did he make a story of one year from the experience of two years," as Shanley noted; "he also used the accounts of experiences of other times"—accounts tallied in the journal—"so long as they were true to the nature and tenor of his days at the pond."[18] And, as Robert Sattelmeyer explains, that story involves a kind of plot: "the journey or quest of the narrator passing through various changes marked by the progress of the seasons and advancing toward some kind of self-knowledge. The book begins to acquire mythic and archetypal dimensions and, in the relative deemphasis of social criticism . . . , becomes less topical and more universal in its reference."[19]

This is to say once again that the "I" of *Walden* is not offering a literal narrative of Henry Thoreau's day-to-day life in the woods between 1845 and 1847. Moreover, he is given lines to speak in the nine later chapters that differ both in content and in tone from those first spoken by the lecturer of 1846 and then incorporated in the 1849 manuscript; they are far less combative than "Economy" and more in the reflective vein of "Where I Lived and What I Lived For" and "Solitude." Thoreau himself had changed in the intervening years, as his journal reveals, and he went to the journal for material used in the latter half of *Walden.*[20] But these late chapters continue to exhibit typical Thoreauvian rhetoric: "puns, irony, redefinition, paradoxes, twisted proverbs, over-statements, Biblical allusions . . . , and gymnastic leaps between the figurative and the literal," as Moldenhauer has characterized Thoreau's inimitable way of writing.[21]

Beginning with the pivotal chapter on "The Ponds," the latter portion of the narrative proceeds to the contrasting subject of "Baker Farm," then on to the pairing of "Higher Laws" with "Brute Neighbors." Next, as summer and fall give way to winter, come four associated chapters: "House-Warming," "Former Inhabitants and Winter Visitors," "Winter Animals," and "The Pond in Winter." The climax of the narrative occurs, appropriately enough, with "Spring," the penultimate chapter, which is followed by a summarizing "Conclusion" that brings together motifs and images that had appeared earlier in the book. Looking back from this retrospective final chapter, we can see how, throughout *Walden,* the narrator has been registering fundamental changes in himself that parallel these seasonal changes in nature.

Readers who are alert to this pattern of gradual change will recognize the beginning of the process in the repeated images of metamorphosis that appear even in the opening pages of the book. "Our moulting season, like that of the fowls, must be a crisis in our lives," we are warned in "Economy" (24). To effect a comparable change, our lives too "must be stripped" of everything nonessential before we can uncover that which is essential, genuine, and true (38). The narrator provides repeated illustrations of change in progress, as in his account of how he spreads out warped boards "to bleach and warp back again in the sun" so that he may use them in building his cabin (44). As in nature, so in mankind. Witness the rites of purification practiced by savage tribes that meet the received definition of a sacrament: an "outward and visible sign of an inward and spiritual grace" (69); the implication for the civilized man—"a more experienced and wiser savage" (40)—should be obvious.

The narrator himself is clearly seeking purification. In "Where I Lived and What I Lived For" he tells us that "Every morning was a cheerful invitation to make my life of equal simplicity, and I may say innocence, with Nature herself" (88). "Morning," he explains, "is when I am awake, and there is a dawn in me" (90), and the theme of awakening to life and all its possibilities is recurrent throughout *Walden.* So too is the figurative search for a firm foundation—a basis on which "you might found a wall or a state, or set a lamp post safely"—which closes this second chapter. In order to gain such a foundation for our lives, the "I" enjoins us, we must work downward, "through the mud and slush of opinion, and prejudice, and tradition, and delusion, and appearance," until we reach "a hard bottom" that we can call *reality*. "Be it life or death, we crave only reality," he declares: "If we are really dying, let us hear the rattle in our throats and feel cold in the extremities; if we are alive, let us go about our business" (97–98).[22]

In "Economy" and in "Where I Lived and What I Lived For," the narrator was establishing a fundamental contrast between the shortcomings of his neighbors—those who are only "*said to live* in New England" (4; emphasis added)—and the advantages he had so far gained by pursuing a different way of living. But he was well aware that any significant change in an individual may bring on a sense of disorientation, as with his own experience of becoming lost in the woods; this brief misadventure prompts him to recall the injunction that we must lose the world, as Scripture tells us, in order to find our true selves (171). We see him withdrawing further from society— into nature and into the self—in the second half of the book. Here the dominant features are the pond, a part of nature from time immemorial, and the cabin, put together in a season with the labor of his hands.

When the narrator first went to the woods he arose every morning and bathed in the pond. "That was a religious exercise," he declares, "and one of the best things which I did," thus renewing himself each day (88). In looking into a lake as clear as Walden Pond, he tells us in a later chapter, "the beholder measures the depth of his own nature" (186). The pond never changes its character; "all the change is in me" (193). Stressing the *purity* of its waters (192, 194), he is "thankful that the pond was made deep and pure for a symbol. While men believe in the infinite some ponds will be thought to be bottomless" (287).[23] As winter approaches, the surface of the pond becomes frozen, but life in its depths is unaffected. The narrator, however, must insulate his cabin against the elements and warm himself by its interior fire. "I withdrew yet farther into my shell," he declares in "House-Warming," "and endeavored to keep a bright fire both within my house and within my breast" (249). So he responds as nature changes with the seasons and winter at last gives way to spring.

As with the seasons, so with the days. "The day is an epitome of the year," says the "I." "The night is the winter, the morning and evening are the spring and fall, and the noon is the summer" (301). "Alert and healthy natures remember that the sun rose clear," we are advised at the very outset (8); its transforming power is continually emphasized. It is the sun that enables the farmer-narrator to make his field "speak beans instead of grass" (157); its burning is the ultimate source of the vital heat that keeps him warm throughout his winter hibernation in the cabin. Morning, "the most memorable season of the day," is "the awakening hour. . . . Morning is when I am awake," he tells us, "and there is a dawn in me" (89–90). After one "still winter night," he "awoke to an answered question, to Nature and daylight" (282). In "Spring" the sun at last frees the pond of its enclosing ice,[24] and as "Walden was dead and is alive again" (311), so too is the narrator awakened and alive. "Only that day dawns to which we are awake," he cautions us at the close of his final chapter, but he is confident nevertheless that "There is more day to dawn" and that "The sun is but a morning star" (333).

Thoreau's consistent but unobtrusive employment of such themes and images depicts for us what Stanley Edgar Hyman rightly called "a vast rebirth ritual, the purest and most complete in our literature."[25] The pattern is a familiar one, as Thoreau himself was well aware. His chapter on "Reading" gives the example of a "solitary hired man on a farm in the outskirts of Concord" who has had just such a "second birth and religious experience." The man "may think it is not true; but Zoroaster, thousands of years ago, travelled the same road and had the same experience." "Being wise," Zoroaster "knew it to be universal, and treated his neighbors accordingly" (108); so too did the author of *Walden*.

iv

In "Conclusion," Thoreau's narrator informs us that he "learned this, at least," by his experiment:

> that if one advances confidently in the direction of his dreams, and endeavors to live the life which he has imagined, he will meet with a success unexpected in common hours. . . . In proportion as he simplifies his life, the laws of the universe will appear less complex, and solitude will not be solitude, nor poverty poverty, nor weakness weakness. If you have built castles in the air, your work need not be lost; that is where they should be. Now put the foundations under them. (323–24)

That these eloquent words coming from the "I" of *Walden* were written deliberately and reservedly for Thoreau's public persona becomes evident when we turn from the book to the private journal. In *Walden* we are told that the narrator went to the woods to learn what life had to teach (90), and that he left "for as good a reason as I went there. Perhaps it seemed to me that I had several more lives to live, and could not spare any more time for that one" (323). Consider now an earlier journal entry of 22 January 1852, where the "I" of the journal would seem to be addressing that aspect of Thoreau's personality that he called not a part of himself but a "spectator" of his experience:

> But Why I changed—? Why I left the woods? I do not think that I can tell. I have often wished myself back— I do not know any better how I came to go there—. Perhaps it is none of my business—even if it is your's. Perhaps I wanted a change— . . .
>
> I must say that I do not know what made me leave the pond— I left it as unaccountably as I went to it. To speak sincerely, I went there because I had got ready to go— I left it for the same reason. (*Journal* 4:275–76)

J. Golden Taylor took Thoreau's words in the journal as a whimsical illustration of "the very extreme to which he allows himself to remain an enigma—even to himself."[26] But John Broderick, looking deeper, has found "pulsations of departure and return" throughout Thoreau's life and writing, even at the level of individual paragraphs. "In style as well as in structure," Broderick writes,

> Thoreau recapitulates the archetypal Romantic theme of rebirth. His significant contribution to the theme is his recognition that the moment of spiritual rebirth is not infinite, that the walk cannot be prolonged indefinitely, that return is inevitable. To death and rebirth, he adds reentry.[27]

In a similar comment, R. W. B. Lewis sees Thoreau returning from the pond to the village much as Plato's enlightened philosophers returned to the cave of conventional life; in *Walden* he would then tell his sleepy-eyed neighbors and his readers that they have been seeing by illumination merely "reflected and derivative" rather than by the true light of the sun that he celebrates throughout the book.[28]

"We should come home from afar," Thoreau himself wrote in "Baker Farm," "from adventures, and perils, and discoveries every day, with new experience and character" (208)—and like Zoroaster, we should proceed to enlighten our neighbors accordingly. The "I" who speaks in Henry Thoreau's journal, it seems to me, is the person he thought he was; the person he *wished to be* is the idealized "I" through whom he addresses the readers of *Walden,* beginning with his as yet unawakened neighbors.[29] And whatever the experience at the pond may have meant to Thoreau himself in after years, his deliberately written account of it, speaking through that idealized "I," has had a powerful effect on others. Indeed, many men and women have even "dated a new era" in their lives (107) from their equally deliberate reading of *Walden.*[30]

14.

Hawthorne's "Autobiographical Impulse"

> . . . we may prate of the circumstances that lie around us, and
> even of ourself, but still keep the inmost Me behind its veil. To
> this extent . . . an author, methinks, may be autobiographical.
> —Hawthorne, "The Custom-House"

"Twice in my life," Nathaniel Hawthorne wrote in 1850, "an autobiographical impulse" had "taken possession of me" (*The Scarlet Letter*, 3). The first occasion was in 1846, when he wrote "The Old Manse: The Author Makes the Reader Acquainted with His Abode" as an introduction to a collection of his stories and sketches, *Mosses from an Old Manse;* the second was in 1850, when he composed "The Custom-House" as an introduction to what was being planned as a similar collection. Both "The Old Manse" and "The Custom-House" are examples of the personal essay, a literary form that readers of the day associated with such nineteenth-century writers as Lamb, Hazlitt, and De Quincey in England and Washington Irving in the United States.

Hawthorne's own writings especially reminded some readers of the essays of Charles Lamb; one newspaper even referred to him in 1849 as "the gentle Elia of our American literature."[1] To examine how he adapted the essay form in "The Old Manse" and "The Custom-House" is to observe him at work during the very time when he was coming into his own as a major American author. Both essays throw considerable light on his own distinctive approach to the writing of fiction.

159

i. "The Old Manse"

Planning for the book that became *Mosses from an Old Manse* began early in 1845, while Hawthorne and his bride were living in Concord, Massachusetts, as the first nonministerial couple to reside in Concord's venerable Unitarian parsonage, where Emerson had once lived. Evert Duyckinck, then an editor for the New York publishing house of Wiley and Putnam, had offered to publish a collection of Hawthorne's short fiction as a successor to his *Twice-Told Tales,* which had appeared first in 1837 and again in a second edition of 1842. Hawthorne agreed, and by the following spring he was projecting a "new story" as "a sort of frame-work" for the book. His original idea was "to make the scene an idealization" of the old parsonage "and of the river close at hand, with glimmerings of my actual life—yet so transmogrified that the reader should not know what was reality and what fancy."[2] As he was later to say of "The Old Manse" itself, "I have appealed to no sentiment or sensibilities, save such as are diffused among us all. So far as I am a man of really individual attributes, I veil my face; nor am I, nor have ever been, one of those supremely hospitable people, who serve up their own hearts delicately fried, with brain-sauce, as a tidbit for their beloved public" (*Mosses from an Old Manse,* 32–33).

"The Old Manse" turns on "idealizations" not only of the parsonage and the nearby river, as Hawthorne had planned, but also of himself, for the "I" who is addressing the reader in the essay is a persona—an image deliberately created for the public, like the "I" of Thoreau's *Walden.* In determining to veil his face, as he put it, Hawthorne meant that he would say nothing to his readers of the joys that he and his wife had shared during their stay at the manse, where their first child, Una, was born in 1844, nor would he complain publicly of his constant worry over money. Hawthorne had continued to write assiduously for American magazines, as he had been doing since the 1830s, but the returns were disappointingly meager and payments were often late if indeed they were made at all.

Meanwhile, Hawthorne's friends had been working to secure a remunerative political appointment for him, and in October of 1845, with a place in the customs service in prospect, he moved his family from Concord to Salem, his birthplace. In the following April he became Surveyor of Customs there at an assured annual salary of $1,200—far more than he had been able to earn as a writer. *Mosses from an Old Manse* at last appeared in July of 1846, the same month in which the Hawthornes' son, Julian, was born. Selecting the pieces to be included and choosing a title for the book had taken much time and thought, and Hawthorne was slow in completing the "story," as he had called the projected introduction. Not until mid-April of 1846, after much of the book was already set in type, did he have it ready to send to Duyckinck.

"The Old Manse" begins very much as Hawthorne had first thought of it, with descriptions of the house and the nearby Concord River. The manse itself, he wrote, was "worthy to have been one of the time-honored parsonages of England," with a comparable "inheritance of sanctity." Conscious of himself as a secular author rather than a clergyman, he "took shame . . . for having been so long a writer of idle stories, and ventured to hope that wisdom would descend upon me . . . and that I should light upon an intellectual treasure in the old Manse." If he could not succeed during his residence in writing some profound work of morality, religion, or history, he "resolved at least to achieve a novel, that should evolve some deep lesson, and should possess physical substance enough to stand alone" (4–5).

To further this design, he assembled his books and pictures in a "most delightful little nook of a study" at the rear of the house, overlooking both the river and the scene of that memorable engagement between Concord yeomen and British regulars that had opened the War for Independence (5–6). "Unexcitable and sluggish" though the Concord River at first appears, "in the light of a calm and golden sunset, it becomes lovely beyond expression. . . . Every tree and rock, and every blade of grass" along its banks "is distinctly imaged, and, however unsightly in reality, assumes ideal beauty in the reflection" (6–7). Thus the river is transformed into a mirror of the ideal, like other reflecting surfaces that appear so frequently in Hawthorne's writings.[3] Far more beautiful than the Concord is its tributary the Asabeth, described in a later passage of the essay: "A more lovely stream . . . has never flowed on earth—nowhere, indeed, except to lave the interior regions of a poet's imagination." It too reflects the scenes through which the current gently takes it:

> Yes, the river sleeps along its course, and dreams of the sky, and of the clustering foliage. . . . Of all this scene, the slumbering river has a dream-picture in its bosom. Which, after all, was the most real—the

picture, or the original?—the objects palpable to our grosser senses, or
their apotheosis in the stream beneath? Surely the disembodied images
stand in closer relation to the soul. (21–22)

Thus the rivers and their reflected images exemplify the very mingling of
reality with fancy that Hawthorne had intended to convey, both here and
in the stories he was introducing.

In the middle section of the essay its author takes the reader inside the
manse. On one rainy day he proceeds upstairs to a huge garret filled with
old books, many of them "transmitted down through a series of consecrated
hands, from the days of the mighty Puritan divines." Though Hawthorne
had sought among these venerable tomes for some "living thought," he
found "no such treasure" there; "all was dead alike"—there and even in
the more recent religious publications that were also stored in the garret.
"Thought grows mouldy," he remarks. "What was good and nourishing
food for the spirits of one generation, affords no sustenance for the next"
(19). By way of contrast, he also mentions other items that he had come
across in the attic: "a few old newspapers, and still older almanacs, which
reproduced, to my mental eye, the epochs when they had issued from the
press, with a distinctness that was altogether unaccountable. It was as if I
had found bits of magic looking-glass among the books, with the images
of a vanished century in them" (20).

This is to say, though Hawthorne himself does not draw the analogy,
that these seemingly ephemeral publications reflect their times much as
the rivers reflect the scenes about and above them. What he does remark
is that the old divines "had been able to produce nothing half so real,
as these newspaper scribblers and almanac-makers had thrown off, in the
effervescence of a moment. . . . It is the Age itself that writes newspapers
and almanacs, which therefore have a distinct purpose and meaning, at
the time, and a kind of intelligible truth for all times" (19–20). Such is
the nature of the source-materials Hawthorne had preferred to consult
when writing his stories of the New England past, and such was the "kind
of intelligible truth for all times" that he himself hoped to reflect and to
convey through his fiction to his contemporary audience.

There is another passage of "The Old Manse" that illuminates its author's
view of contemporary Concord. Elsewhere in the town, he reminds his
readers, was the home of "a great original Thinker," one whose mind "drew

many men upon long pilgrimages, to speak to him face to face" (30). For himself, Hawthorne confessed,

> there had been epochs of my life, when I, too, might have asked of this prophet the master-word, that should solve me the riddle of the universe; but now, being happy, I felt as if there were no question to be put, and therefore admired Emerson as a poet of deep beauty and austere tenderness, but sought nothing from him as a philosopher. It was good, nevertheless, to meet him in the wood-paths, or sometimes in our avenue, with that pure, intellectual gleam diffused about his presence, like the garment of a shining-one; and he so quiet, so simple, so without pretension, encountering each man alive as if expecting to receive more than he could impart. (31)

Unlike Emerson, Hawthorne had before his marriage lived and worked for a time at Brook Farm, the communal enterprise established by a group of so-called Transcendentalists at West Roxbury. Hawthorne's wife, one of the celebrated Peabody sisters of Salem, is said to have once named Emerson as the greatest man alive. But Hawthorne himself was never a Transcendentalist nor even a church-going man; his motive for going to Brook Farm was primarily economic. During his years in the old manse, for all his knowledge and understanding of the New England religious tradition from the Puritans and Quakers through Unitarianism and beyond, he adhered to no body of doctrine or form of worship.

"The Old Manse" concludes with four relatively short paragraphs in which the author turns directly to his audience, posing this question: "Has the reader gone wandering, hand in hand with me, through the inner passages of my being, and have we groped together into all its chambers, and examined their treasures or their rubbish? Not so. We have been standing on the green sward, but just within the cavern's mouth, where the common sunshine is free to penetrate, and where every footstep is therefore free to come" (32). In short, the "I" who has been speaking is a "transmogrified" Hawthorne—an idealized figure who mirrors something of the author's outer life at the manse while veiling not only his "really individual attributes" but also his innermost thoughts.

As for the outer life, this fictionalized Hawthorne acknowledges that Providence "has led me, as the newspapers announce while I am writing, from the Old Manse into a Custom-House! As a storyteller, I have often contrived strange vicissitudes for my imaginary personages, but none like this" (33–34). What then of the ambitious goals as an author he had once sought to realize?

> The treasure of intellectual gold, which I hoped to find in our secluded dwelling, had never come to light. No profound treatise of ethics—no philosophic history—no novel, even, that could stand, unsupported, on its edges. All that I had to show, as a man of letters, were these few tales and essays, which had blossomed out like flowers in the calm summer of my heart and mind. (34)

Of these "fitful sketches," as he called them, he had little to say: "such trifles, I truly feel, afford no solid basis for a literary reputation. Nevertheless, the public . . . will receive them the more kindly, as the last offering, the last collection of this nature, which it is my purpose ever to put forth. Unless I could do better, I have done enough in this kind" (34).

ii. The "Posthumous Papers of a Decapitated Surveyor"

Whatever Hawthorne's true sentiments may have been in 1846 with respect to producing another collection of his "tales and essays," in 1849, during the third year of his new surveyorship, he was facing the need to assemble still another such volume. Once again, as he was to write in "The Custom-House," "Providence had meditated better things for me than I could possibly imagine for myself" (*Scarlet Letter,* 40). A change of administration in Washington following the national elections of 1848 had brought the Whigs into power, and in Massachusetts they began to replace Democratic office-holders with their own partisan appointees. At the Salem Custom-House there were rumors of impending dismissals, and on 8 June 1849 Mr. Surveyor Hawthorne found himself turned out of office. As he put it, "My own head was the first that fell!" (41). Aided by friends in both parties, he fought his dismissal as best he could, but the effort was fruitless. On 28 July his successor was appointed, leaving Hawthorne with no other employment in sight.[4]

Meanwhile, both the local press in Salem and other newspapers through-out New England had taken up Hawthorne's case, pro and con,[5] and for a time, as he recalled with some amusement, their stories kept him

careering through the public prints, in my decapitated state, like
Irving's Headless Horseman; ghastly and grim, and longing to be
buried, as a politically dead man ought. So much for my figurative
self. The real human being, all this time, with his head safely on his
shoulders, had brought himself to the comfortable conclusion, that
every thing was for the best; and, making an investment in ink, paper,
and steel-pens, had opened his long-disused writing-desk, and was
again a literary man. (42–43)

So Hawthorne once more set to work as a writer. "Keeping up the
metaphor of the political guillotine," he remarked that what he produced in
1849 and 1850 could well be thought of as "the POSTHUMOUS PAPERS
OF A DECAPITATED SURVEYOR" (43). Although he publicly claimed
to be happier while composing these pieces "than at any time since he had
quitted the Old Manse," the next few months were admittedly a period of
"still seething turmoil." His mother had died at Salem in July of 1849, and
with a wife and two children to support and a burden of debt remaining
from the idyllic years in Concord, he was once more in pressing need of
money. It was probably September before he was ready to begin writing
the "stern and sombre" story of Puritan Boston, as he called it, that was
to grow into *The Scarlet Letter;* four months later he had finished all but
its last three chapters. By that time he had also completed "The Custom-
House," written to introduce not only this long narrative but also several
shorter pieces. All were to be included in a book called "Old-Time Legends"
that the Boston firm of Ticknor and Fields had agreed to publish, and in
late January of 1850 the firm was advertising the forthcoming volume as
another collection of Hawthorne's tales.

Then came a change in plans. When James T. Fields, a partner in the
firm, first read the still-incomplete *Scarlet Letter,* he was so impressed with
its merits that he persuaded the reluctant author to drop everything else
from the book except "The Custom-House." Fields proceeded to rush the
new work into print while Hawthorne was still hurrying to complete his
manuscript, not giving him an opportunity to revise the references to other
stories in the final paragraphs of his introductory sketch. The volume was
published as *The Scarlet Letter* on 16 March 1850, roughly six months after
Hawthorne had begun to compose its new materials.

How Hawthorne managed in such a short period of time to produce a
narrative at once so beautifully conceived and so densely written cannot be

explained simply by citing his need for money and the pressure to finish his manuscript. He himself once remarked that since *The Scarlet Letter* is "all in one tone, I had only to get my pitch, and could then go on interminably."[6] But there is more to be said—especially about the antecedents of the book. For some years, as we know from "The Old Manse," Hawthorne had wished to produce something of greater magnitude than stories and sketches, but in a very real sense those same tales that he came to deprecate had prepared the way for a book that Henry James was to call "the finest piece of imaginative writing yet put forth" by an American author.[7] As early as the 1820s he had begun to soak himself in the history of colonial New England, the setting of many of his stories; *The Scarlet Letter* is a narrative of seventeenth-century Boston, and both its characters and its themes have their prototypes in history, in his own earlier fiction, or in personal observation.

Through his reading, for example, Hawthorne had encountered several instances of women required to wear the letters *AD* or *A* as their punishment for adultery, and in a story of 1837 that he called "Endicott and the Red Cross" he wrote of just such a person—an obvious forerunner of Hester Prynne. In her appearance and characterization Hester is one of a line of Dark Ladies in Hawthorne's fiction—a type that evidently continued to fascinate him. Hester not only wears her Scarlet Letter openly, she embellishes it with rich embroidery, and her daughter, Pearl, is the letter personified. This "elf-child" whose unpredictable conduct strikes some readers as unrealistic is actually patterned after little Una Hawthorne as Hawthorne had observed her and then described her in his notebooks.

In another story of Hawthorne's earlier years, one with a peculiarly resonant title, "The Minister's Black *Veil*" (emphasis added), a New England clergyman startles his devoted followers by appearing before them with his face hidden beneath a dark cloth—an emblem whose full significance the minister never consents to explain, even though parishioners who know him speculate on what secret he may be concealing. Arthur Dimmesdale in *The Scarlet Letter,* a young minister beloved by his parishioners, wears no veil, but he holds his hand over his heart as though something were hidden there that he cannot bring himself to reveal. As readers soon infer, he is the unacknowledged father of Hester's Pearl. The same inference is drawn by a newcomer to Boston, a misshapen old man calling himself Roger Chillingworth. He soon attaches himself to Dimmesdale in a persistent effort to discover whether the minister too wears a Scarlet Letter on his breast—not openly, as Hester does, but as a hidden stigma.

Chillingworth had already recognized Hester Prynne as the young woman whom he had married years before in England—not for love, as they both knew at the time, though she looked up to him as a respected man of intellectual attainments. Now he enjoins her not to reveal his true identity, and she reluctantly agrees, thus making it possible for the old man to become Dimmesdale's close companion and physician—one who applies himself as a veritable leech to the young minister. In his consuming desire for revenge, Chillingworth manages to destroy both Dimmesdale's bodily frame and what little is left of the spiritual health he had once enjoyed. The minister realizes only too late what he has dimly suspected of Chillingworth's machinations. As he ultimately says, in the course of a late meeting with Hester, Chillingworth "has violated, in cold blood, the sanctity of a human heart"—adding, more or less truthfully, "Thou and I, Hester, never did so!" And Hester whispers her agreement (195).

Two entries in Hawthorne's notebooks of 1841 and 1847 anticipate his creation of Chillingworth in 1850: "To symbolize moral or physical disease by disease of the body" and "A story of the effects of revenge, in diabolizing him who indulges in it."[8] Relevant to Chillingworth's obsessive probing of Dimmesdale is a still earlier sketch of 1831 called "Sights from a Steeple," where Hawthorne's narrator observes that "The most desirable mode of existence might be that of a spiritualized Paul Pry, hovering invisible round man and woman, witnessing their deeds, *searching into their hearts,* borrowing brightness from their felicity, and shade from their sorrow, and retaining no emotion peculiar to himself" (*Twice-Told Tales,* 192; emphasis added). But if the narrator was speaking here for the author, Hawthorne's "Ethan Brand," a kind of cautionary tale written concurrently with *The Scarlet Letter,* illustrates a much different view of such cold-blooded invasion of another human heart. Brand had once looked into the hearts of others with all due reverence, but his subsequent intellectual development disturbs "the counterpoise" between his mind and his own heart so that he gradually loses his respect for the sanctity of others. And he too deteriorates, like Chillingworth, until he also becomes "a fiend" (*The Snow-Image,* 98–99).

There is much of Nathaniel Hawthorne in these characters: not only Chillingworth and Dimmesdale but also Hester Prynne. Both author and character possess "a sympathetic knowledge of the hidden sin in other hearts" (86). Isolated from the Puritan community, Hester takes up her needle as a professional seamstress, much as Hawthorne had again taken up his pen as a professional writer in order to support himself and his family. With her needlework Hester embroiders the letter she must wear and Pearl's elaborate costumes as well, finding in her art "a mode of expressing, and therefore soothing, the passion of her life" (84). So too did Hawthorne, who for many readers reveals more of himself in *The Scarlet Letter* than he was willing to express openly through the "I" who speaks with such conscious discretion in "The Old Manse" and again in the essay that became "The Custom-House."

When Hawthorne composed his introduction to what he was still thinking of as "Old-Time Legends," he began by reminding his readers of the earlier "autobiographical impulse" that had led him to write "The Old Manse." This time, he said, he would proceed as though he were enjoying a talk with "a kind and apprehensive, though not the closest friend." In such company, he continued,

> a native reserve being thawed by this genial consciousness, we may prate of the circumstances that lie around us, and even of ourself, but still keep the inmost Me behind its veil. To this extent and within these limits, an author, methinks, may be autobiographical, without violating either the reader's rights or his own. (4)

Once more, as in "The Old Manse"—and like his protagonist in "The Minister's Black Veil," Hawthorne would be safeguarding his inmost being.

iii. "The Custom-House"

The author of "The Custom-House" had two objectives in mind: to introduce the stories that were to follow and also—as Hawthorne privately intended—to take revenge on political enemies.[9] It was this introductory essay rather than *The Scarlet Letter* that made the new book an immediate best-seller, especially in Salem. The partisan tone in which the "decapitated Surveyor" treated his dismissal from the Custom House angered local Whigs; more than that, he drew readers and scandalized many of them by including word sketches of three former colleagues. One was General

James F. Miller, a military hero who had served as Collector of Customs at Salem for twenty-four years despite shifts in the political winds—a man whom Hawthorne obviously respected and admired in spite of his conservative bent. The two other unnamed officers were a superannuated "permanent Inspector" preoccupied with his past dinners and, by contrast, a fully qualified "man of business" whose talents were needed to keep a faltering enterprise functioning.

Replies from Hawthorne's enemies came quickly and forcefully. One Salem paper, for example, attacked his sketches as "calumnious caricatures of inoffensive men, who could not possibly have given occasion for such wanton insults."[10] But Hawthorne held his fire until a second edition of the new book was called for. There, in an added preface, he noted that reaction to the three sketches "could hardly have been more violent . . . had he burned down the Custom-House." But after carefully reading over what he had written, he continued, he had concluded that the "only remarkable features" of his introductory essay "are its frank and genuine good-humor" and its "general accuracy," and that he was "constrained, therefore," to republish it "without the change of a word" (1–2).

Hawthorne also remarked in his preface that "The Custom-House" "might, perhaps, have been wholly omitted, without loss to the public, or detriment to the book" (1), and indeed there have been printings of *The Scarlet Letter* unaccompanied by the essay. But the historic setting of "The Custom-House" provided him with a plausible basis for explaining "how a large portion of the following pages came into my possession" and thereby establishing "the authenticity of a narrative therein contained" (4)—that is to say, the ensuing story of the Scarlet Letter. In this sense the book as a whole is more of a piece than *Mosses from an Old Manse,* where the introductory essay bears little relation to the other components except that most of them had been written in the house Hawthorne was describing. What the two introductions have chiefly in common is that both are leisurely discourses that profess to be autobiographical, each locating its author in relation to buildings with historical associations.[11]

Here Hawthorne may well have been following the example of Charles Lamb's familiar essay "The South-Sea House"; his controversial sketches of the three Custom-House officers are likewise somewhat reminiscent of Lamb's "Old Benchers of the Inner Temple." The opening pages of "The Custom-House" look back in time from nineteenth-century Salem past its great days as a commercial port to the still earlier colonial settlement where Hawthorne's "first ancestor" had established the family line. This grave progenitor, whose image "haunts" his descendant, was a man of authority, possessing "all the Puritanic traits, both good and evil." He became "a bitter persecutor" of Quakers; his son, who "inherited the persecuting spirit," was a judge in the infamous Salem witchcraft trials. "I, the present writer, take shame upon myself for their sakes," Hawthorne declared, praying for removal from his family of "any curse incurred by them." "Doubtless" these Puritan ancestors would disapprove of their descendant as a mere "writer of storybooks!" (9–10). Thoughts of shame and disapproval were not new for Hawthorne; in "The Old Manse" he had previously admitted that he "took shame" for being merely "a writer of idle stories" (*Mosses,* 4).

By establishing a sense of the interrelation of past and present Hawthorne was preparing for later passages of the essay and in turn for the story of Puritan New England that it was particularly to introduce. Though more recent generations of his family had "sunk almost out of sight" in Salem, he continued, he himself felt destined to return once again to his ancestral home, this time to fill his new post as chief executive officer of the Custom House. There he "found few but aged men" in his department, some of whom "never dreamed of making their appearance" during much of the year. "I must plead guilty to the charge of abbreviating the official breath of more than one of these venerable servants of the republic," he confessed (12–13), thus provoking the ire of his Whig opponents. At this point in the essay come his sketches of General Miller and the two other officers. Only one of these sketches, the unflattering account of the permanent Inspector, strikes a twentieth-century reader as at all likely to provoke the storm that arose when Hawthorne's contemporaries read "The Custom-House," but his portraits served as convenient targets for political attack.

Through this part of the essay Hawthorne was writing in the literary mode that one critic, Nina Baym, has called "surface representation, or 'realism.'" A significant change to the mode of "symbolic narrative" occurs, however, with his shift of scene from the offices on the main floor of the Custom House to the musty attic above[12]—a setting resembling the garret Hawthorne had previously described in "The Old Manse." What he reports finding this time, however, were not sermons and works of theology but secular documents of various kinds that had survived from earlier centuries. Among other papers he supposedly came upon was a commission appointing one of his official predecessors, Jonathan Pue, to be Surveyor of His Majesty's Customs for the colonial port of Salem. Although Surveyor Pue's death in 1760 is a matter of historical record, the objects that his successor purportedly discovered in the Custom-House attic are of course products of Hawthorne's imagination.

Among these fictional discoveries is a bit of faded red cloth, richly embroidered in gold, in the shape of the capital letter *A;* another is a manuscript in the hand of Surveyor Pue explaining why the Scarlet Letter was worn by a woman of seventeenth-century Boston whose story he had supposedly heard in his youth from aged persons who knew her in earlier years. "The main facts" of "the story entitled '*THE SCARLET LETTER,*'" Hawthorne explains, "are authorized and authenticated by the document of Mr. Surveyor Pue," though he has allowed himself "nearly or altogether as much license as if the facts had been entirely of my own invention. What I contend for is the authenticity of the outline" (32–33).

Central to both "The Custom-House" and the story that follows is the Scarlet Letter itself. That "there was some deep meaning in it," their author tells us, he had felt certain when he first came upon it—a meaning

> most worthy of interpretation, and which, as it were, streamed forth from the mystic symbol, subtly communicating itself to my sensibilities, but evading the analysis of my mind.
>
> While thus perplexed, . . . I happened to place it on my breast. It seemed to me,—the reader may smile, but must not doubt my word,—it seemed to me, then, that I experienced a sensation not altogether physical, yet almost so, as of burning heat; and as if the letter were not of red cloth, but red-hot iron. I shuddered, and involuntarily let it fall upon the floor. (31–32)

These words, obviously a part of Hawthorne's effort to set the tone of the narrative to follow, take on added significance if we remember that they were written *before* he completed *The Scarlet Letter.* During a concentrated period of some four months he had been devoting himself to what he called the "positively a h—l f—d story, into which I found it almost impossible to throw any cheering light"[13] (note the recurrent fire imagery), and it is not merely fanciful to suppose that, in his near identification with the characters of both Hester Prynne and Arthur Dimmesdale, he too had figuratively placed the Letter upon his own breast.

At this turning point of the essay Hawthorne has clearly left the ground-floor realities of the old Custom House for the private reality of his imagination, represented by the isolated attic above. There he also imagines that the ghost of Jonathan Pue, a surrogate for his own creative faculties, has supposedly "authorized" him to develop the story of the Scarlet Letter. " 'Do this,' said the ghost,"

> "do this, and the profit shall be all your own! You will shortly need it; for it is not in your days as it was in mine, when a man's office was a life-lease, and oftentimes an heirloom. But, I charge you, . . . give to your predecessor's memory the credit which will be rightfully its due!" And I said to the ghost of Mr. Surveyor Pue,—"I will!" (33–34)[14]

iv. Hawthorne's "neutral ground"

Like "The Old Manse," "The Custom-House" closes with a return to the nineteenth-century present, this time as the discharged Surveyor recalls his enforced resumption of private life. Before concluding the essay, however, Hawthorne was moved to discuss once again the nature of imaginative writing, a subject he addressed only incidentally in the earlier essay. There he had expressed his desire to publish something more substantial than another collection of "tales and essays"; now he was about to complete his most ambitious work to date, *The Scarlet Letter,* and his comments are based on the experience of writing it. Still another objective when he composed "The Custom-House" may well have been to record and communicate what he had learned in the process: about the nature of fiction as he had come to understand it and also about the conditions essential for producing imaginative works.

In "The Old Manse" Hawthorne had written approvingly of an ideal mingling of reality with fancy in images that mirror their surroundings—whether they are reflecting natural objects in a mirror-like stream or the life of a "vanished century" in such "bits of magic looking-glass" as old newspapers and almanacs. But he encountered nothing of the kind in performing his day-to-day duties as a customs officer. Though he had been "as good a Surveyor as need be," his imaginative faculty, "if it had not departed, was suspended and inanimate within me" (26). As he came to realize, "So little adapted is the atmosphere of a Custom-House to the delicate harvest of fancy and sensibility" that had he remained there, he could never have brought forth such a work as *The Scarlet Letter.* When he tried to write, he found his imagination to be but "a tarnished mirror."

> It would not reflect, or only with miserable dimness, the figures with which I did my best to people it. The characters of the narrative would not be warmed and rendered malleable, by any heat that I could kindle at my intellectual forge. They would take neither the glow of passion nor the tenderness of sentiment, but retained all the rigidity of dead corpses. (34)

The Surveyor's imagination failed to quicken even when he sat in his own parlor at home, before a glowing fireplace and with moonlight streaming in through the window. For him, "Moonlight, in a familiar room, . . . is a medium the most suitable for a romance-writer," as he now identified himself, for it so transforms ordinary objects "that they seem to lose their actual substance, and become things of intellect." Thus "the floor of our familiar room" might itself "become a neutral territory, somewhere between the real world and fairy-land, where the Actual and the Imaginary may meet, and each imbue itself with the nature of the other." The "warmer light" of the coal fire is also essential, mingling with "the cold spirituality of the moonbeams" and communicating "a heart and sensibilities of human tenderness to the forms which fancy summons up. It converts them from snow-images into men and women" (35–36).

Though at Concord Hawthorne had "sought nothing" from Emerson as a philosopher, there is something reminiscent of Emerson's teaching in this passage—especially the idea of *converting* ordinary objects into "things of intellect."[15] Here the passage continues with another image of a reflecting mirror:

> Glancing at the looking-glass, we behold—deep within its haunted verge—the smouldering glow of the half-extinguished anthracite, the white moonbeams on the floor, and a repetition of all the gleam and shadow of the picture, with one remove farther from the actual, and nearer to the imaginative. Then, at such an hour, and with this scene before him, if a man, sitting all alone, cannot dream strange things, and make them look like truth, he need never try to write romances. (36)

In this portion of "The Custom-House" Hawthorne has epitomized the kind of writing he had always aspired to produce, most recently and notably in *The Scarlet Letter*. But "during the whole of my Custom-House experience," he went on to say, the "gift" connected with the "susceptibilities" he has thus described "was gone from me." A "different order of composition," he was moved to add, might have been preferable: "The page of life that was spread out before me seemed dull and commonplace, only because I had not fathomed its deeper import. A better book than I shall ever write was there. . . ." But such perceptions, he felt, "have come too late" (36–37). Although this comment about realistic writing may seem surprising, it "chimes in exactly" with Hawthorne's opinion of the novels of Anthony Trollope, as F. O. Matthiessen rightly pointed out. "They precisely suit my taste," Hawthorne was to say of Trollope's novels in later years: "solid and substantial, written on the strength of beef and through the inspiration of ale, and just as real as if some giant had hewn a great lump out of the earth and put it under a glass case, with all its inhabitants going about their daily business, and not suspecting that they were made a show of."[16]

Hawthorne was never to write an entire book in Trollope's novelistic mode, at any stage of his career, though there are passages of realistic "surface representation" throughout his fiction as well as in "The Old Manse" and "The Custom-House." Nor do his later works achieve the remarkable balance between "the Actual and the Imaginary" that made *The Scarlet Letter* the finest of his romances. There, moreover, by identifying so unreservedly with his principal characters but shielding himself behind the veil of third-person narration,[17] he surrendered to his "autobiographical impulse" more fully than he allowed himself to do in his familiar essays and his later prefaces. The one exception may be the passage in "The Custom-House" where he describes the sensation "as of burning heat" that he had experienced in holding the imagined Scarlet Letter to his breast—as though he himself were Hester Prynne or Arthur Dimmesdale. Otherwise, the "I" who speaks for Nathaniel Hawthorne, however much he may "prate" of his circumstances and even of himself, still keeps inviolate his "inmost Me."

15.

Whose Book Is *Moby-Dick*?

I have written a wicked book, and feel spotless as the lamb.
—Melville to Nathaniel Hawthorne, [17?] November 1851

During the early years of the Melville Revival, which began in this country in the aftermath of World War I, roughly a hundred years after Melville's birth in 1819, there was much discussion of *Moby-Dick* as a rediscovered masterpiece. But then as now, many people merely talked about the book instead of actually reading it. When Harold Ross founded the *New Yorker* magazine in 1925, according to James Thurber in *The Years with Ross* (1959), he was "unembarrassed by his ignorance of the great novels of any country," including his own. One day, Thurber reports, "he stuck his head into the checking department of the magazine . . . to ask 'Is Moby Dick the whale or the man?' "[1] But whether or not they've ever read the book, most literate Americans today know that it was Ahab who pursued the White Whale and are also well aware of another character in *Moby-Dick:* the one who speaks that memorable opening line, "Call me Ishmael."

Whose book, then, is *Moby-Dick*? Should we award it to the title character, the invincible whale himself? or to Captain Ahab, who dooms his ship and crew in his desperate quest to slay the monster who had reaped away his leg? or to narrator Ishmael, the one human survivor of the inevitable catastrophe, who alone escapes to tell the story? Since the book was first published in 1851 the question has been posed repeatedly, but the answers to it, as we shall see, have been various indeed. For the entire book is like that gold doubloon, the coin of great value that Ahab nailed to his ship's mainmast, promising it as a reward to the first man who should sight the White Whale. Witness these words of Ahab: "this round gold is but the image of the rounder globe, which, like a magician's glass, to each and every man in turn but mirrors back his own mysterious self" (chap. 99, "The Doubloon," 431). So with the book—and so too with its principal characters. All of them mirror back the reader and whatever he or she has brought to the experience of reading.

But Melville's contemporaries saw little of themselves in either the characters or the book, despite all that he had put into it for those possessing eyes to see. Like two other innovative literary works of the 1850s in America, Thoreau's *Walden* and Whitman's "Song of Myself," Herman Melville's *Moby-Dick* had to wait the better part of a century for the readership that we now think it deserves. What each of the three writers had to say in these works and the unique way in which he said it seemed somehow foreign to their contemporaries, who had other ideas about what literary productions should be and do. We see a similar divergence in our own day between popular taste and the groundbreaking work of new artists in various media, not only in poetry and prose but also in music and painting, or in architecture and interior design. Indeed, every creative artist, if he is "great and at the same time *original*, has had the task of *creating* the taste by which he is to be enjoyed." So Wordsworth, speaking from experience, put it as long ago as 1815, for he and Coleridge as innovators in poetry had faced the same problem in England since publishing their *Lyrical Ballads* in 1798.[2]

Different as they are in both subject matter and form from the poetry of Wordsworth and from one another, *Walden,* "Song of Myself," and *Moby-Dick* as innovative works have much in common with the pervasive Romantic spirit that had animated European art and literature long before its influence was felt on this side of the Atlantic, but they also draw on experience that we recognize immediately as uniquely American. Like much Romantic art, moreover, they are intensely subjective in character. Each of the three employs what Wayne Booth has called a "dramatized narrator," an "I" who not only tells the reader about events of the past but also addresses him directly in the narrative present, as in the opening paragraphs of *Walden:* "In most books, the *I,* or first person, is omitted; in this it will be retained; that, in respect to egotism, is the main difference. . . . I should not talk so much about myself if there were any body else whom I knew as well."[3] Here are the first three lines of "Song of Myself":

I celebrate myself,
And what I assume you shall assume,
For every atom belonging to me as good belongs to you.[4]

And here too are the familiar opening lines of chapter 1 of *Moby-Dick,* also addressed directly to the reader—to "you": "Call me Ishmael. Some years ago—never mind how long precisely—having little or no money in my purse, and nothing in particular to interest me on shore, I thought I would sail about a little and see the watery part of the world. It is a way I have of driving off the spleen, and regulating the circulation" (3).

Again in Romantic fashion, each of the three works proceeds to take both the "I" and the reader into nature and the open air: with Thoreau to "the shore of Walden Pond, in Concord, Massachusetts," there to transact what he calls some private business; with Whitman "to the bank by the wood," there to "loafe and invite my soul"; with Melville's Ishmael, again "waterward"—since "as every one knows, meditation and water are wedded for ever"—and ultimately to sea, motivated chiefly by "the overwhelming idea of the great whale himself," for "only on the profound unbounded sea, can the fully invested whale be truly and livingly found out" (4, 7, 454).

To speak now about Melville's book in particular, are we to read it as a story both by and about its narrator, like *Walden,* or is it about what Ishmael calls "the fully invested whale"—specifically the title character, though Moby Dick himself does not appear until the third chapter from the end? Or is it really about still another character, one linked both to Moby Dick and to Ishmael—Captain Ahab? Ahab, that "grand, ungodly, god-like man," as Captain Peleg describes him to Ishmael (79), makes his entrance only after Melville has given us a hundred pages of Ishmael's story, but he seemingly dominates the action thereafter. Is it then Ahab's book, or the Whale's, or narrator Ishmael's? Contemporary reviewers first raised these questions; twentieth-century readers have raised them again.

On the evidence of the original titles, *The Whale* in the first English edition of 1851 and *Moby-Dick; or, The Whale* in the first American, a reader might well infer that Melville himself thought of whales and especially of one White Whale—Moby Dick—as central to the book. As a persuasive twentieth-century reader put it in 1966, Melville presents Moby Dick as "the crown and consummation of the imperial breed of whales"; moreover, "the logic of the book as a whole works to give whales in general, and him in particular, a mythic and heroic stature. He gains this stature only by having whalers and whaling share it; but because they do, he gains it more triumphantly. . . . Moby Dick *is,* in the most relevant sense, the book's protagonist."[5]

At first hearing you may be inclined to agree with this eloquent statement and say that the book is indeed Moby Dick's. But before you go that far, consider as well these differing opinions from three other twentieth-century essays, also by readers of the 1960s:

> *Second Reader:* "I say 'Call me an Ishmaelite' because I assume that this is primarily Ishmael's book. The drama of Ahab and the whale is most significant when seen in relation to Ishmael experiencing that drama. . . . Ahab never would (nor could) have written this book; Ishmael does (and must)."[6]

> *Third Reader:* "But this is not Ishmael's story. He is a delightful narrator in the beginning, and for a time at sea plays the role admirably, but when Melville becomes truly engrossed in telling the story of Ahab, he pushes Ishmael aside and gives insights denied his first-person narrator."[7]

> *Fourth Reader:* "But is Ahab then the 'hero' of *Moby Dick*? To answer with an unqualified affirmative is to neglect just half of the book. For if it is the tragedy of Captain Ahab, it is also the novel of Ishmael."[8]

On a purely literal level, one must grant, Ahab certainly couldn't have written such a book, if only because it describes his own death, and Ishmael does indeed disappear from our view in later chapters when Ahab comes to the fore and at last encounters Moby Dick. The narrative as we have it gives readers not only "insights" but also basic information that sailor Ishmael could not conceivably have obtained aboard the *Pequod:* for example, Ahab's statements either in his private soliloquies or in exchanges with Stubb, Starbuck, and Pip that no other member of the crew would have easily overheard. To the question "Whose book is *Moby-Dick?*" there is still no generally accepted answer among those who variously name the White Whale, Ishmael, or Ahab as its principal figure. Moreover, there has been further disagreement over the genre and form of *Moby-Dick:* can a book be considered aesthetically unified if it is at once "the tragedy of Captain Ahab," "the novel of Ishmael," and what one early reviewer called it, a

"Whaliad"[9]—meaning a prose epic treating learnedly and exhaustively, or exhaustingly, of whales and whaling?

i

For an indication of how and when these associated questions first arose, let us begin with a glance at aspects of the nineteenth-century response to *Moby-Dick*. None of the three principal figures—Ishmael, Ahab, and the White Whale—attracted many readers to the book during Melville's lifetime—to his deep disappointment, as we know, for he had composed *Moby-Dick* with the sense that a literary masterwork might well be taking form under his hand. The initial reviews had been mixed. Even those British critics who had high praise for some attributes of the book were troubled nevertheless by what they considered its faults of style and structure: for example, they noted that Melville did not consistently maintain Ishmael's first-person point of view and, since the London edition did not include the Epilogue, they complained that the book offered no explanation of Ishmael's survival after the sinking of the *Pequod;* how, they asked, could he be alive to tell his story?

The first American reviewers were less concerned with such technical matters, partly because the first New York edition not only provided the Epilogue but also carried "Etymology" and the "Extracts" on whales and whaling at the beginning of the narrative rather than at the end, where they had appeared in the earlier London edition. But Americans too were uncertain about how to classify the new work, and several of them objected to its general tone. One leading journal, the *New York Literary World,* published by Melville's friends Evert and George Duyckinck, dealt with it as "two if not three books . . . rolled into one." Their two-part review praised Melville's "brilliantly illustrated" account of the great Sperm Whale and identified Moby Dick as his "hero," going on to express reservations about both the characterization of Ahab and the prominence given Ishmael and his inveterate philosophizing.[10] To the Duyckincks, Ahab's story seemed melodramatic rather than tragic, and with other American critics of the 1850s they considered Ishmael's speculations to be shockingly irreverent. Melville, wrote a representative critic in 1857, should give over his "metaphysical and morbid meditations" and return to the vein of *Typee* and *Omoo,* the books of adventure that had so pleased the public a decade earlier.[11]

With the decline of the whaling industry in later years of the century, when petroleum, natural gas, and electricity in turn replaced whale-oil in American and European households, interest in books about whales and whaling declined as well. But a small band of admirers in England kept Melville's name alive there, and with the conclusion of World War I a new generation of American readers found that *Moby-Dick,* along with *Walden* and "Song of Myself," was speaking to them in a way that most nineteenth-century readers had simply failed to understand and enjoy. By 1951, the book's centennial year, *Moby-Dick* had become a standard work on American college reading lists and a subject for proliferating critical and scholarly study.

ii

The one twentieth-century work that in effect legitimated an aesthetic approach to Melville and his American contemporaries was F. O. Matthiessen's *American Renaissance: Art and Expression in the Age of Emerson and Whitman,* first published in 1941.[12] Other scholars writing during the 1950s and 1960s significantly broadened the context of both research and teaching by relating the work of our nineteenth-century authors to the Romantic and symbolist movements in both America and Europe. One example is Morse Peckham, a theorist of Romanticism who dealt with Melville and *Moby-Dick* in terms of the perennial Romantic themes;[13] another is Charles Feidelson, whose *Symbolism and American Literature* (1953) traced the affiliations of American writers not only with their European predecessors but with their modern heirs and successors as well.[14]

These studies and others like them had a remarkable effect on ways of reading *Moby-Dick.* Where some commentators since the 1850s had seen the book as a structural hybrid, an uneasy juxtaposition of epic and essay, or of novel and tragedy, that failed to conform to the accepted rules of any one literary genre, others writing in the spirit of Matthiessen and Peckham were now praising it as a highly successful example of Romantic art, creating its own form not mechanically, after some existing model, but

organically—again like *Walden* and "Song of Myself." As Ishmael puts it at
the beginning of chapter 63, "Out of the trunk, the branches grow; out of
them, the twigs. So, in productive subjects, grow the chapters" (289). And
as Walter Bezanson remarked in his "*Moby-Dick:* Work of Art," a landmark
essay first read as a lecture in the centennial year of 1951, "Organic form is
not a particular form but a structural principle. In *Moby-Dick* this principle
would seem to be a peculiar quality of making and unmaking itself as it
goes. . . . Ishmael's narrative is always in process and in all but the most
literal sense remains unfinished. For the good reader the experience of
Moby-Dick is a participation in the act of creation."[15]

The approach to *Moby-Dick* represented by Bezanson's essay brought
with it a reconsideration of two of the interrelated issues under discussion
here: whether or not the book has a unified structure and whom to identify
as its central character. During the early stages of the Melville revival the
usual emphasis of both readers and critics was clearly on Ahab and his
struggle with the whale, with lesser regard for Ishmael and what were often
objected to as his philosophical "digressions." Interpreters as late as the
1940s tended to see the opposition between Ahab and Moby Dick in
allegorical terms, praising Ahab as a self-reliant, Promethean individual
confronting in Moby Dick the embodiment of all the forces of evil—
physical or metaphysical—that beset oppressed humanity. For Melville,
wrote one representative commentator, "the essence of the world is a
dualism between good and evil," and man's appointed role is "to fight evil
without compromise and without respite." So Ahab is fated "to spend his life
pursuing Moby Dick, knowing that the master of the *Pequod* could never
conquer the whale. In the end Ahab saved his soul, maintained inviolate
his personal integrity by going down in unconquered defeat while Moby
Dick swam on for other Ahabs to pursue. Ahab was the personification of
Melville's philosophy of individualism."[16]

Much can be said for such a reading, as for most serious approaches
to any complex book, but there are also other factors to be considered.
What, for instance, are we to make of a monomaniac captain, repeatedly
denominated as "crazy" or "mad," and his willful dedication of his ship
and her crew to the fulfillment of his private quest for what his chief mate
calls "vengeance on a dumb brute" (163)? Isn't Melville offering an implied
criticism of self-reliant individualism—perhaps of capitalist entrepreneurs
generally—rather than an endorsement? Even so, Ishmael's admiration of

the man informs the portrait he is essaying. As a "tragic dramatist who would depict mortal indomitableness in its fullest sweep and direst swing," he must acknowledge that Ahab lacks "all outward majestical trappings and housings." Therefore, "what shall be grand" in the resulting portrait "must needs be plucked at from the skies, and dived for in the deep, and featured in the unbodied air!" (148).

Melville's presentation of Ahab through Ishmael's words shows him as a commanding figure of tragic stature, flawed by "fatal pride" (519) yet not incapable of compassion, as we see in his treatment of Pip and even of Starbuck; he is no mere cardboard "personification." As Leon Howard wrote as long ago as 1950, when critics were beginning to deal with the book in a more searching and understanding way, "It was the author's emotional sympathy" for Ahab as "a character of whom he intellectually disapproved which gave *Moby Dick* much of its ambiguity and dramatic intensity."[17]

In the newer readings of *Moby-Dick* the White Whale emerged as more than that fixed allegorical embodiment of pure evil which Ahab persisted in seeing; instead, critics after the 1950s came to write of the whale's function in the overall structure of the book as that of a dynamic and ever-changing symbol, a cynosure that gradually accumulates not only meaning but multiple significance. From "Etymology" and "Extracts" through what Howard Vincent called its "cetological center"[18] to its concluding Epilogue, the book is filled with the lore of whales and whaling, showing how whales have figured in time and place over the centuries, how they appear not only to artists and scientists but to men actually risking their lives in the whale fishery. As a former whaleman, Melville well knew that "the only mode in which you can derive even a tolerable idea of [the whale's] living contour, is by going a whaling yourself; but by so doing, you run no small risk of being eternally stove and sunk by him" (264).

As Ishmael revealed at the outset, "the overwhelming idea of the great whale" had been a leading motive for his own decision to go a whaling. But as his narrative progresses we learn with him how Captain Ahab had projected his rage and hate upon one particular White Whale, and we begin to understand as well how Ishmael came first to share and later to distance himself from Ahab's obsession. And in due course, as initiated readers we are at last prepared to confront Moby Dick himself, in all his magnitude and surpassing beauty:

Not the white bull Jupiter swimming away with ravished Europa clinging to his graceful horns . . . ; not Jove, not that great majesty Supreme! did surpass the glorified White Whale as he so divinely swam. . . . No wonder there had been some among the hunters who namelessly transported and allured by all that serenity, had ventured to assail it; but had fatally found that quietude but the vesture of tornadoes. Yet calm, enticing calm, oh whale! thou glidest on, to all who for the first time eye thee, no matter how many in that same way thou may'st have bejuggled and destroyed before. (548)

However any one critic may view Moby Dick—as "the deepest blood being of the white race," in the words of D. H. Lawrence, or the Freudian superego, as Henry A. Murray suggested,[19] or Deity, or Death, or Nature, or the universe itself, to cite some other interpretations—there is likely to be no more agreement about his ultimate meaning than there was among the crews aboard the various ships we as readers encounter in the nine gams of the *Pequod.* "Shall we ever identify Moby Dick?" Harry Levin once asked. "Yes," he answered—"when we have sprinkled salt on the tail of the Absolute; but not before."[20]

iii

During the 1950s, while critics were still thinking of Ahab as Melville's protagonist confronting his antagonist in Moby Dick, Bezanson and other scholars had also begun to write of Ishmael and his point of view as the unifying center of the story. Although there was minimal reference to *Moby-Dick* in Wayne Booth's influential book of 1961, *The Rhetoric of Fiction,*[21] Booth's work inspired others to undertake a close examination of the technical aspects of Melville's fiction—notably his use of narrative point of view and his employment of dramatized narrators. With *Moby-Dick* in particular this approach of course involved a reappraisal of Ishmael's role.

Bezanson had already distinguished between the younger Ishmael who had once sailed aboard the *Pequod* and the older Ishmael who is telling his story; in 1962 Warner Berthoff in *The Example of Melville*—the best book to date on Melville as a literary craftsman—demonstrated how artfully Melville used Ishmael first to set the nautical scene and then to prepare us for both Ahab and the whale. As Berthoff explained, Ishmael conducts us as readers through "four distinct 'worlds.'" We meet him first in the world of "the dry land, or at least the thronged edges of it: New York, New Bedford, Nantucket." Next, Melville and Ishmael take us aboard the *Pequod*, herself "a virtual city of the races and talents of men," and there, through a great opening-out, into "the non-human world of the sea and the indifferent elements." Then at last we are prepared to enter "the final, furthest 'world' set out in *Moby Dick*," one that "communicates to men only in signs, portents, and equivocal omens, and seems intelligible only to madmen like Ahab and Pip."[22]

Into the fourth of these worlds, the realm beyond physical nature, it is fair to add that Melville himself could never have conducted us directly. Instead, speaking by indirection—first through Ishmael's voice and later through Ahab's—he "craftily says, or sometimes insinuates," what would be "all but madness" for an author to utter or even to hint to us "in his own proper character." So Melville himself had once written of Shakespeare, at the very time when *Moby-Dick* was taking form; so Emily Dickinson would enjoin us to "Tell all the Truth but tell it slant— / Success in Circuit lies."[23] Even as truth-teller Ishmael is leading us out of our everyday world into the world of ships and the sea, where at last we meet Ahab and ultimately Moby Dick, he is at the same time securing for Melville the needed aesthetic distance from those two antagonists that as their creator he had to establish and maintain.

When any writer becomes "identified with the objects of [his] horror or compassion," as in our own century Scott Fitzgerald would declare in *The Crack-Up*, the result, as Fitzgerald had learned, to his own cost, is "the death of accomplishment."[24] An author who fails to guard against such identification risks artistic disaster, and perhaps a psychological crisis as well—witness Melville in his next book, *Pierre, or the Ambiguities* (1852), where there is no Ishmael to stand between him and his title character: reviewers unanimously condemned *Pierre,* and some readers and critics even questioned its author's sanity. In *Moby-Dick,* by contrast, Ishmael as intervening narrator had provided Melville with essential insulation, as Nick Carraway would do for Fitzgerald in *The Great Gatsby* and Marlow for Joseph Conrad in *Heart of Darkness,* each narrator distancing the creator from his creation. Were there no Ishmael in *Moby-Dick,* we may feel sure, Melville would never have been able to give us his protagonist and antagonist—or to purge himself of his own pity and terror by doing so.

That is why he could say, with relief, to Hawthorne, "I have written a wicked book, and feel spotless as the lamb" (*Correspondence,* 212).

iv

Ishmael's dual role as narrator and as actor has been profitably explored by several critics since Bezanson distinguished between "the enfolding sensibility . . . , the hand that writes the tale, the imagination through which all matters of the book pass," and that "young man of whom, among others, narrator Ishmael tells us in his story." The older narrator looking back upon his younger self had been a feature of Melville's earlier works, the differences between the two growing sharper in *Redburn* (1849) and *White-Jacket* (1850), the immediate predecessors of *Moby-Dick.* Now in a fully dramatized Ishmael, we witness "the narrator's unfolding sensibility," Bezanson observed. "Whereas forecastle Ishmael drops in and out of the narrative . . . , the Ishmael voice is there every moment."[25]

The fullest exploration of "the Ishmael voice" is Paul Brodtkorb's "phe-nomenological reading" of the book, *Ishmael's White World* (1965), which presupposes that narrator Ishmael is not only "the vessel that contains the book," but "in a major sense he *is* the book."[26] In 1961 Glauco Cambon had written of Ishmael as "the artist in the act of telling us, and struggling to understand, his crucial experience";[27] in 1970 Barry A. Marks further pointed out that like other "retrospective narrators" in Thoreau and Whitman, Ishmael is in fact presenting two stories simultaneously: one, his "past-time story," is about his recollected experience that is now over and done; the other, his "writing-time story," is about experience still in progress—an ongoing story of "a narrator's *telling* about his past."[28]

Like speakers in Thoreau and Whitman, Ishmael too addresses his reader directly; he frequently pauses in his narration to consider the larger implications for the narrative present of something in the past that he had just described or related. "Yes, there is death in this business of whaling," he remarks after telling of the memorial tablets in Father Mapple's chapel (37). Again, in concluding his chapter on "The Line," he observes that "All men live enveloped in whale-lines. All are born with halters round their necks; but it is only when caught in the swift, sudden turn of death, that mortals realize the silent, subtle, ever-present perils of life" (281). And at the end of "The Try-Works" he specifically warns the reader: "Give not thyself up, then, to fire, lest it invert thee, deaden thee; as for the time it did me. There is a wisdom that is woe; but there is a woe that is madness" (425).

As for his ongoing story, Ishmael makes us fully aware of the challenge facing "a whale author like me" who is presently engaged in "writing of this Leviathan" and earnestly striving "to produce a mighty book" on such "a mighty theme" (456). So daunting an enterprise, he contends, demands "a careful disorderliness" as "the true method" (361). "I promise nothing complete," he tells us in his chapter on "Cetology"; he holds the typical Romantic view that "any human thing supposed to be complete, must for that very reason infallibly be faulty. . . . God keep me from ever completing anything. This whole book is but a draught—nay, but the draught of a draught" (136, 145).

Concerning Ishmael's several departures from his original first-person point of view, that unconventional practice that so troubled nineteenth-century reviewers and twentieth-century formalist critics as well, and other instances of what have been called "formal discontinuities" in *Moby-Dick*, Cambon has argued that Ishmael's supposed disappearance from the story is a legitimate rhetorical device that has its parallels both in the classical poets and historians and in twentieth-century fiction. Thus Ishmael's "imaginative reconstruction" of the other characters anticipates what Quentin Compson was to do in Faulkner's *Absalom, Absalom!*, where "memory modulates into imagination," and where once again the reader "share[s] the experience of creation in progress."[29]

v

Emphasis on Ishmael as narrator rather than actor—and on Ishmael-like observers in contemporary American criticism, fiction, and intellectual life generally—has dismayed other commentators. "Ahab and the whale do not appear in our novels," one of them complained in 1959; "we write only about Ishmael."[30] A decade later, in the midst of the campus activism of the late 1960s, an angry black contributor to *Partisan Review* blasted narrator Ishmael as "the precursor of the modern white liberal-intellectual" that he found infesting American universities. If Ishmael were really an active "character" in the story, according to Cecil Brown, he "would have repelled Ahab"![31]

More recently, historicist and contextualist critics of *Moby-Dick* have indeed been shifting their focus from Ishmael back to Ahab, at the same time exploring what they see as the book's political implications rather than the cetological, metaphysical, and literary elements that variously engaged their predecessors. Meanwhile, scholars investigating the origins and textual development of the book have once again cast doubt on its artistic unity, citing a panoply of minor inconsistencies in Melville's text and even suggesting "unnecessary duplicates" among his characters.[32] Such instances of apparent disunity in the book can of course be cited against Bezanson and other champions of organic form—a concept which its opponents in an age of deconstruction dismiss as a convenient mask for hiding both minor and major artistic failings.[33]

To the degree that the Ishmaels of this world overshadow its Ahabs and White Whales, the anti-Ishmaelites do indeed have a point. But it also seems fair to say that in the last analysis the book is not the story of any one or even two of its characters. The only feasible way *to* Ahab and at last to the White Whale is *through* Ishmael, Melville's necessary surrogate and the reader's veritable guide, philosopher, and friend; and *all three figures* are equally indispensable to the author, to his book, and to its readers. As for the question of unity or disunity, the real test comes in the very act of responsive reading. In Brodtkorb's words, "literary unity is in the mental set of the reader as much as in the literary work,"[34] and in the case of *Moby-Dick* that "mental set" is powerfully influenced and shaped by Ishmael—favorably so, as for Bezanson and his followers, or unfavorably, as for Cecil Brown.

For further guidance from Ishmael himself, consider his distinctions in chapter 89 between Fast-Fish and Loose-Fish, based on "the laws and regulations of the whale fishery" with respect to harpooned whales:

> I. A Fast-Fish belongs to the party fast to it.
> II. A Loose-Fish is fair game for anybody who can soonest catch it.
> (395–96)

Whose book, then, *is* this much-hunted Loose-Fish? It cannot be just Ahab's, or the whale's, or Ishmael's, nor is it entirely Melville's, since you and I as individual readers have genuine claims of our own as well. "There is then creative reading, as well as creative writing," as Emerson long ago observed,[35] and modern critics such as Bezanson and Cambon have applied his idea to *Moby-Dick*. "For the good reader," Bezanson told us, "the experience of *Moby-Dick* is a participation in the act of creation." In Cambon's phrasing, such a reader "will share the experience of creation in progress"—the same experience that Barry Marks has illustrated for us in Melville along with Thoreau and Whitman.

Once you as reader share that experience, then you have indeed made fast to *Moby-Dick,* and in a real sense it has become *your* book—*your* Fast-Fish, as I feel it to be very much mine. But if this comment sounds like an endorsement of what is now called reader-response criticism, we must nevertheless remember that there is a reciprocal corollary: Melville, reaching out through Ishmael as his surrogate, has at the same time figuratively harpooned *us* as his readers, making us fast to his book and therefore belonging to it. As narrator Ishmael, once again turning directly to each of us, pointedly asks, "What are you, reader, but a Loose-Fish, and a Fast-Fish, too?" (398).

At the conclusion of *Moby-Dick,* the fated *Pequod* has been lost—lost with all her crew save one. Protagonist Ahab has met his lonely death on lonely life, while the White Whale, his invincible antagonist, swims on victorious. It is Ishmael, survivor of the *Pequod*'s wreck, who escapes alone to tell their story. And by addressing us indirectly through Ishmael's omnipresent voice, Melville himself persuades us, like the authors of *Walden* and "Song of Myself," to assume what he has assumed in this mighty book and to celebrate, with him and with Ishmael, its mighty theme.

Postscript

[By way of conclusion, I transcribe my remarks at the annual luncheon of the American Literature Section, Modern Language Association of America, at New York City on 28 December 1992.]

To My Colleagues in American Literature:

In mid-March of 1941 a young graduate student in New Haven received a letter from the chairman of the editorial board of *American Literature* telling him that his very first submission had been accepted by the board for printing in the May number. The chairman was Jay B. Hubbell of Duke University and I was the delighted graduate student. Now, more than fifty years later, I am once again delighted: this time to be honored as the 1992 recipient of the Jay B. Hubbell medal. I never supposed that the election might someday light on me, and I thank those who decided that in this year of 1992 I should join the august line of worthies that began with Professor Hubbell himself in 1964.

The kindness of both Jay Hubbell and his managing editor, Clarence Gohdes, in welcoming me as a contributor to our still-flourishing journal is typical of the encouragement I received from the generation of scholars that preceded mine. My mentors at Wooster and Yale not only awakened my interest in literature and the life of the mind but—equally important— inspired me to continue learning on my own initiative and to develop my own strategies as a scholar and teacher. Along with the incomparable Stanley Williams, with whom I studied at Yale, other Americanists such as Willard Thorp, Perry Miller, Bruce McElderry, Leon Howard, Arlin Turner, and my late Wisconsin colleagues Henry Pochmann and Harry Hayden Clark—I could go on—stood as exemplars of the best in American literary scholarship and became my generous sponsors and good friends as well.

None of us can ever repay the debts we owe to predecessors such as these, but we can at least strive to do the best we can with what talents we have—and certainly we should help and encourage our successors

189

just as our elders generously helped and encouraged us when our own careers were developing. Now that I can look back over more than half a century as a student and teacher, it seems clear to me that for those truly professional men and women I have admired most, there has been no essential dichotomy between their teaching and their scholarship, that scholarship meant for them not only distinguished original research but at the same time keeping abreast of the research and interpretations of others, and that their teaching and learning took place both in the classroom and beyond it, as they spoke to and wrote for members of the public as well as their students and professional colleagues.

When I decided, in the late 1930s, to concentrate chiefly on American rather than on British literature, which had been the staple of my formal study, it was still the fashion in some quarters to regard American writings as aesthetically inferior cultural artifacts, to be treated as historical documents rather than as literary works. But as the so-called New Criticism taught us the value of close reading, the significance of metaphor and symbol, the importance of structure and tone, emphasis among Americanists began to shift from historical backgrounds and biographies of authors to the literary qualities of the texts we were reading and teaching. Scholars of today have come to think that the pendulum of change actually swung too far at that time. Even so, when Matthiessen's *American Renaissance* appeared in 1941 it struck many of us as a powerful vindication—not only of the aesthetic values of the works it dealt with but of our own widening and deepening understanding of our practice as professionals.

Continual openness to enlightenment, from whatever quarter it may come, should mark every true teacher and scholar. In the changing climate of scholarship in the 1990s, with New Criticism replaced by New Historicism, close reading transformed into deconstruction, and aesthetic considerations giving way—for some at least—to various cultural, ideological, and even overtly political goals, I can only hope that the pendulum of change has not once more swung too far, lest our professional widening and deepening be foreclosed, either by too-narrow specialization or by shallow propagandizing for extra-literary causes. Being first and last a lover of literature as literature, I still hold firmly to a more open and liberal conception of our challenging role, now and in the future.

Appendix 1

Questions concerning Herman Melville's "Bartleby"

From *Resources for Discussing Herman Melville's Tale, "Bartleby, the Scrivener,"* prepared by Merton M. Sealts, Jr. (Madison: Wisconsin Humanities Committee, 1982), 17–19; reprinted here with minor revisions.

The most important consideration in approaching "Bartleby" is this: all we know about the setting, the characters, and the action of the story is given us in the words of *the attorney who narrates it.* Melville as author never comes between the attorney and the reader; he never interrupts what his narrator is saying to qualify, interpret, or evaluate. The attorney is therefore the lens through which the reader must view everything in the story, the attorney himself included. Does he speak clearly and fairly, or must the reader make allowances for his disposition or temperament, for his point of view as a legal specialist (Master in Chancery), for his worldly success, for his age ("not far from sixty")?

1. How, specifically, does the lawyer introduce and characterize himself at the opening of the story? Can you accept this self-portrait at face value, or is it qualified by his later words and actions as the story unfolds?

2. The lawyer is a Master in Chancery, with chambers located on the second floor of a building on Wall Street in New York City; he makes reference to events of the 1840s, thus placing the action at that period or shortly thereafter. How do the time, place, and circumstances of his professional life bear on the story? Is the setting, for instance, to be taken only literally, or are the *walls* that he so frequently mentions to be read metaphorically as well, as some critics have suggested?

3. How, specifically, does the lawyer present his three employees—Turkey, Nippers, and Ginger Nut? What does his account of them, individually and collectively, suggest to you about the lawyer himself as an employer and as a human being? Does this segment of his narration

in any way prepare the reader for the lawyer's subsequent response to Bartleby?

4. After Bartleby begins working for the lawyer, he withdraws more and more into himself, finally declining to exert himself at all ("I would prefer not to"). Is the cause of his withdrawal inherent in Bartleby? Is it to be sought somewhere in his previous experience of life? Does it lie within the lawyer's office? Or do we know enough about Bartleby even to address such questions?

5. Undeterred by the reader's limited knowledge, which is circumscribed by what the lawyer knows and/or tells, some critics have gone *outside* the lawyer's story in an effort to "explain" Bartleby. They have identified him variously with Melville himself, with some friend of Melville's or someone he knew about, such as Henry Thoreau, and even with Jesus Christ; they have interpreted him as a "type": the neglected artist; the "alienated" worker victimized (say Marxist critics) by the capitalist system; the saint martyred on the altar of materialism. To what degree will the lawyer's words support any or all of these readings?

6. At the other extreme, psychologically oriented critics have seen Bartleby as simply pathological—for example, as a schizophrenic. Is this a better explanation?

7. If Bartleby is a social or psychological misfit who is either unable or unwilling to perform the duties for which he was hired, why should the lawyer put up with him? Consider such comments as these:

a. "I think I should kick him out of the office," says Nippers, his fellow employee.

b. In legal terms, a *contract,* verbal or understood, is at issue here. (If so, *who* has violated it?)

c. As Bartleby's employer, as a fellow citizen, as a church-going Christian, the lawyer is *responsible* for a human being less fortunate than himself. ("Am I then my brother's keeper?") Note the tenor of the comment addressed to him by a fellow lawyer.

d. Not the lawyer but organized society—a church or charity, a labor union, the government itself—must take care of the Bartlebys of this world.

e. The invention of copying machines and word processors has eliminated the need for scriveners as the nineteenth-century law office employed them, and hence the problem of Bartleby. (But machines of all kinds also get out of order—and they aren't customers who will pay for goods and services.)

f. What if Bartleby were *a woman?*

8. In much recent criticism the focus is less on Bartleby than on his employer—the lawyer himself. Consider such comments as these:

a. Bartleby may be taken as a projection or objectification of some element within the lawyer's psyche; the two are really psychological "doubles," like Dr. Jekyll and Mr. Hyde, and Bartleby may represent the negative element of perversity or refusal or rebellion that is present in everyone.

b. Bartleby is the lawyer's *conscience.* ("Something from within me upbraided me," says the lawyer at one point.)

c. Bartleby is an emissary from Heaven, sent to test or perhaps to sanctify the lawyer. ("These troubles of mine, touching the scrivener, [were] all predestinated from eternity, and Bartleby was billeted upon me for some mysterious purpose of an all-wise Providence.") Compare Matthew 24:40: "Inasmuch as ye have done it unto one of the least of these my brethren, ye have done it unto me."

d. Bartleby is an emissary from Hell, a Tempter.

9. Even those who emphasize the role of the lawyer disagree over the question of whether he is *changed* in any way—for the better or for the worse—through his encounter with Bartleby. In addressing this perplexing issue, consider:

a. The various phases or stages of his response to Bartleby, up through his decision to move his office to another place, leaving Bartleby behind.

b. The various reasons—or rationalizations—he gives himself and the reader for his words and actions at any given point.

c. His various references to current events, religious sanctions, the writings of Jonathan Edwards and Joseph Priestley, the "unsolicited and uncharitable remarks" of his "professional friends."

d. His ultimate offer to take Bartleby home with him.

10. What further light is thrown on this issue by subsequent events, including the following:

a. The lawyer's visit to Bartleby in the Tombs, where Bartleby "want[s] nothing to say" to him?

b. His remark after Bartleby is found dead "at the base of the wall" of the prison: Bartleby is now sleeping "With kings and *counselors.*" (The phrasing echoes Job 3:14.)

c. The "sequel" in which he reports the rumor that Bartleby "had been a subordinate clerk in the Dead Letter Office at Washington." Does this element of the story tell you more about the lawyer or about Bartleby? Is it relevant? sentimental? mawkish?

d. His concluding comment: "Ah, Bartleby! Ah, humanity!"

As these questions suggest, the twentieth-century reader may take "Bartleby" in a variety of ways—as a period piece dealing with Wall Street in the 1840s; as a psychological study of an enigmatic scrivener, his troubled employer, or both; as a "parable of the walls" encompassing Herman Melville; as social criticism; as religious allegory; as a personal Rorschach test reflecting one's own predispositions. Possibly it is *all* of the above.

Appendix 2

Questions concerning Herman Melville's "Benito Cereno"

Not previously published; adapted from study material I prepared and distributed in 1984 and again in 1992.

Note that Melville's fictionalized characters must be distinguished from the living persons described by the real-life Amasa Delano in chapter 18 of his *Narrative of Voyages and Travels* (Boston, 1817; reprinted in *"The Piazza Tales" and Other Prose Pieces,* 810–47). Delano's chapter of some 14,000 words, written in the first person, tells of his experiences aboard his own ship, the *Perseverance,* and a Spanish ship, the *Tryal,* in 1804; in "Benito Cereno" a third-person narrator tells in about 34,000 words how an imagined Captain Delano responded to imagined persons and events aboard his own ship, now called the *Bachelor's Delight,* and a Spanish ship, now called the *San Dominick,* in 1799. The other leading characters— the Spanish captain, Don Benito Cereno, and especially the slave Babo— differ appreciably from their prototypes in the *Narrative;* as one critic has remarked, "Melville does three things to his source study: he enlarges Amasa Delano, he creates Babo, and he transforms Benito Cereno."

The topics for consideration in reflection upon "Benito Cereno" are grouped under four headings: the narrator and his narration, the characters, theme and interpretation, and evaluation.

The Narrator and His Narration

1. What did Melville gain—or lose—by shifting from first-person narration, as in Delano's chapter, to third-person narration?

2. Why did he rechristen Delano's ship, changing the *Perseverance* to the *Bachelor's Delight?*

195

3. Evaluate these contrasting suggestions: (a) The *Tryal* becomes the *San Dominick* to fit Melville's description of that ship in terms of similes drawn from monastic life; for example, the reference to "Black Friars" is an allusion to the Dominican order. (b) Melville changed both the date of Delano's adventure and the name of Cereno's vessel so as to invoke the violent slave revolt which occurred on the isle of *Santo Domingo* in 1799.

4. Locate passages in which the narrator makes value judgments concerning any or all of the three principal characters and their conceptions of race and slavery. Does the narrator agree or disagree with their respective views, or does he remain noncommittal?

5. The narrator's extended quotation, near the end of his story, of "extracts . . . from one of the official Spanish documents," a passage adapted from Delano's *Narrative,* has been a bone of contention among critics. Does Cereno's deposition impede narrative continuity, as some readers have charged; does it actually constitute "the key to fit into the lock of the complications which precede it," as the narrator claims; or does it "miss the truth as widely as did Delano in his complete innocence," as one writer (Allen Guttmann) would have it?

6. Why does the narrator wait until *after* he has quoted the extracts to report the earlier conversations between Cereno and Delano during their "long, mild voyage" from Santa Maria to Lima?

7. Once you have read and reflected on the story, what do you make of (a) the *San Dominick*'s "shield-like stern-piece," remembering the episode in the boat where Delano's foot is upon Babo's head; and (b) its figurehead and motto (*"Sequid vuestro jefe"*—follow your leader), which are referred to repeatedly throughout the narration?

The Characters

1. Is Don Benito Cereno, the title character of the story, an abused victim of an evil conspiracy, or is he himself a figure of evil? Does he represent a race, a class, an attitude of mind? Is "Benito Cereno" primarily *his* story?

2. Is the perplexed Amasa Delano, the "central intelligence" whose uncertainty we share as the action unfolds, simply an "innocent," as Allen Guttmann calls him; is he rather an average human being; or is he really the utter fool depicted in Robert Lowell's version of Delano's *Narrative*?

Does *he* represent a race, a class, an attitude of mind? Is "Benito Cereno" primarily *his* story?

3. The character of Babo, almost entirely Melville's invention, has been variously interpreted by twentieth-century critics: first as a bloodthirsty savage, but more recently as "the one person in the story to struggle against a moral wrong"—slavery (Allen Guttmann again). Does *he* represent a race, a class, an attitude of mind? Is "Benito Cereno" primarily *his* story, as certain critics since the 1960s have argued?

4. Melville either expanded or actually invented the roles of certain minor characters such as Atufal and Francesco, the hatchet-polishers and the oakum-pickers, the black woman nursing her child ("There's naked nature, now; pure tenderness and love, thought Captain Delano"), and the several Spaniards who try to communicate with the American captain. How do these various characters contribute to the characterization, plot, and theme of "Benito Cereno"?

Theme and Interpretation

"Benito Cereno" has been interpreted in various ways over the years. On the basis of your own reading and your answers to the foregoing questions, decide which of the following statements is most applicable to Melville's story as you see it.

1. Melville simply intended to write a saleable, readable suspense story, making it as long as he could because he was paid by the page and badly needed the money.

2. Melville in the 1850s was preoccupied with the problem of knowledge: how can we know? whom can we trust? (Witness *The Confidence-Man,* which he published in 1857.) Delano's uncertainties in the story reflect the author's own preoccupations.

3. Ever since he wrote *Moby-Dick* (1851) Melville had wrestled with the problem of evil in the world; the confrontation of Cereno with Babo reflects this concern. (Which of the two, then, represents "evil"? Does such a representation involve a slur on that character's race?)

4. Melville wrote "Benito Cereno" for *Putnam's Monthly Magazine* (whose editors were opposed to slavery) at a time when the controversy over slavery was dividing the nation and threatening the very existence of

the Union. He intended his story to be read as an indictment of slavery, of slaveholders, and of those too blind to see the dangers ahead for the United States.

5. Melville was less concerned with contemporary issues than with perennial religious and philosophical questions; his supposed attitudes towards blacks and slavery—whether pro or con—are really the inventions of twentieth-century readers who mistakenly attribute their own outlooks to writers of earlier periods.

6. I don't find any of these statements altogether adequate because ———.

Evaluation

Finally, *how good a story* is "Benito Cereno"?

Appendix 3

Questions concerning Herman Melville's *Billy Budd, Sailor*

From *Innocence and Infamy: Resources for Discussing Herman Melville's "Billy Budd, Sailor,"* prepared by Merton M. Sealts, Jr. (Madison: Wisconsin Humanities Committee, 1983), 23–33; reprinted here with minor revisions.

Although a relatively short work, *Billy Budd, Sailor* is tightly packed, allusive, and open to a variety of interpretations. Written over a period of some five years, between 1885 and 1891, it draws upon both Melville's experience at sea and his later thinking and writing. The comments and questions that follow are intended to assist the individual reader and to raise issues suitable for group discussion. The topics for consideration are grouped under seven headings: the narrator, the narration, the characterization of Billy Budd, the characterization of John Claggart, the characterization of Edward Fairfax Vere, other characters and events, and legal aspects of *Billy Budd, Sailor.*

The Narrator

In Melville's earlier fiction through 1851 and in most of his shorter tales the story is told by a first-person narrator—an "I"—who had supposedly been directly involved in the events he is recounting: for example, Ishmael in *Moby-Dick* or the lawyer in "Bartleby." But in *Billy Budd* the "I" who tells the story assumes the air of a detached historian reporting what he calls "facts"; he denies knowing what took place between Billy Budd and Captain Vere in chapter 22; and he but rarely takes the reader into the mind of any of his characters. Only on occasion does he offer analysis of what he reports in this "inside narrative," as he calls it. What authority and what credibility are we to allow such a narrator?

1. If he is in effect a projection of Melville himself, are their views essentially the same? Critics who answer affirmatively tend to give *Billy Budd* a "straight" reading.

2. If he is in effect a character in his own right, are their views essentially different? Critics who answer affirmatively tend to give *Billy Budd* an "ironist" reading.

The Narration

Melville's narrator makes several pointed comments about the form and character of his own storytelling. The digression on Horatio Nelson in chapters 4 and 5 he calls "a literary sin." Billy's story, the narrator insists in chapter 2, is "no romance"; "though properly" it "ends with [Billy's] life," he observes later, he goes on to say at the beginning of chapter 28 that three concluding chapters "in way of sequel" to that life "will not be amiss." Here he also makes this further statement: "The symmetry of form attainable in pure fiction cannot so readily be achieved in a narration having less to do with fable than with fact. Truth uncompromisingly told will always have its ragged edges; hence the conclusion of such a narration is apt to be less finished than an architectural finial." The implication of these various remarks is that the narrator (and/or Melville himself) is more concerned with "fact," with "truth uncompromisingly told," than with artistic finish.

1. Are such observations to be taken only as the conventional assurances of the historical novelist to his reader that a trustworthy version of past events is being presented?

2. The issue is crucial to readers and critics troubled by the narrator's occasional inaccuracies and outright errors, and especially by what he tells us of Vere's handling of Billy's trial and execution: the captain proceeds contrary to statutes governing the British fleet at the time of the story (see "Legal Aspects of *Billy Budd, Sailor*" below). Are these discrepancies merely incidental mistakes that any author might well have made but would have noticed and corrected had he invested more time in his research and writing; are they actually something that Melville *purposely* introduced (as one "ironist" critic has argued) so as to discredit the narrator and undercut

his presentation of Vere; or are they simply beside Melville's main point in composing this "inside narrative" (as the subtitle calls it)?

The Characterization of Billy Budd

Billy, it appears, is both a type figure, the "Handsome Sailor," and a unique individual.

1. According to the narrator, however, he "is not presented as a conventional hero." In what specific way, then, is he unconventional?

2. Aged twenty-one, Billy is still inexperienced and immature, as both the name "Budd" and the nickname "Baby" may well suggest. In some respects his story involves an initiation, a rite of passage from youth into maturity and from innocence to experience. Given his particular background, how do his individual attributes, both inherited and acquired, affect the course of his development? For example, consider the factors of strength and beauty, physical force and vocal hesitancy, in his successive encounters with "the Red Whiskers" aboard the *Rights-of-Man* (chapter 1), with the afterguardsman aboard the *Bellipotent* (chapter 14), and later, in the captain's cabin, with John Claggart (chapter 19).

3. When Billy first enters the King's service, "something about him" is said to provoke "an ambiguous smile" among the "harder faces" of the *Bellipotent*'s crew (chapter 2). What is that "something"?

4. Both in chapter 15 and again in chapter 21 the question is raised whether Billy should have reported to a superior his encounter with the afterguardsman. To whom would such a report have been made? Would the outcome of Billy's trial have been different had he disclosed the incident?

5. At the opening of chapter 3 the narrator speaks of his account as "restricted . . . to the inner life of one particular ship"—the *Bellipotent*—"and the career of an individual sailor"—Billy Budd. How does this statement square with his previous introduction of Billy in chapter 1 as an example of the "Handsome Sailor," a type figure to be found in both "the military and merchant navies" in "the time before steamships"?

6. Some readers and critics have seen Billy as a Christ figure, though the narrator never explicitly draws such an analogy; instead, he links Billy with "young Alexander" (chapter 1), "young Achilles" (chapter 9), "young

David" (chapter 12), "young Joseph" (chapter 18), "young Isaac" (chapter 22), and especially "young Adam before the Fall" (chapter 18). How do such analogies affect your response to Billy and his fate?

The Characterization of John Claggart

Claggart is difficult to study apart from Billy, since the two are obviously antithetical; comparisons and contrasts between them are therefore in order, beginning with the narrator's inability to tell much about the previous life of either character.

1. Are the characters, then, exact opposites as the narrator actually presents them?

2. After Claggart's public and private responses to the incident of the spilled soup described in chapter 10, two further chapters of analysis pose and at least partly answer the question "What was the matter with the master-at-arms?" How, specifically, does the narrator address the question? Will his speculations really solve Claggart's "mystery of iniquity"?

3. Claggart, we are told, can hide but cannot annul his innate evil; he must express what he *is* by what he *does,* and "like the scorpion . . . , act out to the end" his "allotted part" (chapter 12). The narrator by his analogy would appear to deny free will to a nature like Claggart's, which is admittedly "exceptional"—but both Billy Budd and Captain Vere are likewise viewed as exceptional. Do they exhibit a power of choice denied Claggart, or are their characters and actions also to some degree determined or at least conditioned?

4. With free will presumably goes responsibility. Are Billy and Vere then responsible for what *they* do after Claggart falsely accuses Billy of mutiny? Or does the responsibility lie with Claggart, for putting in motion the whole train of events that follows? Or, if "the Creator alone" is responsible for making scorpions and, by inference, Claggarts, is the *ultimate* responsibility then His? As lawyers would put it, what is the proximate cause of Claggart's death? Of Billy's?

5. Though Claggart is "depraved according to nature," he is nevertheless said to be "without vices or small sins" (chapter 11). The narrator goes on to deny anything "sordid or sensual" in his depravity, and to assert in a later passage that his envy of Billy's innocence is "no vulgar form of the passion"

(chapter 12). How do such observations bear on the theory that Claggart must be a thwarted homosexual?

The Characterization of Edward Fairfax Vere

The narrator's introduction of Vere, captain of the *Bellipotent,* occurs in chapter 6, immediately following a sequence of three background chapters: in chapter 3, his discussion of mutinies in the British fleet earlier in 1797, the year of the story, and in chapters 4 and 5 his digression on Horatio Nelson. "Whatever [Vere's] sterling qualities," the narrator tells us in chapter 6, he "was without any brilliant ones," yet in chapter 7 we learn that he is another "exceptional" character. He has little part in the story until chapter 18, when Claggart approaches him with accusations against Billy; in the remaining chapters he appears only intermittently, his death being reported in chapter 28 with two other chapters still to follow.

1. How, specifically, does the narrator characterize Vere in these respective chapters?

2. At the conclusion of chapter 5 the narrator observes that the mutinies of 1797 at Spithead and the Nore caused anxiety within the British navy, leading to "precautionary vigilance" at sea—particularly in view of possible engagements with French ships. How do we learn that Vere too shares this anxiety? What weight should be given this fear of mutiny in evaluating both Vere's reasoning with respect to the drumhead court and the court's ultimate decision concerning Billy?

3. In the aftermath of the Great Mutiny, as the narrator tells us in chapter 5, Nelson won the allegiance of *his* men "by force of his mere presence and heroic personality"; Vere, however, is no Nelson, and he feels obliged to exercise command by much different methods. In deciding to include the digression on Nelson in his manuscript, was Melville then offering an oblique comment on Vere and on his course of action?

4. "Something exceptional" in Vere's "moral quality" makes him a keen judge of human nature, the narrator declares in chapter 18. But though he has noticed Billy favorably and has his doubts about Claggart, he feels it necessary to "test" Claggart and his accusation through a private confrontation of accuser and accused. Later, after Claggart's death, he maintains secrecy aboard ship until after Billy is tried and convicted. "Here

he may or may not have erred" (chapter 21). Should Vere have made the whole affair public? If so, at what stage and by what means?

5. During the confrontation between Claggart and Billy, when Billy has difficulty speaking, Vere's "fatherly" encouragement actually seems to prompt Billy's fatal blow—after which "the father" in Vere is immediately "replaced by the military disciplinarian" (chapter 19). What does this dichotomy suggest about Vere? How does it again come to the fore in the course of the trial that follows?

6. "Struck dead by an angel of God!" Vere exclaims "vehemently," immediately adding, "Yet the angel must hang!" The "prudent" surgeon, hearing "these passionate interjections" and observing Vere's agitation after Claggart's death (chapter 19), is led to question Vere's mental condition (chapter 20); the noncommittal narrator, after pondering what he takes to be the narrow line between sanity and insanity, simply refers the question of "any degree of aberration" in Vere to the reader (chapter 21). *Was* Vere really "unhinged"?

7. Vere's decision to appoint a drumhead court to try Billy forthwith strikes the surgeon as "impolitic, if nothing more"; the naval and marine officers of the *Bellipotent* agree with him that "such a matter should be referred to the admiral" (chapter 20); Vere would willingly have awaited the admiral's judgment, we are told, had not a sense of "urgency" led him to act immediately in accordance with naval "usage" (chapter 21). None of these characters raises the issue that has so concerned certain twentieth-century scholars, aware that in point of historical fact Vere had no legal right to try Billy because only admirals had convening authority in capital cases (see "Legal Aspects of *Billy Budd, Sailor*" below). Why this departure from historical accuracy?

8. Vere's conduct of the trial (chapter 21) has provoked much discussion, turning upon such matters as his prejudgment of the case, his testimony from the windward side of the cabin—looking down upon the court, his assertion that military officers are no longer "natural free agents" and that in serving the King they must rule out compassion, his insistence that in military law Billy's "intent or non-intent is nothing to the purpose," and his conclusion that the court has but two alternatives: condemn Billy to hang, as he is manifestly urging, or else let him go. Is the trial scene then to be read as (1) simply an engrossing event, (2) a revelation, whether friendly or hostile, of Vere and all that he stands for in terms of class, profession,

and worldview, or (3) a dispassionate presentation in dramatic form of basic issues such as the competing demands of freedom and commitment, natural impulses and societal obligations, tolerance and discipline, compassion and rational judgment, motivation and consequences?

9. What took place when Vere privately told Billy of the court's verdict "was never known," the narrator states in chapter 22, though "in view of the character of the twain" he is led to offer certain highly qualified conjectures. Why isn't *this* scene rendered dramatically? Are the narrator's conjectures plausible? Is he suggesting, as some have thought, that Billy was Vere's natural son? Did Billy really suffer less than Vere, as "apparently indicated" by his blessing of Vere in chapter 25?

10. What further insights into Vere's character are afforded by his address to the crew (chapter 23), his reported rigidity after receiving Billy's blessing before the execution (chapter 25), his subsequent handling of the crew through "forms, measured forms" (chapter 27), and by what the narrator tells us of his fatal wound and dying words (chapter 28)?

Other Characters and Events

Throughout the narrative there is mention of other individuals, some a part of the action and others wholly outside it, who deserve the reader's attention.

1. The Dansker, with his "pithy guarded cynicism" (chapter 9), not only speculates about Billy's prospects aboard the *Bellipotent* but soon divines that Claggart is "down" on Billy. He thus alerts the reader as he tries to alert Billy himself; should he have taken a more active role in Billy's behalf, as some critics have thought? Or does he function primarily as a narrative device—or even as a surrogate for the author?

2. The surgeon, originally introduced solely to pronounce Claggart dead, was later given an enlarged role: to cast doubt upon Vere's actions and sanity after Claggart's death (chapters 19, 20, 21) and to direct and afterwards comment upon Billy's "hanging scientifically conducted" (chapter 26). Considering who and what the surgeon is, and what he says and does, how much weight should be given his interpretation of persons and events?

3. Among other minor characters, the various members of the court (chapter 21) and the ship's chaplain (chapter 24) are most prominent.

What light do they throw upon Billy and Vere, and upon the little world of the *Bellipotent?* Note particularly the chaplain's visit to Billy and the narrator's subsequent comments (chapter 24).

4. As the narrator notes, his account might well have ended with Billy's death (chapter 28). But he reports a number of subsequent events: the conversation of the purser and surgeon (chapter 26), the crew's responses to Billy's execution and burial (chapter 27), the later death of Captain Vere (chapter 29), the erroneous report in "a naval chronicle of the time" concerning Billy and Claggart—though not the captain (chapter 29), and, last but not least, the sailors' tributes to Billy, epitomized in "Billy in the Darbies" (chapter 30). To borrow a phrase from *Moby-Dick,* how do these "unequal cross-lights" contribute to the overall effect of *Billy Budd, Sailor,* and how do they influence your views of the narrative, the principal characters, and the theme of the story? Whose book, in your judgment, is *Billy Budd?*

Legal Aspects of *Billy Budd, Sailor*

1. The Chicago edition of *Billy Budd, Sailor* (1962), in its "Notes and Commentary" on the text of the story, includes discussion of certain contemporary documents—the Articles of War, the Mutiny Act, and *Statutes Relating to the Admiralty, Navy, Shipping, and Navigation*—that were current in Great Britain at the time of the action of Melville's narrative, 1797, and may have some bearing on interpretation. The following catch phrases quoted from the text of chapters 19–21 identify corresponding notes in the Chicago edition, pages 175–83, that concern relevant historical and legal issues.

a drumhead court: for corresponding note, see 175–76.

the individuals composing it: see 178–79.

the heaviest of penalties: see 179.

According to the Articles of War: see 180–81.

the Mutiny Act: see 181.

the U.S. brig-of-war Somers: see 181–83.

follows without delay: see 183.

2. Among published articles that also deal with legal aspects of the story are the following:

C. B. Ives. "*Billy Budd* and the Articles of War." *American Literature* 34 (March 1962): 31–39.

> Notes that "Billy Budd's offense was punishable by death under the Articles, but . . . Vere was wrong in asserting that the Articles required him to hang Billy forthwith. They . . . provided nowhere for such summary court-martial as was held by Captain Vere" (33).

Charles A. Reich. "The Tragedy of Justice in *Billy Budd*." *Yale Review* 56 (Spring 1967): 368–89.

> Distinguishes three issues: How, and by what standards, should Billy and his deed be judged? How does Vere perceive the problem and respond to it? How adequate are society's standards of judgment? Through Vere, the novel asks what is wrong with the law and its progenitor, society.

Jack W. Ledbetter. "The Trial of Billy Budd, Foretopman." *American Bar Association Journal* 58 (June 1972): 614–19.

> Billy "was falsely accused of one crime, mutiny. He was then guilty of at least two crimes, striking a superior officer and murder, and possibly a third, mutiny. He was improperly tried and convicted for his crimes and was illegally sent to his death by hanging." Vere "violated fundamental principles of due process in the conduct of the court and in his personal domination over its deliberations and decision. . . . In ordering Billy's execution without opportunity for appeal and review" Vere "clearly violated the express statutory rules of the British navy" (619).

Richard H. Weisberg. "How Judges Speak: Some Lessons of Adjudication in *Billy Budd, Sailor* with an Application to Justice Rehnquist." *New York University Law Review* 57 (April 1982): 1–69.

> "Vere's articulation and application of the law in many respects were erroneous, and . . . Melville intended his reader both to realize this fact and to consider its broader implications" (5). Through Vere's deceptive argument to his court Melville is casting into doubt "adjudicatory communication, at its highest level of articulateness and sophistication" (42). Weisberg's article has been revised and reprinted as "The Creative Use of Statutes for Subjective Ends" in *The Failure of the Word: The Protagonist as Lawyer in Modern Fiction* (New Haven, Conn.: Yale University Press, 1984), 131–76, 206–14.

Lawry, Robert P. "Justice in *Billy Budd*." *The Gamut* (Cleveland State University) 6 (Spring/Summer 1982): 76–86; reprinted in *In Brief* (Case Western Reserve University School of Law) 31 (June 1984): 13–19.

For Lawry, Billy's case presents a "paradox" that leads him to a "tentative conclusion": "no injustice was done; yet the absence of injustice is insufficient to warrant the further conclusion that justice was done" (76). Melville, he argues, "chose only those features of the law [the British Articles of War as of 1797] that would set up the moral dilemma that [he] wanted to dramatize" (78). His story is grounded "on the possibility of mutiny and the Navy's concern that sailors in wartime not be allowed to think that they could strike an officer with impunity" (80), and Vere as a naval commander is faced with a situation in which to " 'condemn or let go' was the only legal choice" in Billy's case (83). Thus "we cannot say Vere's decision was unjust" (82), but Melville suggests that Admiral Nelson—a greater man than Vere—"would have behaved differently" (83). Even though "legal justice" may indeed have been done, "this notion of justice seems inadequate to many," as indeed it does to Vere himself (81).

Appendix 4

The Melvilles, the Gansevoorts, and the Cincinnati Badge

From *Melville Society Extracts* 70 (September 1987): 1, 4; the accompanying notes have been somewhat revised in order to take account of later scholarship. I include this brief paper in the present volume because it corrects factual errors in two articles of the 1950s that were included in my previous collection of chapters and essays, *Pursuing Melville* (1982). A comment by Stanton Garner encouraged me to write the original version of the paper; he kindly read an early draft and shared additional information concerning both the Gansevoorts and the Melvilles that he had acquired in the course of his research for *The Civil War World of Herman Melville* (Lawrence: University Press of Kansas, 1993).

Although Herman Melville's paternal grandfather, the senior Major Thomas Melvill (1751–1832), served as a commissioned officer during the American Revolution, he did not meet the specific requirements for original membership in the founders of the Society of the Cincinnati, comprising officers who had fought against the British in the American Revolution. Right to membership was defined to exist in those

> officers of the Line (regular army), holding commissions from the Continental Congress, who were in any of the following classes:
> (a) Those in service at the time of the institution of the Society in May, 1783.
> (b) Those officers previously deranged (retired) by act of the Continental Congress.
> (c) Those who served three years as commissioned officers of the Continental Line.[1]

Major Melvill, who had originally served in an artillery regiment raised by the colony of Massachusetts, was in Continental service just short of the three years required for membership.

Hereditary membership in the Society has since passed from the original members through eldest sons in each succeeding generation; in addition, state societies have also elected honorary members. The names Melvill and Melville do not appear in either of the *Memorials of the Society of the Cincinnati of Massachusetts* published by the Massachusetts Society in 1873 and 1890,[2] nor are they to be found in William S. Thomas's 1929 compilation of national members. But Gilbert Stuart's portrait of General Peter Gansevoort (1749–1812), Herman Melville's maternal grandfather, shows the Cincinnati badge affixed to the general's left lapel,[3] and Thomas lists him as an original member, together with three of his descendants (p. 64): Peter's son Herman (1779–1862) was admitted in 1813 following his father's death; the second Peter Gansevoort (1789–1876), a younger brother of Herman, was admitted in 1868,[4] and Edward Gansevoort Curtis, a great grandson of the first Peter Gansevoort, was admitted in 1907.

Herman Melville's own "double Revolutionary descent" was an attribute that he shared with the title character of his *Pierre* (1852) and the Jack Gentian of his later Burgundy Club sketches, written in the 1870s and 1880s, which depict Gentian as proudly wearing the Cincinnati badge. In one of the sketches, "Major Gentian and Colonel Bunkum," an unnamed speaker, identified only as "the eldest son of a Revolutionary officer and as such the inheritor of the Cincinnati badge," is quoted as saying that "if ever there is a recognized order of nobility in this land it will be formed of the sons of the officers of the Revolution." Here his remark is directed to "his own son then a stripling"; another version of the same episode occurs in "Note: The Cincinnati," where the unnamed speaker addresses "the writer of this note" as his "Nephew."[5]

Since none of the Melvills (or Melvilles) qualified for membership in the Society, this "eldest son of a Revolutionary officer and as such the inheritor of the Cincinnati badge" was presumably Herman Gansevoort— not the junior Thomas Melvill, with whom I mistakenly identified him in two articles of the 1950s, "The Ghost of Major Melvill" and "Melville's Burgundy Club Sketches."[6] By the same token, Herman Melville was evidently associating Jack Gentian's military prowess not with that of his paternal relatives but rather with the exploits of the elder Peter Gansevoort, the Revolutionary "Hero of Fort Stanwix," and of Melville's cousin Henry Sanford Gansevoort (1834–1871), grandson of the first Peter, a Union officer whom Melville had visited at the front during the Civil War.[7]

Notes

1.

Emerson as Teacher

From *Emerson Centenary Essays,* ed. Joel Myerson (Carbondale: Southern Illinois University Press, 1982), 180–90, 210–12; previously reprinted in *Ralph Waldo Emerson: A Collection of Critical Essays,* ed. Lawrence Buell (Englewood Cliffs, N.J.: Prentice Hall, 1993), 199–210; reprinted here with added references to later scholarship and with minor stylistic revisions. Some of the quotations are from texts of *CW* and *JMN* that were not yet available when this essay was first drafted and published. It began as an invited lecture at the College of Wooster in 1974 in honor of Professor Lowell William Coolidge on the occasion of his retirement from teaching (but not from further service to the College). He was my mentor when I was an undergraduate and he remained a valued friend until his death in 1995. The lecture was intended to embody ideals of teaching which I share with both Emerson and Bill Coolidge. I have read the present text on a number of other campuses since 1974; a somewhat shorter version, "The Scholar as Teacher," appears as the Epilogue to my *Emerson on the Scholar* (Columbia: University of Missouri Press, 1992), 267–76, 301–2.

1. See also *JMN* 10:300–301 and "Culture," *W* 6:147.

2. Henry James to Emerson, 3 October 1843, as printed in Ralph Barton Perry, *The Thought and Character of William James,* 2 vols. (Boston: Little, Brown, 1935), 1:51.

3. See Matthew Arnold, "Emerson," in *Discourses in America* (London: Macmillan, 1885), 138–207.

4. Thomas Carlyle, *Sartor Resartus: The Life and Opinions of Herr Teufelsdröckh,* ed. Charles Frederick Harrold (Garden City, N.Y.: Doubleday, Doran, 1937), 18.

5. See Andrews Norton, "A Discourse on the Latest Form of Infidelity," an address delivered before the alumni of Harvard Divinity School on 19 July 1839 and subsequently printed as a pamphlet. The address is excerpted in Perry Miller, *The Transcendentalists: An Anthology* (Cambridge: Harvard University Press, 1950), 210–13, along with other documents in the controversy which Emerson's address of 1838 provoked.

6. "Why has never the poorest country college offered me a professorship of rhetoric? I think I could have taught an orator, though I am none" (*JMN* 15:246). Moncure Daniel Conway, *Emerson at Home and Abroad* (Boston: James R. Osgood, 1882), 55, reports that Emerson once told him that when he graduated from Harvard "his ambition was to be a professor of rhetoric and elocution."

7. Henry D. Thoreau, *Journal,* vol. 1, *1837–1844,* 5, in *The Writings of Henry D. Thoreau* (Princeton, N.J.: Princeton University Press, 1971–).

8. Twice reported by James Townsend Trowbridge: in his "Reminiscences of Walt Whitman," *Atlantic Monthly* 89 (1902): 163–75, and again in *My Own Story* (Boston: Houghton Mifflin and Co., 1903), 360–401; Jerome Loving quotes Trowbridge with evident reservations in his *Emerson, Whitman, and the American Muse* (Chapel Hill: University of North Carolina Press, 1982), 11, 195 n. 5.

9. Nathaniel Hawthorne, "The Old Manse," in *Mosses from an Old Manse* (1846), ed. J. Donald Crawley, vol. 10 of the Centenary Edition of *The Works of Nathaniel Hawthorne,* 20 vols. (Columbus: Ohio State University Press, 1974), 31.

10. Melville to Evert Duyckinck, Boston, 3 March 1849 (*Correspondence,* 122).

11. Perry Miller, *The Golden Age of American Literature* (New York: George Braziller, 1959), 12.

12. Review of *American Renaissance: Art and Expression in the Age of Emerson and Whitman,* by F. O. Matthiessen, *Time,* 2 June 1941, 84.

13. Lyon N. Richardson, "What Rutherford B. Hayes Liked in Emerson," *American Literature* 17 (March 1945): 28.

14. Hayes, letter of 5 December 1889, quoted in Richardson, "What Hayes Liked in Emerson," 23, from *Diary and Letters of Rutherford B. Hayes,* ed. Charles Richard Williams.

15. "Lecturing was his business," Emerson's daughter Ellen said of her late father in 1902; "he had to work at it as other men do at their business. He said he wished he could give it up, that Mrs. [Caroline Sturgis] Tappan was ashamed to have him travel peddling lectures all over the country. But we told him we weren't ashamed, we felt he was trying to benefit and to teach his country, as well as to make his living." See Edith Emerson Webster Gregg, "Emerson and His Children: Their Childhood Memories," *Harvard Library Bulletin* 28 (October 1980): 413.

16. James Russell Lowell, "Emerson the Lecturer," in *My Study Windows* (Boston: James R. Osgood, 1871), 375.

17. See David Mead, *Yankee Eloquence in the Middle West: The Ohio Lyceum, 1850–1870* (East Lansing: Michigan State College Press, 1951), 24–27.

18. Carl Bode, *The American Lyceum: Town Meeting of the Mind* (New York: Oxford University Press, 1956), 201.

19. See Eleanor Bryce Scott, "Emerson Wins the Nine Hundred Dollars," *American Literature* 17 (March 1945): 75–85, which illustrates Emerson's western experiences with an account of his reception in Rock Island, Illinois, on New Year's Day 1856.

20. Lowell, "Emerson the Lecturer," 375.

21. George William Curtis, "Emerson Lecturing," in *From the Easy Chair* (New York: Harper and Brothers, 1892), 22.

22. Lowell, "Emerson the Lecturer," 378.

23. Oliver Wendell Holmes, *Ralph Waldo Emerson* (Boston: Houghton, Mifflin, 1884), 363–64.

24. Curtis, "Emerson Lecturing," 26.

25. Conway, *Emerson at Home and Abroad,* 55.

26. Henry James, Sr., "Emerson," *Atlantic Monthly* 94 (December 1904): 741 (written ca. 1868).

27. Holmes, *Ralph Waldo Emerson,* 363. Holmes also remarked that "the music of his speech pleased those who found his thought too subtle for their dull wits to follow" (376).

28. Edwin Percy Whipple, "Some Recollections of Ralph Waldo Emerson," *Harper's Magazine* 65 (September 1882): 580.

29. Julian Hawthorne, *The Memoirs of Julian Hawthorne,* ed. Edith Garrigues Hawthorne (New York: Macmillan, 1938), 99.

30. Quoted in C. E. Schorer, "Emerson and the Wisconsin Lyceum," *American Literature* 24 (January 1953): 468.

31. "Often there were very funny stories and remarks in his lectures," according to Emerson's daughter Ellen, "and he would read them over and over at home—sometimes, he said, twenty times—to get through laughing at them himself, that he might be sure not to laugh at the lecture" (Gregg, "Emerson and His Children," 413).

32. Curtis, "Emerson Lecturing," 22.

33. Lowell, "Emerson the Lecturer," 382.

34. Curtis, "Emerson Lecturing," 23–24.

35. Henry Adams, *The Education of Henry Adams* (Boston: Houghton Mifflin, 1961), 300.

36. His lectures in Edinburgh occasioned a pamphlet entitled *Emerson's Orations to the Modern Athenians; or, Pantheism.* See Ralph L. Rusk, *The Life of Ralph Waldo Emerson* (New York: Charles Scribner's Sons, 1949), 338.

37. Mead, *Yankee Eloquence in the Middle West,* 60.

38. Yvor Winters, "The Significance of *The Bridge,* by Hart Crane," in *In Defense of Reason* (New York: Swallow Press and William Morrow, 1947), 587.

39. Randall Stewart, *American Literature and Christian Doctrine* (Baton Rouge: Louisiana State University Press, 1958), 55.

40. D. H. Lawrence, "Model Americans," review of *Americans,* by Stuart P. Sherman, *Dial* 74 (May 1923): 507.

41. I first discussed this subject in "The American Scholar and Public Issues: The Case of Emerson," *Ariel: A Review of International English Literature* 7 (July 1976): 109–21. In *Emerson on the Scholar* (1992) I offered an expanded treatment in chapters 11–13 emphasizing Emerson's changing response to the issue of slavery and his relations with the Abolitionists.

42. As early as 1830 Emerson remarked in a sermon on the "vast difference between the power of two teachers," one of whom speaks "*living* truth" while the other presents "*dead* truth, . . . passively taken and taught at second hand; it lies like a lump of foreign matter in his intellectual system, separate and inoperative. It is, compared with the same truth quickened in another mind, like a fact in a child's lesson in geography, as it lies unconnected and useless in his memory, compared with the same fact, as it enters into the knowledge of the surveyor or the traveller" (Sermon LXXVI); see Teresa Toulouse and Andrew H. Delbanco, eds., vol. 2 of *The Complete Sermons of Ralph Waldo Emerson,* ed. Albert J. von Frank (Columbia: University of Missouri Press, 1990), 194. The parallel with Whitehead's "inert ideas" is striking.

43. The teacher's "capital secret," Emerson liked to say, is "to convert life into truth" (*EL* 2:202; *CW* 1:86). On the relation between life and truth, see also *JMN* 5:324 and *CW* 1:55.

44. Conway, *Emerson at Home and Abroad,* 298; cf. "Education" (1840), *EL* 3:295.

45. Conway, *Emerson at Home and Abroad,* 297.

46. Henry David Thoreau, *Walden,* ed. J. Lyndon Shanley (Princeton, N.J.: Princeton University Press, 1971), 71.

47. Walt Whitman, "Song of Myself," lines 1210–11, in *"Leaves of Grass": Comprehensive Reader's Edition,* ed. Harold W. Blodgett and Sculley Bradley (New York: New York University Press, 1965), 83. "The best part of Emersonianism," Whitman wrote later in his essay "Emerson's Books, (The Shadows of Them.)," is that "it breeds the giant that destroys itself. Who wants to be any man's mere follower? lurks behind every page. No teacher ever taught, that has so provided for his pupil's setting up independently—no truer evolutionist." See Whitman, *Prose Works 1892,* ed. Floyd Stovall, 2 vols. (New York: New York University Press, 1964), 2:517–18.

48. Herman Melville, *Moby-Dick,* 264.

2.

Melville and Whitman

From *Melville Society Extracts* 50 (May 1982): 10–12; here revised and expanded.

1. Unsigned notice in the *Brooklyn Daily Eagle,* 15 April 1846, quoted in *Log,* 1:211.

2. Unsigned notice in the *Brooklyn Daily Eagle,* 5 May 1847, reprinted in Watson G. Branch, ed., *Melville: The Critical Heritage* (Boston: Routledge & Kegan Paul, 1974), 95.

3. Thomas L. Brasher, *Whitman as an Editor of the Brooklyn Daily Eagle* (Detroit: Wayne State University Press, 1970), 250 n. 9. Brasher quotes Whitman's words on Melville from Horace Traubel's *With Walt Whitman in Camden,* 7 vols. to date (Boston, New York, and Carbondale, Ill., 1906–1992), 5:446.

4. Quoted from *Academy,* 15 August 1885, in *Log,* 2:792.

5. Quoted from *Universal Review,* 15 May 1889, in *Log,* 2:787.

6. On Buchanan and the Stedmans, see Merton M. Sealts, Jr., *The Early Lives of Melville: Nineteenth-Century Biographical Sketches and Their Authors* (Madison: University of Wisconsin Press, 1974), 23–24.

7. Whitman to William Sloane Kennedy, 3 February 1891, in *The Correspondence of Walt Whitman,* ed. Edwin Haviland Miller, 5 vols. (New York: New York University Press, 1951–1969), 5:159.

8. Laura Gould Stedman, "Concerning Herman Melville and the Stedmans," quoted in Sealts, *The Early Lives of Melville,* 49.

9. Lawrence Buell, "Transcendentalist Catalogue Rhetoric: Vision versus Form," *American Literature* 40 (November 1968): 325–39. This essay was incorporated in his *Literary Transcendentalism: Style and Vision in the American Renaissance* (Ithaca, N.Y.: Cornell University Press, 1973).

3.

Herman Melville's "Bartleby"

From *Resources for Discussing Herman Melville's Tale, "Bartleby,"* prepared by Merton M. Sealts, Jr. (Madison: Wisconsin Humanities Committee, 1982); reprinted here with some shortening and other revision. The pamphlet incorporates material that I had prepared for an all-day seminar on Melville's story held on 27 February

1982 for approximately one hundred lawyers from south-central Wisconsin; participants also viewed a videotaped dramatization of "Bartleby," produced in 1979 by the Maryland Center for Public Broadcasting. The seminar was sponsored by the Wisconsin Humanities Committee (now the Wisconsin Humanities Council), which is funded primarily by the National Endowment for the Humanities. The Committee later published the pamphlet "to make possible the replication of this seminar in other parts of the country." As a demonstration project later in 1982 I again led discussion of the story at an NEH Regional Conference at St. Louis.

The lawyers attending the seminar in Madison had already read "Bartleby" and had received the study questions printed here in Appendix 1. My introductory remarks to them were intended simply to provide background for the story rather than to influence the ensuing discussion by setting forth any particular line of interpretation. The present version of my introduction omits a section of purely biographical material, "The Profile of Melville's Career" (pp. 6–10 of the 1982 pamphlet); a more detailed treatment of the nature and reception of his various writings is available to the reader here in essay 11, " 'The Flower of Fame.' "

1. The fullest treatment of the criticism and scholarship discussed in this and the following paragraphs is in Lea Bertani Vozar Newman, *A Reader's Guide to the Short Stories of Herman Melville* (Boston: G. K. Hall, 1986), 205–14.

2. Reproduced in *"The Piazza Tales" and Other Prose Pieces 1839–1860*, 574.

3. Nathaniel Hawthorne to William D. Ticknor, 19 January 1855, *The Letters, 1853–1856*, ed. Thomas Woodson et al., in the Centenary Edition of *The Works of Nathaniel Hawthorne*, 20 vols. (Columbus: Ohio State University Press, 1962–1988), 17:304.

4. Lewis Mumford, *Herman Melville* (New York: Harcourt, Brace, 1929), 259.

5. Donald Yannella, in "Writing 'the *other* way': Melville, the Duyckinck Crowd, and Literature for the Masses" (in John Bryant, ed., *A Companion to Melville Studies* [New York, Westport, and London: Greenwood Press, 1986], 63–81), suggests that the supporting characters Standard and Hautboy may be patterned after Melville's New York friends Evert Duyckinck and Cornelius Mathews.

4.

Melville's "Benito Cereno"

This essay, which has not been published previously, is based on notes I prepared on Melville's much-debated story for discussions that I led on three separate occasions: first—in sequence with treatment of Melville's "Bartleby" and *Billy Budd, Sailor*— at the Alumni College of the College of Wooster in the summer of 1984; later, as a visitor in a classroom at Indiana State University in September of 1991; and most recently, in the Elderhostel course "Melville Centennial Reflections," which I offered at Edgewood College, Madison, Wis., in the summer of 1992.

Study questions concerning the story, first posed in 1984 and used again in 1992, are printed here in Appendix 2. On the sources, composition, and dating of "Benito Cereno," see Lea Bertani Vozar Newman, *A Reader's Guide to the Short Stories of Herman Melville* (Boston: G. K. Hall, 1986), 95–153; the editors' notes in *"The Piazza Tales" and Other Prose Pieces 1839–1860* (1987), 581–82; and a comment in my own Historical Note in *"The Piazza Tales" and Other Prose Pieces,* 495 n.

Concerning the time of composition, when I wrote "The Composition of Melville's Short Fiction" (1980) I assumed that a letter to his publishers dated by Melville as 1 April 1855 referred to proofs of "Benito Cereno"; Alma A. MacDougall subsequently demonstrated that Melville's dating of the letter was in error: the correct date is 1 April 1856 and his reference was actually to proofs of his own *Piazza Tales* volume, published later that year. Thus my article of 1980 and its reprinting in my *Pursuing Melville, 1940–1980: Chapters and Essays* (Madison: University of Wisconsin Press, 1982) should both be emended accordingly. (For a correction of two other items in *Pursuing Melville,* see Appendix 4, "The Melvilles, the Gansevoorts, and the Cincinnati Badge.")

5.

Innocence and Infamy: Melville's *Billy Budd, Sailor*

This essay is from a chapter of the same title contributed to *A Companion to Melville Studies,* ed. John Bryant (Westport, Conn.: Greenwood Press, 1986; an imprint of Greenwood Publishing Group, Inc., Westport, Conn.), 407–30; reprinted with minor revision and restyling. The chapter incorporates material from an earlier pamphlet that I prepared, *Innocence and Infamy: Resources for Discussing Herman Melville's "Billy Budd, Sailor"* (Madison: Wisconsin Humanities Committee, 1983), and from an unpublished lecture, "Melville's Sense of the Past," which I read in 1984 at North Texas State University, the University of Texas at Arlington, and the University of Texas at Austin, and in 1986 at the University of Wisconsin–Milwaukee.

The pamphlet of 1983 contains material I had prepared for an all-day seminar on Melville's story, held on 22 January 1983 for a group of lawyers from south-central Wisconsin. The seminar was sponsored by the Wisconsin Humanities Committee (now the Wisconsin Humanities Council), which is funded primarily by the

National Endowment for the Humanities. The Committee then published this pamphlet, like the earlier pamphlet of 1982 on Melville's "Bartleby," to encourage replication of similar discussions in other parts of the country. Study questions used in the seminar and included in the pamphlet are printed here in Appendix 3.

The present essay quotes from Melville's late writings in both prose and verse that have not yet been included in the Northwestern-Newberry edition of *The Writings of Herman Melville*. Quotations here from *Billy Budd* are from the Reading Text of *Billy Budd, Sailor (An Inside Narrative)*, by Herman Melville (Reading Text and Genetic Text, edited from the manuscript with Introduction and Notes, by Harrison Hayford and Merton M. Sealts, Jr. [Chicago: University of Chicago Press, 1962], 41–132), and are cited parenthetically in the text. Quotations of Melville's Burgundy Club sketches are from *Great Short Works of Herman Melville*, Introduction by Warner Berthoff (New York: Harper & Row, 1969); page numbers in this text are indicated parenthetically: (*Great Short Works,* 000). Quotations from Melville's *John Marr and Other Sailors* are from *Collected Poems of Herman Melville*, ed. Howard P. Vincent (Chicago: Hendricks House, 1946); page numbers in this text are indicated parenthetically: (*Poems,* 000).

1. See the Editors' Introduction to the Chicago edition of *Billy Budd*, 25–27, which I draw upon here and below; I also cite various parts of this edition throughout the notes. Both Hayford and I contributed to the Introduction.

2. In Melville's copy of *The Life of Nelson*, by Robert Southey, now in the Melville Collection of the Harvard College Library, is a notation in his wife's hand: "This book is kept for reference from 'Billy Budd'—(unfinished)"; see "Check-List of Books Owned and Borrowed," no. 481, in Sealts, *Melville's Reading* (rev. and enlarged ed., Columbia: University of South Carolina Press, 1988), 216.

3. See leaf 344 of the Genetic Text, *Billy Budd*, Chicago edition, 422.

4. Vern Wagner, "Billy Budd as Moby Dick: An Alternate Reading," in A. Dayle Wallace and Woodburn O. Ross, eds., *Studies in Honor of John Wilcox* (Detroit: Wayne State University Press, 1958), 174.

5. Edward Stessel, "Naval Warfare and Herman Melville's War against Failure," *Essays in Arts and Sciences* 10 (May 1981): 75.

6. Editors' Introduction, *Billy Budd*, Chicago edition, 30.

7. F. O. Matthiessen, *American Renaissance: Art and Expression in the Age of Emerson and Whitman* (New York: Oxford University Press, 1941), 501.

8. Michael Paul Rogin, *Subversive Genealogy: The Politics and Art of Herman Melville* (New York: Alfred A. Knopf, 1983), 288–316.

9. Brook Thomas, "The Legal Fictions of Herman Melville and Lemuel Shaw," *Critical Inquiry* 11 (September 1984): 24–51.

10. See leaf 87 of the Genetic Text, *Billy Budd*, Chicago edition, 315.

11. Peter L. Hays and Richard Dilworth Rust, " 'Something Healing': Fathers and Sons in *Billy Budd*," *Nineteenth-Century Fiction* 34 (December 1979): 326–36.

12. Whether or not Melville even saw the magazine articles is simply unknown. For a collection of earlier documentary materials concerning the *Somers* case, see Harrison Hayford, *The Somers Mutiny Affair* (Englewood Cliffs, N.J.: Prentice-Hall, 1959). The Chicago edition of *Billy Budd* includes a survey of commentary up to 1962 on the relation of the case to *Billy Budd, Sailor;* see Editors' Introduction, 27–30, and Notes & Commentary, 181–83. Michael Rogin has discussed larger implications of the analogue afforded by the *Somers* case: see "The Somers Mutiny and *Billy Budd:* Melville in the Penal Colony" (1980), reprinted in his *Subversive Genealogy* (1983), 288–316. Among other considerations, Rogin argues that Melville's treatment of the *Somers* affair in *White-Jacket* "discredited his family" in the person of Guert Gansevoort and that " 'filial duty' now obliged him to make reparation" in *Billy Budd* (294).

13. See note 2 above.

14. B. R. McElderry, Jr., "Three Earlier Treatments of the *Billy Budd* Theme," *American Literature* 27 (May 1955): 251–57; Richard and Rita Gollin, "Justice in an Earlier Treatment of the *Billy Budd* Theme," *American Literature* 28 (January 1957): 513–15.

15. John Bryant, "Melville and Charles F. Briggs: *Working a Passage* to *Billy Budd*," *English Language Notes* 22 (June 1985): 48–54.

16. Editors' Introduction, *Billy Budd*, Chicago edition, 30–33.

17. Ibid., 176.

18. See Notes & Commentary in the Chicago edition, 175–83: notes on "a drumhead court," "the individuals composing it," "the heaviest of penalties," "according to the Articles of War, a capital crime," "the Mutiny Act," and "follows without delay." For more extended commentary, see C. B. Ives, "*Billy Budd* and the Articles of War," *American Literature* 34 (March 1962): 31–39; Jack W. Ledbetter, "The Trial of Billy Budd, Foretopman," *American Bar Association Journal* 58 (June 1972): 614–19; Richard H. Weisberg, "How Judges Speak: Some Lessons of Adjudication in *Billy Budd, Sailor* with an Application to Justice Rehnquist," *New York University Law Review* 57 (April 1982): 1–69, revised and reprinted as "The Creative Use of Statutes for Subjective Ends" in *The Failure of the Word: The Protagonist as Lawyer in Modern Fiction* (New Haven: Yale University Press, 1984), 131–76, 206–14; and Robert P. Lawry, "Justice in *Billy Budd*," *The Gamut* (Cleveland State University) 6 (Spring/Summer 1982): 76–86, reprinted in *In Brief* (Case Western Reserve University School of Law) 31 (June 1984): 13–19. For a different approach to the trial scene, see Charles A. Reich, "The Tragedy of Justice in *Billy Budd*," *Yale Review* 56 (Spring 1967): 368–89.

19. Weisberg, "How Judges Speak," 32, 32 n. 92, 5. The version of Weisberg's essay published in his *Failure of the Word* somewhat revises his position.

20. Stanton Garner, "Fraud as Fact in Herman Melville's *Billy Budd*," *San Jose Studies* 4 (May 1978): 85. In a further extension of his logic, Garner argues, with the Chicago Reading Text as his target, that, in view of Melville's "confidence man tricks" in his narrative, "all textual emendations in *Billy Budd* made in the sole interest of factual accuracy are unwarranted" (100).

21. Stanton Garner, "Melville's Scout toward Aldie," *Melville Society Extracts* 51 (September 1982): 12–13; see Garner's revised and enlarged treatment of the episode in *The Civil War World of Herman Melville* (Lawrence: University Press of Kansas, 1993), 307–8.

22. Raymond Weaver, Introduction to *Shorter Novels of Herman Melville* (New York: Horace Liveright, 1928), xi.

23. Corrections of Freeman's transcription made by Elizabeth Treeman were published in 1953 by Harvard University Press in a pamphlet, *Corrigenda,* and used as the basis for the text of *Billy Budd* published in a college anthology in 1956. For more detailed discussion of the Weaver and Freeman editions and of other texts deriving from them, see "History of the Text" in the Editors' Introduction to the Chicago edition of 1962, 12–24.

24. Textual Notes to the Reading Text of *Billy Budd,* Chicago edition, 213.

25. Milton R. Stern, ed., *Billy Budd, Sailor (An Inside Narrative),* by Herman Melville (Indianapolis: Bobbs-Merrill, 1975).

26. Harrison Hayford, ed., Note on the Texts, *Herman Melville: Pierre, Israel Potter, The Piazza Tales, The Confidence-Man, Uncollected Prose, Billy Budd, Sailor* (New York: Library of America, 1984), 1448.

27. J. Middleton Murry, "Herman Melville's Silence," *Times Literary Supplement,* no. 1173 (10 July 1924), 433, reprinted in *"John Clare" and Other Studies* (London: Peter Neville, 1950), 209–12; E. L. Grant Watson, "Melville's Testament of Acceptance," *New England Quarterly* 6 (June 1933): 319–27.

28. Raymond Short, Introduction to *Four Great American Novels* (New York: Henry Holt & Co., 1946), xxxii.

29. T. T. E. [George Arms], "Melville's *Billy Budd,*" *Explicator* 2 (December 1943): query 14.

30. Joseph Schiffman, "Melville's Final Stage, Irony: A Re-examination of *Billy Budd* Criticism," *American Literature* 22 (May 1950): 128–36.

31. Leonard Casper, "The Case against Captain Vere," *Perspectives* 5 (Summer 1952): 146–52.

32. Phil Withim, "*Billy Budd:* Testament of Resistance," *Modern Language Quarterly* 20 (June 1959): 115–27.

33. Editors' Preface, *Billy Budd*, Chicago edition, v.

34. Kingsley Widmer, "The Perplexed Myths of Melville: *Billy Budd*," *Novel* 2 (Fall 1968): 25–35.

35. Charles Mitchell, "Melville and the Spurious Truths of Legalism," *Centennial Review* 12 (Winter 1968): 110–26.

36. Richard Harter Fogle, "*Billy Budd*—Acceptance or Irony," *Tulane Studies in English* 8 (1958): 107–13.

37. Paul Brodtkorb, Jr., "The Definitive *Billy Budd:* 'But Aren't It All Sham?'" *PMLA* 82 (December 1967): 600–612.

38. Barbara Johnson, "Melville's Fist: The Execution of *Billy Budd*" (1979), as reprinted in her *The Critical Difference: Essays in the Contemporary Rhetoric of Reading* (Baltimore: Johns Hopkins University Press, 1980), 84–85. Brook Thomas, in an avowedly Marxist essay, not only takes issue with Johnson's nonjudgmental reading of the story but also attacks deconstructionists generally for what he sees as their conservative ideology. Both Melville and his reader, according to Thomas, "are in the position to judge Vere's judgment according to the direction history has taken. When we do so," Thomas argues, "Vere's judgment seems clearly to support a dead order." See Thomas's "*Billy Budd* and the Judgment of Silence," *Bucknell Review* 27 (1982): 70.

39. Here I adapt a paragraph from my own essay-review of Melville scholarship published in 1971; see chapter 3, "Melville," of *American Literary Scholarship: An Annual / 1969,* ed. J. Albert Robbins (Durham, N.C.: Duke University Press, 1971), 52. This observation was originally prompted by reflections on the comments of two critics who had dealt with essentially the same issue in *Billy Budd* but reached opposite conclusions.

40. Stanton Garner, "The Melville Who Awaits Discovery," *Melville Society Extracts* 53 (February 1983): 2.

41. What can be done by an informed critic who has assimilated what the Genetic Text and the accompanying analysis reveal has since been demonstrated in Hershel Parker's provocative chapter-by-chapter reading of the novel in his *Reading "Billy Budd"* (Evanston, Ill.: Northwestern University Press, 1990).

42. Leon Howard, Introduction to *Moby Dick or, The Whale,* by Herman Melville (New York: The Modern Library, 1950), xiii.

43. Joyce Sparer Adler, "*Billy Budd* and Melville's Philosophy of War and Peace" (1976), as reprinted in her *War in Melville's Imagination* (New York: New York University Press, 1981), 177–78.

44. "The reader must reject or sanctify Vere's action," according to Jon M. Kinnamon, but in doing so he "exposes his own nature—the very depth of his mind and the strength of his compassion. In pondering this problem, the reader

walks the deck," since like Vere he too "is called on to make a decision that is not within his human capacity to make," for "he is above all a mortal." See "*Billy Budd:* Political Philosophies in a Sea of Thought," *Arizona Quarterly* 26 (Summer 1970): 172.

6.

An Author's Self-Education: Herman Melville's Reading

From *Wisconsin Academy Review* 35 (September 1989): 11–16, reprinted with some restyling and revision to include references to later developments. I read earlier versions of this paper—all intended to convey to general audiences something of the nature of my research and the findings I reported to Melville scholars in my *Melville's Reading*—during the 1980s as lectures at the Kendall Whaling Museum in Sharon, Massachusetts, at the College of Wooster, and before the Madison Literary Club.

1. Alan Gribben, "Private Libraries of American Authors: Dispersal, Custody, and Description," *The Journal of Library History* 21 (Spring 1986): 300–314; *Mark Twain's Library: A Reconstruction,* 2 vols. (Boston: G. K. Hall, 1980).

2. Robert Sattelmeyer, *Thoreau's Reading: A Study in Intellectual History with Bibliographical Catalogue* (Princeton, N.J.: Princeton University Press, 1988).

3. Nancy Craig Simmons, "Why an Enthusiast? Melville's *Pierre* and the Problem of the Imagination," *ESQ: A Journal of the American Renaissance* 33 (3d Quarter 1987): 147.

4. Stuart M. Frank, *Herman Melville's Picture Gallery: Sources and Types of the "Pictorial" Chapters of "Moby-Dick"* (Fairhaven, Mass.: Edward J. Lefkowicz, Inc., 1986); Christopher Sten, ed., *Savage Eye: Melville and the Visual Arts* (Kent, Ohio: Kent State University Press, 1991); Robert K. Wallace, *Melville and Turner: Spheres of Love and Fright* (Athens: University of Georgia Press, 1992).

5. The figures are derived from "A Second Supplementary Note to *Melville's Reading* (1988)," *Melville Society Extracts* 100 (March 1995): 2–3.

6. F. O. Matthiessen, *American Renaissance: Art and Expression in the Age of Emerson and Whitman* (New York: Oxford University Press, 1941), 122.

7.

Melville's Reading, 1853–1856

From Merton M. Sealts, Jr., *Melville's Reading: Revised and Enlarged Edition* (Columbia: University of South Carolina Press, 1988), chapter 6, 85–96. Both text and notes have been expanded to provide additional information and documentation, and both have been somewhat restyled.

Melville's Reading (1988) is a sequel to an extended study listing the books that Melville is known to have owned or borrowed, which I first published serially in the *Harvard Library Bulletin* in 1948–1950 and then revised and expanded into book form in 1966. The 1988 edition lists still more titles that had become known as other books that once were Melville's continued to turn up. In addition, responding to suggestions from readers, I also included nine new chapters that bring together what scholars have been able to establish about Melville's most significant reading during successive periods of his life and professional career.

The primary orientation of these new chapters is neither biographical nor critical in the manner of my earlier essays on such individual writings as "I and My Chimney" and *Billy Budd, Sailor.* They serve to document the reciprocal relationship between Melville's reading and his writing—one that became all-important in the late 1840s, when the young author of *Typee* and *Omoo,* whose reading had turned from books about the sea to classics of general literature and philosophy, began the ambitious experiment of writing and publishing *Mardi* (1849).

This essay reflects two of my long-standing interests as a student of Melville: his reading and his shorter fiction. The treatment here of known sources for his magazine pieces of the years 1853 to 1856 (apart from *Israel Potter*) is based primarily on materials I collected between 1965 and 1978, during my service as volume editor for the Northwestern-Newberry edition of *"The Piazza Tales" and Other Prose Pieces 1839–1860* (1987); other editors completed work on this volume after my service was terminated. In addition to their notes to individual prose pieces, see also Lea Bertani Vozar Newman, *A Reader's Guide to the Short Stories of Herman Melville* (Boston: G. K. Hall, 1986), previously cited in notes to my discussions of "Bartleby" and "Benito Cereno" above.

1. See Hershel Parker, "Herman Melville's *The Isle of the Cross:* A Survey and a Chronology," *American Literature* 62 (March 1990): 1–16. The work remained unpublished; the manuscript has not survived.

2. For the chronology of Melville's writing during the years 1851 to 1856, see my Historical Note, *"The Piazza Tales" and Other Prose Pieces,* 476–99.

3. Sealts, Historical Note, 494.

4. Quoted in Sealts, Historical Note, 503.

5. Sealts, Historical Note, 513.

6. Part II of *Melville's Reading* (1988) includes a detailed "Check-List of Books Owned and Borrowed" by Melville (149–228), cited here as "Check-List." The numbering corresponds to that of earlier versions.

7. Her letter is among the Melville Family Papers, Gansevoort-Lansing Collection, New York Public Library (Astor, Lenox and Tilden Foundations).

8. On the theme of failure in four stories of 1853, see essay 3, "Herman Melville's 'Bartleby,' " above.

9. Donald Yannella, "Writing 'the *other* way': Melville, the Duyckinck Crowd, and Literature for the Masses," in John Bryant, ed., *A Companion to Melville Studies* (Westport, Conn.: Greenwood Press, 1986), 63–81.

10. Melville did not acquire his surviving copy of Spenser until 1861 (Check-List, no. 483). Penny L. Hirsch, after making a line-by-line collation between the epigraphs and editions of Spenser available in 1854, reports in "Melville's Spenser Edition for *The Encantadas*," *Melville Society Extracts* 50 (May 1982), 15–16, that "he used a text based on that of John Upton's two-volume edition of *The Faerie Queene* (London, 1758). The closest such text . . . was the one in Volume II of Robert Anderson's *Poets of Great Britain* (London and Edinburgh, 1792–93). Very possibly the edition Melville actually had in hand was some later one, perhaps American, based on Anderson."

11. Walter E. Bezanson, Historical Note, *Israel Potter* (1982), 184. See also *The Piazza Tales*, 605.

12. Sealts, Historical Note, 186–87.

13. Jay Leyda, ed., *The Complete Stories of Herman Melville* (New York: Random House, 1949), xxvi.

14. Leyda, *Complete Stories*, xxvii n.

15. G. Thomas Tanselle, "Two Melville Association Copies: The Hubbard *Whale* and the Jones *Moby-Dick*. Part I: The Hubbard Whale," *The Book Collector: Collector's Piece* 8 (Summer 1982): 170–86.

16. Evert Duyckinck had described Broadhall in 1850 as "an old family mansion, wainscoted and stately, with large halls & chimneys—quite a piece of mouldering rural grandeur. . . . Herman Melville knows every stone & tree & will probably make a book of its features" (*Log*, 1:383). As I have pointed out in "The Ghost of Major Melvill" (1957; reprinted in *Pursuing Melville, 1940–1980: Chapters and Essays* [Madison and London: University of Wisconsin Press, 1982]), Melville's description of the house in "Jimmy Rose" anticipates his description of Broadhall itself in his later "Sketch of Major Thomas Melville, Jr.," quoted in *The History of Pittsfield* (1876). The "Sketch" is printed in full in my "Thomas Melvill, Jr., in *The History of Pittsfield*," *Harvard Library Bulletin* 35 (Spring 1987): 201–17.

17. Sealts, *The Early Lives of Melville: Nineteenth-Century Biographical Sketches and Their Authors* (Madison: University of Wisconsin Press, 1974), 169.

18. On the relation of the story both to family "secrets" that Melville had alluded to in *Pierre* and to concern for his own mental health, see my "Herman Melville's 'I and My Chimney' " (1941) and "Melville's Chimney, Reexamined" (1969), both of which are reprinted in *Pursuing Melville*, 11–22 and 171–92.

19. Pamela R. Matthews, "Four Old Smokers: Melville, Thoreau, and Their Chimneys," *ATQ: American Transcendental Quarterly* 51 (Summer 1981): 151–64.

20. Helmbrecht Breinig, "The Destruction of Fairyland: Melville's 'Piazza' in the Tradition of the American Imagination," *ELH: A Journal of English Literary History* 35 (June 1968): 254–83.

8.

"Pulse of the Continent": The Railroad in American Literature

From *Wisconsin Academy Review* 36 (March 1990): 26–32; adapted from a paper read earlier before the Madison Literary Club.

1. Leo Marx, *The Machine in the Garden: Technology and the Pastoral Ideal in America* (New York: Oxford University Press, 1964). See also his essay "The Railroad-in-the Landscape: An Iconological Reading of a Theme in American Art," in Susan Danly and Leo Marx, eds., *The Railroad in American Art: Representations of Technological Change* (Cambridge: MIT Press, 1988), 183–208. For an interview with Marx on "a deeply American conflict concerning technology and the memory of a lost way of life," see "Paradise Limited," *American Heritage of Invention & Technology* (Fall 1988): 34–39.

2. Passages from "Song of the Exposition" and "To a Locomotive in Winter" (below) are reprinted by permission of New York University Press from *"Leaves of Grass": Comprehensive Reader's Edition,* ed. Harold W. Blodgett and Sculley Bradley (copyright © 1965 by New York University).

3. Reprinted by permission of the publishers and the Trustees of Amherst College from *The Poems of Emily Dickinson,* ed. Thomas H. Johnson (Cambridge: Harvard University Press, Belknap Press, copyright 1951, © 1955, 1979, 1983 by the President and Fellows of Harvard College). The poem is also included as no. 585 in *The Complete Poems of Emily Dickinson,* ed. Thomas H. Johnson (Boston: Little, Brown, 1960).

4. From *Chicago Poems* (1916); see *The Complete Poems of Carl Sandburg: Revised and Expanded Edition* (New York: Harcourt Brace Jovanovich, Inc., 1970), 17.

5. From *Chicago Poems;* see *Complete Poems of Carl Sandburg,* 20.

6. Lines from "The Egg and the Machine" and "The Oven Bird" (below) are reprinted from *The Poetry of Robert Frost,* ed. Edward Connery Lathem (copyright 1916, 1928, © 1969 by Holt, Rinehart and Winston; copyright 1944, © 1956 by Robert Frost), by arrangement with Henry Holt and Co. and (for the British Commonwealth) Random House UK Limited.

9.

Emerson Then and Now

From *Wisconsin Academy Review* 38 (Summer 1992): 29–32; adapted from an earlier talk given by invitation at Unity Chapel, Spring Green, Wisconsin, and again at a Sunday service of the First Unitarian Society in Madison. Written for a general audience, this paper draws on my experience as an editor of Emerson's *Journals and Miscellaneous Notebooks* and more specifically on both my essay "Emerson as Teacher" (1982), essay 1 here, and my subsequent preparation of *Emerson on the Scholar* (Columbia: University of Missouri Press, 1992).

10.

The Scholar Idealized

From Merton M. Sealts, Jr., *Emerson on the Scholar* (Columbia: University of Missouri Press, 1992), 3–7 (the book's Introduction) and 261–63 (the conclusion of chapter 16). As Emerson wrote in "Circles" (1841), there is in every man's thought "a helm which he obeys, the idea after which all his facts are classified" (*CW* 2:180). The premise of my book is that Emerson's own governing idea was his ideal conception of "the Scholar," initially developed over a period of some four years preceding his address of 1837 on "The American Scholar": see my "Emerson on the Scholar, 1833–1837," *PMLA* 85 (March 1970): 185–95. In a series of five other published essays (1975, 1976, 1979, 1982, 1985) I explored further implications of Emerson's idea of the Scholar, primarily in his writings of the late 1830s. All six of these essays were subsequently incorporated into *Emerson on the Scholar,* which was gradually taking form in my own thinking between 1970 and 1992. The book continues my study of Emerson's conception into his later years, noting his increasingly more secular and activist interpretation of the Scholar's role in society as he responded to events in his own life and in the world around him.

    1. Robert E. Spiller, "From Lecture into Essay: Emerson's Method of Composition," *Literary Criterion* 5 (Winter 1962): 28.

    2. Henry James, "Emerson" (1887), in *Partial Portraits* (London: Macmillan, 1888), 20.

    3. Henry Nash Smith, "Emerson's Problem of Vocation: A Note on 'The American Scholar,'" *New England Quarterly* 12 (March 1939): 58, 59.

    4. Ibid., 62.

5. These studies were characteristic of the 1950s and early 1960s: see, respectively, Sherman Paul on "correspondence" in *Emerson's Angle of Vision: Man and Nature in American Experience* (Cambridge: Harvard University Press, 1952); Stephen E. Whicher, *Freedom and Fate: An Inner Life of Ralph Waldo Emerson* (Philadelphia: University of Pennsylvania Press, 1953; 2d ed., 1971); Paul Lauter, "Truth and Nature: Emerson's Use of Two Complex Words," *ELH: A Journal of English Literary History* 27 (March 1960); Philip L. Nicoloff, *Emerson on Race and History: An Examination of English Traits* (New York: Columbia University Press, 1961); James Emanuel, "Emersonian Virtue: A Definition," *American Speech* 36 (May 1961): 117–22; Henry F. Pommer, "The Contents and Basis of Emerson's Belief in Compensation," *PMLA* 77 (June 1962): 248–53; Jonathan Bishop, *Emerson on the Soul* (Cambridge: Harvard University Press, 1964).

6. Smith, "Emerson's Problem of Vocation," 66.

11.

"The Flower of Fame": A Centennial Tribute to Herman Melville

From *ESQ: A Journal of the American Renaissance* 38 (2d Quarter 1992): 89–117; reprinted with minor stylistic changes. This paper was read as the Joseph S. Schick Lecture at Indiana State University, 19 September 1991, and again as part of the "Herman Melville Centennial: A Day of Events," at the University of Wisconsin–Madison, 26 October 1991.

Except as noted, the texts of quotations are from named volumes of the Northwestern-Newberry edition of *The Writings of Herman Melville*. Some of Melville's writings in both verse and prose have not yet appeared in that edition, however. Quotations from Melville's *Battle-Pieces* (1867) and from minor verse of his later years are therefore taken from *Collected Poems of Herman Melville*, ed. Howard P. Vincent (Chicago: Packard and Co., Hendricks House, 1947), identified in the text as *Poems,* and quotations from *Billy Budd, Sailor* are from the Reading Text of the Chicago edition, ed. Harrison Hayford and Merton M. Sealts, Jr. (Chicago: University of Chicago Press, 1962).

1. *New York Press,* quoted in *Log,* 2:836.

2. *New York Daily Tribune,* quoted in *Log,* 2:837.

3. In "Hawthorne and His Mosses," Melville had written, "It is not so much paucity, as superabundance of material that seems to incapacitate modern authors" (*Piazza Tales,* 246).

4. *London Atlas,* quoted in Hershel Parker and Harrison Hayford, eds., *Moby-Dick as Doubloon: Essays and Extracts (1851–1970)* (New York: W. W. Norton, 1970), 16, 13. *Moby-Dick as Doubloon,* as its editors remark, "contains most of the best and some of the worst that has been written about *Moby-Dick*" (xv). Parker's survey of the reception of the book in Historical Note, Northwestern-Newberry edition of *Moby-Dick,* section VII, also draws on the full listing of reviews and criticism in Brian Higgins, *Herman Melville: An Annotated Bibliography . . . 1846–1930,* and *Herman Melville: A Reference Guide, 1931–1960* (Boston: G. K. Hall, 1979, 1987). See also Higgins and Parker, eds., *Critical Essays on Herman Melville's "Moby-Dick"* (New York: G. K. Hall, 1992).

5. *London Examiner,* quoted in Parker and Hayford, eds., *Moby-Dick as Doubloon,* 24.

6. Hershel Parker, Historical Note, *Moby-Dick,* 716.

7. *New York Commercial Advertiser,* quoted in *Moby-Dick as Doubloon,* 53.

8. *Literary World* (New York), quoted in *Moby-Dick as Doubloon,* 50–51, 35. In Hawthorne's judgment, as he told Evert Duyckinck in a letter, the review "hardly . . . did justice" to Melville's book, which had given him "an idea of much greater power than his preceding ones" (*Log,* 1:438).

9. Hawthorne, journal entry of 12 November 1856 (*Log,* 2:529).

10. The phrase occurs in a passage that the Northwestern-Newberry editors, in one of their "more significant emendations," assign to Ahab, though they acknowledge in their note on the passage that there is no indication to that effect in either the first English or the first American edition (901).

Melville characteristically regarded both individual lives and the course of history in terms of repetitive cycles rather than of forward movement onward and upward, knowing that "civilizations" both rise and fall. In his earlier prose he had deplored the fates of Polynesian "savages" and Native Americans at the hands of supposedly civilized whites, and in his later *Battle-Pieces* he would call human slavery "man's foulest crime" ("Misgivings," in *Poems,* 3). In a letter to George William Curtis, Pittsfield, 15 September 1857, he ironically proposed as "a good, earnest subject" for a lecture "*Daily progress of man towards a state of intellectual & moral perfection, as evidenced in history of 5th Avenue & 5 Points*" (*Correspondence,* 314), and he continued to counter the notion of "Adam's alleged advance" in his subsequent lectures and other later writings.

11. Ann Douglas, *The Feminization of American Culture* (New York: Avon Books, 1978), 7.

12. Emily Dickinson to T. W. Higginson, 25 April 1862, *The Letters of Emily Dickinson,* ed. Thomas H. Johnson, 3 vols. (Cambridge: Harvard University Press, Belknap Press, 1958), 2:404.

13. Nathaniel Hawthorne to William D. Ticknor, 19 January 1855, *The Letters, 1853–1856,* ed. Thomas Woodson et al., in the Centenary Edition of *The Works of Nathaniel Hawthorne,* 20 vols. (Columbus: Ohio State University Press, 1962–1988), 17:304.

14. G. Thomas Tanselle, "The Sales of Melville's Books," *Harvard Library Bulletin* 17 (April 1969): 213; see statement no. 9. Only 500 copies of the first English edition were printed; 217 were still on hand as of 4 March 1852 (p. 198).

15. James D. Hart, *The Popular Book: A History of America's Literary Taste* (New York: Oxford University Press, 1950), 93, 112, is the source of information on sales of *Fern Leaves* and *Uncle Tom's Cabin.*

16. *New York Day Book,* summarized in Higgins, *Herman Melville: An Annotated Bibliography,* 123. Melville "was really supposed to be deranged," according to this paper, and was to be placed "under treatment."

17. There is a family tradition that Melville was given a mental examination, presumably during the early 1850s; in 1867 Elizabeth Melville's relatives urged a separation on grounds of his supposed insanity, but she remained at his side.

18. Parker, Historical Note, *Moby-Dick,* 728.

19. Fitz-James O'Brien, "Our Authors and Authorship: Melville and Curtis," *Putnam's Monthly Magazine* 9 (April 1857): 390.

20. Elizabeth Shaw Melville, Memoranda, in Merton M. Sealts, Jr., *The Early Lives of Melville: Nineteenth-Century Biographical Sketches and Their Authors* (Madison: University of Wisconsin Press, 1974), 169.

21. See Hershel Parker, "Herman Melville's *The Isle of the Cross:* A Survey and a Chronology," *American Literature* 62 (March 1990): 1–16.

22. Arthur Stedman, " 'Marquesan' Melville" (1891), in Sealts, *The Early Lives of Melville,* 109.

23. Arthur Stedman, Introduction to *Typee* (1892), in Sealts, *The Early Lives of Melville,* 166.

24. Ibid.

25. Prose headnote to "The American Aloe on Exhibition," *Poems,* 278.

26. Quoted from Melville's copy of *The Wisdom of Life* in *Log,* 2:832–33.

27. As Hershel Parker acknowledges in the Historical Note to *Moby-Dick,* "The significance of the year 1919 as precipitating the Melville revival may sometimes seem overstated, given the interest already manifested in the preceding decades, but as a public forum for diverse manifestations of interest it was incalculably important" (749).

Even while Melville was still alive he had enjoyed what Willard Thorp appropriately called a "subterranean reputation" among British admirers; see "Melville's Reputation" in his *Herman Melville: Representative Selections* (New York: American

Book Co., 1938), cxxvi. But as Mary A. Taylor has recently observed, "Current scholars may not yet have an accurate sense of what the reputation of *Moby-Dick* was in the United States in the 1910s and early 1920s"; see her "More Evidence of H. M. Tomlinson's Role in the Melville Revival," *Studies in American Fiction* 20 (Spring 1992): 113. The article reprints a *New York Evening Post* column of 5 February 1921 in which Christopher Morley responded to a charge by Tomlinson that American critics had neglected *Moby-Dick*: "Melville, like Dana, has so long been accepted as a classic over here," Morley wrote, "that he is more or less taken as a matter of course (as a matter of college course too often, we fear) and too little mentioned" (112).

For consideration of just *how* and particularly *why* in the United States during the 1920s Melville "was transformed . . . from an obscure teller of South Sea Island tales into the pre-eminent American novelist—at least for many reputable critics," see Paul Lauter, "Melville Climbs the Canon," *American Literature* 66 (March 1994): 1–24.

28. Matthew Josephson, "The Transfiguration of Herman Melville," *Outlook* 150 (19 September 1928): 809.

29. Hawthorne, review of *Typee* in the *Salem (Mass.) Advertiser,* 25 March 1846, quoted in *Log,* 1:207.

30. Viola Meynell, Introduction to the World's Classics edition of *Moby-Dick* (1920), quoted in Higgins, *Herman Melville: An Annotated Bibliography,* xiii and 273.

31. Information given here and below on the various editions, abridgments, and adaptations of *Moby-Dick* is based on G. Thomas Tanselle, *A Checklist of Editions of Moby-Dick, 1851–1976* (Evanston and Chicago: Northwestern University Press and the Newberry Library, 1976); other editions and adaptations have since appeared.

32. Between 1923 and 1976, well over a hundred abridgments and adaptations for a general audience were published, including "school editions" for younger students, simplified comic books, and even a Moby Dick coloring book. As might be expected, the abridgments concentrate on Ahab and his pursuit of the White Whale; in some abbreviated versions Ishmael's role is greatly reduced or even omitted altogether.

33. Rupert C. Clift, Introduction to *The Whaling Story from Moby Dick* (1927), quoted in Tanselle, *A Checklist of Editions,* 29 (no. 60). As Earl Maltby Benson, another editor, remarked in 1929, the book as originally written "contains many long, uninteresting philosophical digressions" which in the twentieth century "would not be appreciated even by the majority of adult readers"; see Tanselle, *A Checklist of Editions,* 29 (no. 62).

In 1946 the editors of *Life* magazine, taking note of the growing interest in *Moby-Dick* at that time but granting that "many readers have found it hard to get through," commissioned Samuel Eliot Morison, the distinguished maritime historian, to contribute the essay "How to Read 'Moby Dick' "; see *Life* 40 (25 June 1946): 57–58, 61–62, 67–68. Advising beginners to read for the story, Morison listed those chapters he considered essential to the action and others that might well be skipped. Three years later, an abridgment by the British novelist W. Somerset Maugham also emphasized the story line. As a note explained, Maugham had selected *Moby-Dick* as one of the "ten greatest novels of the world" to be edited "for modern reading enjoyment" by "eliminating cumbersome dissertations."

Maugham himself justified his resulting abridgments on aesthetic grounds. It would be "stupid," he asserted, to regard Melville's narrative as well constructed. To emphasize the action of the story, much as Morison had recommended, and at the same time to tighten the structure, he cut Ishmael's opening "Etymology" and "Extracts" altogether and reduced the remaining chapters from 135 to 99, omitting all "digressions which impede the narrative." This meant eliminating not only Ishmael's disquisitions on cetology but also the key chapter, "The Whiteness of the Whale," which struck Maugham as merely "absurd." See *Moby Dick or The White Whale,* by Herman Melville, ed. W. Somerset Maugham (Philadelphia and Toronto: John C. Winston Co., 1949), v, xxvii.

The critic Harvey Breit was appalled by Maugham's treatment of *Moby-Dick*—especially by his elimination of "The Whiteness of the Whale," which Breit called "one of the most brilliantly imaginative speculations in all modern literature"; see his "Nibbled Whale," *New York Times Book Review,* 10 July 1949: 2. A later column in the issue of 31 July objects to the "extraordinary audacity" of another editor, Maxwell Geismar, in publishing his Pocket Books abridgment without justifying or even indicating what he chose to leave out (16).

34. See Parker and Hayford, *Moby-Dick as Doubloon,* 60, 86.

35. "Hawthorne and His Mosses," *Piazza Tales,* 246.

36. John Barrymore, *Confessions of an Actor* (1926), quoted in Higgins, *Herman Melville: An Annotated Bibliography,* 316.

37. The Introduction to a 1925 edition of the book, "illustrated with scenes from the photoplay," posits a need to account for what it delicately calls Ahab's "derangement" on something other than metaphysical grounds. The filmmakers accordingly

> looked for other motivation and found it in the faintest hint. A woman, mentioned as having played a part in Ahab's early life, was vitalized and her influence upon him and his fortunes given deserved emphasis. The construction of this early history, which shows that the loss of

his leg had cost Ahab the woman he loved because an envious brother had suggested that her love for Ahab would thenceforth be mere pity, is not presumptuous meddling. It is, on the contrary, a laudable act of critical explanation.

See S. R. Buchman, "*Moby Dick*—the Book and *The Sea Beast*—the Picture: An Appreciation," in *Moby Dick or The White Whale* (New York: Grosset & Dunlap, 1925), x.

38. The first doctoral dissertation to deal with Melville's writings was accepted as early as 1924; by 1940, 13 had been written; in each of the next 4 decades the existing total approximately doubled or more than doubled, rising by 1980 to more than 500. See John Bryant, *Melville Dissertations, 1924–1980: An Annotated Bibliography and Subject Index* (Westport, Conn.: Greenwood Press, 1983). The totals are as follows: 1924–1940, 13; 1941–1950, 24; 1951–1960, 57; 1961–1970, 146; 1971–1980, 291; grand total, 531 (p. 129). My own dissertation (Bryant, no. 18) was submitted in 1942, just as I was reporting for military service. Two of the later dissertations (Bryant, nos. 43 and 121) discuss the Melville revival itself: that by Bernard M. Wolpert (Ohio State, 1951) stresses its British origins; that by Michael P. Zimmerman (Columbia, 1963) begins with movements of the 1890s and 1910s.

For published books and articles on Melville, see Higgins's *Annotated Bibliography . . . 1846–1930* and *Reference Guide 1931–1960* (note 4 above); for more recent listings, see the annual MLA Bibliography published by the Modern Language Association of America and the chapters on Melville in *American Literary Scholarship: An Annual,* ed. James Woodress et al., published for the years beginning with 1963 (Durham, N.C.: Duke University Press, 1965–). Also valuable are the chapters on Melville by Stanley T. Williams and Nathalia Wright in successive editions of *Eight American Authors: A Review of Research and Criticism,* ed. Floyd Stovall (New York: Modern Language Association of America, 1956) and James Woodress (New York: W. W. Norton, 1971).

39. Harry Levin, *The Power of Blackness: Hawthorne, Poe, Melville* (New York: Alfred A. Knopf, 1958), vi. In 1949 Malcolm Cowley, a shrewd observer of the literary scene, had remarked on the special appeal of Melville and T. S. Eliot, then at the height of his influence. At some universities, Cowley wrote facetiously, almost every member of the English department was either working on Eliot or had "written or planned a book on Herman Melville"; see Cowley, "The New Age of the Rhetoricians," reprinted in his *The Literary Situation* (New York: Viking Press, 1954), 19.

In 1951 Cowley wrote for the *New Republic* "a sort of market letter" on the current "literary stock exchange," reporting, "Among the American classics Melville continued to be the most active and once again ended the period with a net gain, but for the first time there was indication of short selling. Market insiders were saying that Melville backers had become overextended and that a reaction was certain to follow"; by 1952, he subsequently noted, "There was less activity in American blue-chip stocks, and notably in Melville, but the limited trading was still at high prices. Overproduction led to a steep decline in Melville Critical Products." See his "Hardbacks or Paperbacks" in *The Literary Situation*, 128, 130.

40. Quoted from an anonymous contribution to the *ACLS Newsletter*, published by the American Council of Learned Societies, 2 (May 1951): 16–17. The author regrets "the enthusiasm of younger scholars and critics for criticism and for certain contemporary tastes," specifically mentioning their devotion to "that idol of the academic world, T. S. Eliot" and "the T. S. Eliot–Reinhold Niebuhr view of man."

41. Cowley, "The New Age of the Rhetoricians," in *The Literary Situation*, 14–15.

42. The phrase is Stanton Garner's; see *Melville Society Extracts* 53 (February 1983): 2.

43. In a recent letter to *Time* magazine, 20 May 1991, pp. 9–10, Stanley Fish of Duke University, a defender of the new disciplines against their conservative opponents, remarked that conservative literary scholars attacked American literature in our century and English literature even earlier; nevertheless, each new field ultimately gained its legitimacy. "No matter how far back one looks," Fish wrote, "the pattern is the same. Yesterday's rebels become today's preservers of orthodoxy and spend time beating back the challenge they once represented. It was ever thus."

44. Noted by William A. Henry III, "Upside Down in the Groves of Academe," *Time*, 1 April 1991, 66–67. Some feminist critics would go even further in order to extend the canon beyond "an almost entirely male white elite": Lillian S. Robinson, who named *Moby-Dick* ("my own bête noire") as "one Great Unreadable among the Great Books," has observed that "no one seems to be proposing—aloud— the elimination of *Moby-Dick* and *The Scarlet Letter*, just squeezing them over somewhat to make room for another literary reality, which, joined with the existing canon, will come closer to telling the poetic truth." See her "Treason Our Text," *Tulsa Studies in Women's Literature* 2 (Spring 1983): 88, 89.

12.

The Presence of Walt Whitman

This paper, which has not been published previously, was first read in its present form at Edgewood College, Madison, Wis., on 25 October 1994 as part of

Edgewood's "Living and Learning" lecture series; a different version with the same title was presented at Madison General Hospital on 28 January 1982 as part of the hospital's William Osler lecture series. As the following notes indicate, I have quoted from several reprinted editions of *Leaves of Grass,* preferring in each case what I regard as the best text of the poem under discussion.

1. This and the following quotations are from the chapter on Whitman in Logan Pearsall Smith, *Unforgotten Years* (Boston: Little, Brown, 1939), 92–102, copyright © 1953, 1965 by John Russell, executor, Estate of Logan Pearsall Smith; used by permission of the executor.

2. *Leaves of Grass by Walt Whitman,* Facsimile Edition of the 1860 text with an Introduction by Roy Harvey Pearce (Ithaca: Cornell University Press, 1961), 344–46 (emphasis added). These lines, untitled in the third edition, made up the third of Whitman's "Calamus" poems. This edition will be cited hereafter as "1860 ed."

In later editions Whitman used the initial line as a title: "Whoever You Are Holding Me Now in Hand"; at one time he had considered calling the poem "These Leaves Conning, You Con at Peril." A student of mine, after thinking about the obvious ambiguities in its lines, once suggested that Whitman should have shifted his comma to make the projected title read "These leaves *conning you,* con at peril." The student was punning on the multiple meanings of the word *con,* which as a verb can mean "to peruse carefully," "to study," "to fix in the memory"—but can also mean "to deceive," and even "to swindle." He was suggesting, of course, that Whitman is a kind of "*con* man": one who *cons* his victim after first gaining his confidence. (Melville, author of *The Confidence-Man,* would have appreciated the pun!)

The Whitman of 1860, I should add, differs markedly from the poet of 1855 and 1856 whose work I am emphasizing here. As noted in Pearce's Introduction to his facsimile edition, Whitman thought of his new volume as offering "a religion of man" with himself as the "poet-priest" that Emerson had called for (xviii–xix). "I . . . inaugurate a Religion," he announces in "Proto-Leaf," section 25 (p. 11), and "I alone would expect to be your God, sole and exclusive," as he says in the third "Calamus" poem, section 3 (p. 345). I have omitted the latter statement in quoting from that poem, as it seems quite tangential to the present discussion.

3. "How Solemn as One by One," from "Drum Taps" in the edition of 1865–1866; quoted from *"Leaves of Grass": Comprehensive Reader's Edition,* ed. Harold W. Blodgett and Sculley Bradley (New York: New York University Press, 1965), 322.

4. "So Long!" concluded the third and subsequent editions of *Leaves of Grass;* see section 20 in the 1860 ed., 455, and an editors' note in the Comprehensive Reader's Edition, 502–3.

5. Carl Sandburg, Introduction to the Modern Library Edition of *Leaves of Grass* (1921), quoted in *Walt Whitman: The Measure of His Song,* ed. Jim Perlman, Ed Folsom, and Dan Campion (Minneapolis: Holy Cow! Press, 1981), 53. The latter volume is made up of "representative statements" about the poet and his poetry "from poets and writers from Whitman's day to our own" (xvi).

6. *The Presence of Walt Whitman: Selected Papers from the English Institute,* ed. R. W. B. Lewis (New York: Columbia University Press, 1962), vii. See also *The Continuing Presence of Walt Whitman: The Life after the Life,* ed. Robert K. Martin (Iowa City: University of Iowa Press, 1992).

7. "There Was a Child Went Forth" (as it has been known since 1871), in Walt Whitman, *"Leaves of Grass": The First (1855) Edition,* ed. Malcolm Cowley (New York: Viking Press, 1959), 138–39. Also useful are (1) a facsimile of the first edition, with an Introduction by Richard Bridgman (San Francisco: Chandler Publishing, 1968); and (2) *Whitman's "Song of Myself"—Origin, Growth, Meaning,* ed. James E. Miller, Jr. (New York and Toronto: Dodd, Mead, 1964). Miller's book includes early notebook versions of selected passages plus the 1855 and 1892 texts of the poem, printed on facing pages so as to make Whitman's revisions readily apparent to the reader. Also included are essays offering six "varied critical perspectives" on "Song of Myself."

8. Quotations here are again from the 1855 edition as edited by Malcolm Cowley (1959), 25–86 (using the line numbers—lacking in the first edition—supplied by the editor); unspaced ellipses follow Whitman's usage, while spaced ellipses show my omissions.

9. Cowley, Introduction to his edition (1959), x, xxxii, viii.

10. John Berryman, " 'Song of Myself': Intuition and Substance," as extracted in *Walt Whitman: The Measure of His Song,* ed. Perlman, Folsom, and Campion, 155–56.

11. Changing fashions in Whitman criticism are evident to anyone who compares the earlier books, cited in notes 5, 6, and 8 above, with the essays collected in *Walt Whitman: The Centennial Essays,* ed. Ed Folsom (Iowa City: University of Iowa Press, 1994). See especially Betsy Erkkila, "Whitman and the Homosexual Tradition," 153–71, and Robert K. Martin, "Whitman and the Politics of Identity," 172–81, in the section headed "The Culture: Politics and Sexuality"—discussions that contrast strongly with such earlier essays as those by Malcolm Cowley and James E. Miller, Jr., which deal with Whitman and religious experience.

12. Included as "Some Lines from Whitman" in Randall Jarrell, *Poetry and the Age* (1953), as quoted in Miller, ed., *"Song of Myself"—Origin, Growth, Meaning,* 130. I would especially recommend Jarrell's stimulating essay to any reader coming to Whitman for the first time.

13. I quote from Whitman's final text as it is given in the Comprehensive Reader's Edition of 1965, using the line numbers provided by the editors. In their words, the poem is "philosophical in theme . . . yet profoundly personal," comprising Whitman's "own daily experience made illustrious" (159 n).

14. Calamus no. 44, 1860 ed., 377; "Here the Frailest Leaves of Me," Comprehensive Reader's Edition, 131.

13.

The "I" of *Walden*

This paper has not been published previously. It was first read on 10 April 1995 before the Madison Literary Club. Unless otherwise noted, quotations from *Walden* and from Thoreau's *Journal* are from designated volumes of the Princeton edition currently in progress, *The Writings of Henry D. Thoreau,* ed. Walter Harding et al. (Princeton, N.J.: Princeton University Press, 1971–), and are cited parenthetically by page number in the text. Quotations from Thoreau's lecture of 1846 on his life in the woods are from the text of his 1849 draft of *Walden,* in which it was incorporated; this text, designated in notes and parenthetically in the text as FV (First Version), was recovered by J. Lyndon Shanley from the manuscript of *Walden* in its entirety (now in the Huntington Library) and was published in full in *The Making of "Walden," with the Text of the First Version* (Chicago: University of Chicago Press, 1957), 103–208.

Shanley's meticulous work with the manuscript of *Walden* became a model for later textual studies of other authors' works, such as the Hayford-Sealts edition of Melville's *Billy Budd, Sailor* (1962), with its Reading Text and Genetic Text; in 1967 Ronald Clapper extended Shanley's work in his doctoral dissertation at the University of California, Los Angeles: "The Development of Thoreau's *Walden:* A Genetic Text."

1. Problems facing the Princeton editors and the ways in which various earlier editors and critics have grappled with them are analyzed and evaluated by Leonard Neufeldt (coeditor of vol. 4) in "*Praetextus* as Text: Editor-Critic Responses to Thoreau's Journal," *Arizona Quarterly* 46 (Winter 1990): 27–72.

2. Richard Lebeaux, *Young Man Thoreau* (Amherst: University of Massachusetts Press, 1977), 209–13.

3. Note Thoreau's reference here to "this lecture" and compare the opening paragraphs of *Walden,* 3.

4. See FV 126, 128–30, and compare *Walden,* 49, 55, 59–60.

5. The quoted phrase is from Joseph Moldenhauer, "Paradox in *Walden*" (1964, 1968), as revised by the author in Wendell Glick, ed., *The Recognition of Henry David Thoreau: Selected Criticism since 1848* (Ann Arbor: University of Michigan Press, 1969), 360.

In his lecture and again in "Economy," the opening chapter of *Walden*, Thoreau was countering not only his townsmen's economic assumptions but the antecedents of their thinking. As early as the 1920s V. L. Parrington termed *Walden* "the handbook of an economy that endeavors to refute Adam Smith and transform the round of daily life into something nobler than a narrow gospel of plus and minus"; see *Main Currents in American Thought*, 3 vols. (New York: Harcourt, Brace, 1927–1930), 2:400. Herbert F. Smith has since argued that Thoreau "consciously chose to have his work considered within the great tradition of economic thought of Adam Smith, Malthus, and Ricardo"; see his "Thoreau among the Classical Economists," *ESQ: A Journal of the American Renaissance* 23 (2d Quarter 1977): 114–22.

One of my students, Eugene Bodzin, examined Thoreau's oblique treatment in "Economy" of sayings from Franklin's *The Way to Wealth;* see his University of Wisconsin doctoral dissertation, "The American Popular Image of Benjamin Franklin, 1790–1868" (1969). More recently, Leonard Neufeldt has identified Thoreau's parodies of the advice to would-be entrepreneurs he had found in contemporary handbooks of conduct for young men; see his book *The Economist: Henry Thoreau and Enterprise* (New York: Oxford University Press, 1989).

6. Shanley, *The Making of "Walden,"* 65–66.

7. Ibid., 94.

8. See Emerson, "Nominalist and Realist," *CW* 3:143.

9. Before Thoreau divided his manuscript into chapters, the remark on love of society had preceded that on love of solitude (FV 165, 166).

10. Sherman Paul, "Resolution at Walden," *Accent* 12 (1953): 109. In 1917 Norman Foerster had written of Thoreau as "a *Doppelgänger* with a difference," calling the part of him that was spectator "the universal spirit"; see "The Humanism of Thoreau," *Nation* 105 (5 July 1917): 11. The idea of becoming a spectator of one's self is not unique to Thoreau; the "I" of Whitman's "Song of Myself" speaks of being "both in and out of the game, and watching and wondering at it" (line 70 of the 1855 text).

11. At one time he had thought of the phrase "Addressed to My Townsmen" as part of his working title. With the motto of 1854 compare this passage from "Economy": "If I seem to boast more than is becoming, my excuse is that I brag for humanity rather than for myself; and my shortcomings and inconsistencies do not affect the truth of my statement" (49).

12. Moldenhauer, "Paradox in *Walden*," 355–56.

13. Lebeaux, *Young Man Thoreau*, 115. See also Thomas Vishanoff, "Rhetoric and Rebirth: Persona and Audience in *Walden*," *Thoreau Journal Quarterly* 8 (January 1976): 22–30. Vishanoff's discussion, which includes references to a few earlier critics and reviewers, emphasizes changes in tone as the narrative progresses—a point to be considered below.

14. E. B. White, "Walden—1954," *The Yale Review* 44 (September 1954): 16. There is more self-revelation in the second half of the book—notably in the chapter "Higher Laws," a late addition, which deals with the conflict between "an instinct toward a higher, or, as it is named, spiritual life, . . . and another toward a primitive rank and savage one. . . . I reverence them both" (210). Thoreau's ensuing treatment of hunting and fishing and particularly his perplexing references to "chastity" and "impurity" (220–21) have invited much recent speculation.

15. Thoreau incorporated phrasing from his journal entries of 5 and 6 July 1845, made immediately following his move to the pond; see *Journal* 2:155–56. Thomas Woodson, "The Two Beginnings of *Walden*: A Distinction of Styles," *ELH: A Journal of English Literary History* 35 (1968): 440–73, sees these entries as one of the starting points of the book, the other being the lecture of 1846.

16. F. O. Matthiessen, *American Renaissance: Art and Expression in the Age of Emerson and Whitman* (New York: Oxford University Press, 1941), 95. Matthiessen examines this passage as an illustration of Thoreau's "thinking in images"—a concept that influenced a whole generation of critics and teachers.

17. On the relation between the cycle of the seasons and the structure of the book, see A. E. Elmore, "Symmetry out of Seasons: The Form of *Walden*," *South Atlantic Bulletin* 37 (November 1972): 18–24. Robert D. Richardson, Jr., holds that "We have made too much of the seasonal structure, easily assuming that the book's message is to accept the seasonal cycle of nature as final wisdom," and Robert Sattelmeyer agrees: "Thoreau developed the seasonal emphasis . . . not because it was the logical structure for his book but because he was interested in the seasons of his own life." See Richardson, *Thoreau: A Life of the Mind* (Berkeley and Los Angeles: University of California Press, 1986), 310, and Sattelmeyer, "The Remaking of *Walden*," in James Barbour and Tom Quirk, eds., *Writing the American Classics* (Chapel Hill: University of North Carolina Press, 1990), 64.

18. Shanley, *The Making of "Walden*," 62.

19. Sattelmeyer, "The Remaking of *Walden*," 64.

20. Changes over the years in Thoreau's conception of the *Journal* had their parallel in his developing conception of *Walden*. How the editors of the new Princeton edition have characterized each of the first four volumes of the *Journal* published to date, covering the years 1837–1852, is admirably summarized by

Wesley T. Mott in "'A Daily Life Rich Enough to be Journalized': Thoreau's *Journal Volume 4*," *Documentary Editing*, June 1994, 38–42.

21. Moldenhauer, "Paradox in *Walden*," 357.

22. See Joseph Allen Boone, "Delving and Diving for Truth: Breaking through to Bottom in Thoreau's *Walden*," *ESQ: A Journal of the American Renaissance* 27 (3d Quarter 1981): 135–46.

23. Melvin E. Lyon's "Walden Pond as Symbol," *PMLA* 82 (May 1967): 289–300, is an extended treatment of its subject. The pond, Lyon contends, objectifies aspects of Thoreau's own personality. "It is a part of me which I have not prophaned," Thoreau himself wrote in 1852 in a draft of the verse that now appears in the published text of "The Ponds" (*Walden*, 193). See line 7 of his second version, as printed and discussed by Elizabeth Witherell in "An Editor's Nightmare: 'It Is No Dream of Mine' in the Princeton Edition of Thoreau's Poetry," *Concord Saunterer* 12 (Fall 1977): 6.

24. In an extended passage of "Spring" (304–9) that has drawn considerable attention in recent commentary, Thoreau also wrote of his delight in observing "the forms which thawing sand and clay assume in flowing down the sides of a deep cut on the railroad" that runs along the pond (304). The passage illustrates Thoreau's increasingly sharp eye as an observer of natural phenomena. Robert Sattelmeyer, taking note of the author's "radical revision and amplification" of the passage, goes further, reading it in conjunction with "Higher Laws" as evidence of Thoreau's mature recognition "that nature and the human self in which it is reflected have depths heretofore unplumbed but needing to be faced"; see "The Remaking of *Walden*," 66–67.

25. Stanley Edgar Hyman, "Henry Thoreau in Our Time," in *The Promised End* (Cleveland, Ohio: World Publishing Company, 1963), 30. Hyman's comments, like Matthiessen's, have greatly influenced later discussion, the present essay included.

26. J. Golden Taylor, *Neighbor Thoreau's Critical Humor* (Logan: Utah State University Monograph Series, 6 [January 1958]), 19. Using the 1906 text, Taylor printed a somewhat longer extract from the first of the two paragraphs quoted above (he did not discuss the second paragraph); he then contrasted Thoreau's "oracular assurances about his purposes" (20) in "Where I Lived and What I Lived For."

27. John Broderick, "The Movement of Thoreau's Prose," *American Literature* 33 (May 1961): 134, 141.

28. R. W. B. Lewis, *The American Adam* (Chicago: University of Chicago Press, 1955), 21.

29. I am indebted here to a review of recent books on the novelist E. M. Forster by Ann Hulbert: "The Soul and Discretion," *New Republic*, 22 and 29 August

1994, 40–45. Hulbert quotes an interview in which Forster said he had written of "three types of people: the person I think I am, the people who irritate me and the people I would like to be." Among the people who irritated Thoreau were certainly the would-be philanthropists he scorns in "Economy," 72–79, where he assures us, "If I knew for certain that a man was coming to my house with the conscious design of doing me good, I should run for my life" (74).

30. For a stimulating book about reading *Walden* that speaks not only to those first encountering the book but to experienced Thoreauvians as well, I would especially recommend Martin Bickman, *"Walden": Volatile Truths* (New York: Twayne Publishers, 1992).

14.

Hawthorne's "Autobiographical Impulse"

This paper was first read on 13 July 1995 to an Elderhostel class at Edgewood College; it has not been published previously. Unless otherwise indicated, all quotations from Hawthorne's fiction and letters are from named volumes of the Centenary Edition: *The Works of Nathaniel Hawthorne,* 20 vols. (Columbus: Ohio State University Press, 1962–1988). "The Old Manse," it should be noted, introduces *Mosses from an Old Manse* and "The Custom-House" introduces *The Scarlet Letter.*

1. *Albany (New York) Atlas,* 17 June 1849, as quoted in C. E. Frazer Clark, Jr., " 'Posthumous Papers of a Decapitated Surveyor': *The Scarlet Letter* in the Salem Press," *Studies in the Novel* 2 (Winter 1970): 400.

2. Hawthorne to Evert A. Duyckinck, 1 July 1845 (*The Letters, 1843–1853,* 105).

3. See Malcolm Cowley, "Hawthorne in the Looking Glass," *Sewanee Review* 56 (Autumn 1948): 545–63.

4. For the standard account of Hawthorne's dismissal and its immediate consequences, see Hubert H. Hoeltje, "The Writing of *The Scarlet Letter,*" *New England Quarterly* 27 (September 1954): 326–46. (See also note 9 below.)

5. Clark's " 'Posthumous Papers of a Decapitated Surveyor' " surveys the newspaper coverage, reproducing a number of items.

6. Hawthorne to James T. Fields, 3 November 1850 (*The Letters, 1843–1853,* 371). At that time Hawthorne was already at work on *The House of the Seven Gables* (1851).

7. Henry James, *Hawthorne* (London: Macmillan, 1879), 111.

8. *The American Notebooks,* 222, 278.

9. See Hawthorne to Henry Wadsworth Longfellow, 5 June 1849 (*The Letters, 1843–1853,* 269): "If they succeed in getting me out of office, I will surely immolate one or two of them." His particular target in "The Custom-House," the unnamed "permanent Inspector" (16–19), was William Lee, aged seventy-nine at the time of the census of 1850; see Benjamin Lease, "Hawthorne and 'A Certain Venerable Person,'" *Jahrbuch für Amerikastudien* 15 (1970): 201–7. The prototype of Judge Pyncheon in *The House of the Seven Gables* (1851) is thought to be Rev. Charles W. Upham of Salem, another of Hawthorne's political opponents, though Hawthorne never admitted it. Norman Holmes Pearson, "The Pynchons and Judge Pyncheon," *Essex Institute Historical Collections* 100 (October 1964): 235–55, discusses the aftermath of Hawthorne's dismissal and his response to suggestions that he had particular individuals in mind when he portrayed Judge Pyncheon; concerning Hawthorne and Upham, see 237–40.

10. *Salem Register,* 21 March 1850, as quoted in Clark, "'Posthumous Papers of a Decapitated Surveyor,'" 402. Later in the article the author especially objected to what Hawthorne had written of the "permanent Inspector" but did not identify the man as William Lee.

11. On the continuity between the two essays, see James M. Cox, "*The Scarlet Letter:* Through the Old Manse and the Custom House," *Virginia Quarterly Review* 51 (Summer 1975): 432–47. Cox wrote of "The Old Manse" as "the fulfillment of the sketch form" in Hawthorne's writing (436) and "The Custom-House" as his initial linking of that form with the third-person tale—in this instance *The Scarlet Letter* (440). Hawthorne's "adroitness" in his use of the first person, as Cox perceptively remarked, "lies in his capacity to establish an intimacy of tone without being confessional" (437).

12. See Nina Baym, "The Romantic *Malgré Lui:* Hawthorne in 'The Custom House,'" *ESQ: A Journal of the American Renaissance* 19 (2d Quarter, 1973), 16.

13. Hawthorne to Horatio Bridge, 4 February 1850 (*The Letters, 1843–1853,* 312).

14. Cox, "*The Scarlet Letter:* Through the Old Manse and the Custom-House," 443, compares the Surveyor's "I will!" and the "memorable words" of General Miller: "I'll try, Sir!" (23).

15. See my discussion of "Conversion" in *Emerson on the Scholar* (Columbia: University of Missouri Press, 1992), 90–92, and compare Hawthorne's terminology here with that of such a representative passage in Emerson as the conclusion of chapter 5 of *Nature* (1836): when a friend has "become *an object of thought*" and his character "is *converted* in the mind into solemn and sweet wisdom," Emerson wrote, it is "a sign to us that his office is closing" (*CW* 1:29; emphasis added). (He was thinking of the death of his brother Charles; cf. *JMN* 5:174).

16. F. O. Matthiessen, *American Renaissance: Art and Expression in the Age of Emerson and Whitman* (New York: Oxford University Press, 1941), 235; Hawthorne to James T. Fields, 11 February 1960 (*The Letters, 1857–1864,* 229). Discussing Hawthorne's theory of romance-writing, in a section entitled "The Imagination as Mirror," Matthiessen remarked that here in "The Custom-House" he "showed his full understanding of his creative process" (261).

17. My discussion of "The Custom-House" turns on two considerations: (1) it was written while Hawthorne was still at work on *The Scarlet Letter* and reflects the immediate experience of composing the story; (2) in its employment of guarded first-person narration it is actually less "confessional" (Cox's term; see note 11 above) than *The Scarlet Letter* itself, where he had already expressed much of his own inner feelings and compulsions through his characterizations of Hester Prynne, Arthur Dimmesdale, and Roger Chillingworth.

When I came to examine previous treatments of the relation between "The Custom-House" and *The Scarlet Letter,* I realized that a number of critics had proceeded in another direction—*from* the essay *to* the narrative, taking "The Custom-House" at face value as no more than a conventional introduction to a longer story. Among his other objectives, Hawthorne intended both "The Old Manse" and "The Custom-House" to be familiar essays, an established nineteenth-century genre, and his quite intentional shifts of scene and tone are characteristic of the form—*not* evidence of a lack of artistic unity, as some twentieth-century writers have charged.

Moreover, simply to identify the "I" of "The Custom-House" as the "narrator" of *The Scarlet Letter*—an assumption of several previous studies—is to overlook the subtler implications facing an author when he or she decides whether to be a relatively straightforward first-person speaker, or to address the reader through an "I" who is a created persona, or to assume an ostensibly objective stance as a third-person narrator. Paradoxically, the third alternative may prove more revealing than the first, as I have concluded in this study of Hawthorne's practice in three interrelated compositions of 1846–1850.

15.

Whose Book Is *Moby-Dick*?

This paper, previously unpublished, is appearing concurrently in *The Ever-Moving Dawn: Essays in Celebration of the Melville Centennial,* published by Kent State University Press. It was first read in its present form on 12 December 1993 as part of an emeritus faculty lecture series, "Eloquence and Eminence," sponsored by the Division of University Outreach, University of Wisconsin–Madison; an earlier version was presented on 8 May 1985 during my service as Thomas Lamont Visiting Professor at Union College, Schenectady. I have found the related questions of characterization and structure to be unfailingly useful in generating lively classroom discussion of *Moby-Dick.* Quotations from *Moby-Dick* are from the Northwestern-Newberry edition and are cited parenthetically by page number in the text.

1. James Thurber, *The Years with Ross* (Boston: Little, Brown, 1959), 77.

2. William Wordsworth, "Essay Supplementary to Preface (1815)," in *Wordsworth's Literary Criticism,* ed. Nowell C. Smith (London: Humphrey Milford, 1905), 195. Wordsworth credited the idea to Coleridge.

3. Henry D. Thoreau, *Walden,* ed. J. Lyndon Shanley (Princeton, N.J.: Princeton University Press, 1971), 3.

4. Walt Whitman, *"Leaves of Grass": The First (1855) Edition,* ed. Malcolm Cowley (New York: Viking Press, 1959), 25.

5. Vincent Buckley, "The White Whale as Hero," *Critical Review* (Melbourne) no. 9 (1966): 12.

6. Gordon Roper, "On Teaching *Moby-Dick,*" *Emerson Society Quarterly* no. 28, pt. 3: Melville Supplement (1962): 2, 3.

7. William Braswell, "The Main Theme of *Moby-Dick,*" *Emerson Society Quarterly* no. 28, pt. 3: Melville Supplement (1962): 16–17.

8. John Halverson, "The Shadow in *Moby-Dick,*" *American Quarterly* 15 (Fall 1963): 444.

9. *New York Daily Tribune,* quoted in Hershel Parker and Harrison Hayford, eds., *Moby-Dick as Doubloon: Essays and Extracts (1851–1970)* (New York: W. W. Norton, 1970), 47. *Moby-Dick as Doubloon,* as its editors remark, "contains most of the best and some of the worst that has been written about *Moby-Dick*" through 1970 (xv). A full listing of reviews and criticism through 1960 will be found in Brian Higgins, *Herman Melville: An Annotated Bibliography, 1846–1930,* and *Herman Melville: A Reference Guide, 1931–1960* (Boston: G. K. Hall, 1979, 1987).

10. See *Moby-Dick as Doubloon,* 50–51, 35, or the Norton *Moby-Dick,* 613–15. For other contemporary identifications of the Whale as "hero," see *Moby-Dick as Doubloon,* 24, 39, 56, and 61. Another reviewer chose Ahab (11) and still others named Ishmael, or Melville (4, 53, 85, 87); for Ishmael, see also Hershel Parker, "Five Reviews Not in *Moby-Dick as Doubloon,*" *English Language Notes* 9 (March 1972): 183.

11. Fitz-James O'Brien, "Our Authors and Authorship: Melville and Curtis," *Putnam's Monthly Magazine* 9 (April 1857): 390.

12. F. O. Matthiessen, *American Renaissance: Art and Expression in the Age of Emerson and Whitman* (New York: Oxford University Press, 1941).

13. See in particular Morse Peckham, "Toward a Theory of Romanticism," *PMLA* 66 (March 1951): 5–23; R. P. Adams, "Romanticism and the American Renaissance," *American Literature* 23 (January 1952): 419–32; and Morse Peckham, "Hawthorne and Melville as European Authors," in *Melville and Hawthorne in the Berkshires,* ed. Howard P. Vincent (Kent, Ohio: Kent State University Press, 1968), 42–62. In the last essay cited, pp. 58–59, Peckham surveys "the great Romantic themes" as they appear in *Moby-Dick,* suggesting that by 1851 "Melville had absorbed . . . all stages of Romanticism up to his own time, and had presented them in *Moby-Dick* in inextricable confusion." This is the reason, he speculates, that "the interpretation of *Moby-Dick* is so difficult and why in all probability it will never be understood with clarity or agreement."

14. Charles Feidelson, Jr., *Symbolism and American Literature* (Chicago: University of Chicago Press, 1953). Feidelson observes that mid-nineteenth-century American writers "inherited the basic problem of romanticism: the vindication of imaginative thought in a world grown abstract and material . . . ; their solution . . . is closer to modern notions of symbolic reality than to romantic egoism" (4). He credits Edmund Wilson as the first critic to note their affinity with "the symbolist aesthetic that produced modern literature."

15. Walter E. Bezanson, "*Moby-Dick:* Work of Art," in Tyrus Hillway and Luther S. Mansfield, eds., *Moby-Dick: Centennial Essays* (Dallas: Southern Methodist University Press, 1953), 56. Bezanson's essay is reprinted in part in the Norton Critical Edition of *Moby-Dick,* ed. Harrison Hayford and Hershel Parker (New York: W. W. Norton, 1967), 651–71, and in *The Merrill Studies in Moby-Dick,* comp. Howard P. Vincent (Columbus, Ohio: Charles E. Merrill, 1969), 87–103.

16. Ralph H. Gabriel, *The Course of American Democratic Thought: An Intellectual History since 1815* (New York: Ronald Press, 1940), 74. For other representative comments which regard Moby Dick as symbolizing evil, see Yvor Winters, "Herman Melville and the Problems of Moral Navigation" (1938), reprinted in his *In Defense of Reason* (New York: Swallow Press and William Morrow and Co., 1947), 201: "the chief symbol and spirit of evil"; Henry Alonzo Myers, "The Meaning of *Moby Dick,*" in his *Tragedy: A View of Life* (Ithaca, N.Y.: Cornell University Press, 1956), 77: "the white whale of evil."

17. Introduction to *Moby Dick* in the Modern Library Edition (New York: The Modern Library, 1950), xiii.

18. See Howard P. Vincent, *The Trying-Out of Moby-Dick* (Boston: Houghton Mifflin, 1949), part IV.

19. D. H. Lawrence, "Herman Melville's 'Moby Dick'" (1923), and Henry A. Murray, "In Nomine Diaboli" (1951), as reprinted in Vincent, *Merrill Studies in Moby-Dick,* 50, 61.

20. Harry Levin, *Symbolism and Fiction* (1956), quoted in *Moby-Dick as Doubloon,* 265.

21. Wayne C. Booth, *The Rhetoric of Fiction* (Chicago: University of Chicago Press, 1961). Booth's book was immediately influential, especially among younger scholars. John Bryant, *Melville Dissertations, 1924–1980: An Annotated Bibliography and Subject Index* (Westport, Conn.: Greenwood Press, 1983), singled out "the shift to rhetorical criticism, narrative, and point of view" as perhaps the most significant trend among dissertators of the 1960s (xvii).

22. Warner Berthoff, *The Example of Melville* (Princeton, N.J.: Princeton University Press, 1962), 79–86 passim.

23. Melville in "Hawthorne and His Mosses" (1850), as reprinted in *"The Piazza Tales" and Other Prose Pieces 1839–1860,* 244; Dickinson in *Complete Poems,* ed. Thomas H. Johnson (Boston: Little, Brown, 1960), 506 (no. 1129).

24. F. Scott Fitzgerald, "Pasting It Together" (1936), as reprinted in *The Crack-Up* (1945), ed. Edmund Wilson (New York: New Directions, 1956), 81.

25. Bezanson, *"Moby-Dick:* Work of Art," 36, 41.

26. Paul Brodtkorb, Jr., *Ishmael's White World: A Phenomenological Reading of "Moby Dick"* (New Haven: Yale University Press, 1965), 4.

27. Glauco Cambon, "Ishmael and the Problem of Formal Discontinuities in *Moby Dick," Modern Language Notes* 76 (June 1961): 523.

28. Barry A. Marks, "Retrospective Narrative in Nineteenth Century American Literature," *College English* 31 (January 1970): 366–67. This neglected essay, which is especially valuable for classroom teachers and is well worth the attention of literary critics as well, contains a provocative analysis of the "two stories" that Ishmael tells in *Moby-Dick.* According to Marks,

> The shape, and finally the meaning also, . . . stems from the fact that Ishmael's changing manner of narration is more than mere aimlessness; rather it is a significantly patterned search for efficacious speech. . . . The writing-time story of the retrospective narrative parallels the essential shape and meaning of its related past-time story. The narrative present is a metaphoric or mimetic version of the narrative past.
>
> . . . The writing-time story is a means of showing directly and immediately meanings which the author despairs of being able to communicate by conventional language and literary forms. (374)

29. Cambon, "Ishmael and the Problem of Formal Discontinuities," 523.

30. Robert Hazel, speaking at the December 1959 meeting of the Modern Language Association of America.

31. Cecil M. Brown, "The White Whale," *Partisan Review* 36 (1969): 459, 457. "The white whale" in Brown's view "is none other than you, Ishmael—the white, disembodied, overliterate, boring, snobbish, insipid, jew-bastard, nigger-lover, effete, mediocre, assistant-professor type, liberal" (454).

32. See Harrison Hayford, "Unnecessary Duplicates: A Key to the Writing of *Moby-Dick*," in Faith Pullin, ed., *New Perspectives on Melville* (Edinburgh: Edinburgh University Press; Kent, Ohio: Kent State University Press, 1978), 128–61, and "Discussions of Adopted Readings" in the Northwestern-Newberry *Moby-Dick*, 809–906 passim.

After beginning *Moby-Dick* with high hopes for its success, Melville finished writing it only under great difficulties, complaining to Hawthorne of his "ditcher's work" with the book and his fear that all his books were "botches" (*Correspondence*, 212, 191). Although some present-day critics profess to discuss *Moby-Dick* as a virtually seamless narrative web—one, Paul Brodtkorb, going so far as to charge Ishmael rather than Melville himself with the "mistakes and inconsistencies" observable in the narrative (*Ishmael's White World*, 4–5, 7)—others such as Hayford have taken such occurrences as possible clues to the compositional history of the book. For a succinct review of various theories concerning its genesis and development, see section 5 of Historical Note, Northwestern-Newberry edition, 648–59.

33. In 1951, the centennial year of *Moby-Dick*'s publication, when Walter Bezanson first described the book as a work of organic art, James Benziger remarked that "modern organic critics use their theory to check the pretensions of the biographical and historical critics," adding that *any* theory must be "applied with judgment"; see his "Organic Unity: Leibniz to Coleridge," *PMLA* 66 (March 1951): 48. His caution is applicable today, now that successive generations of historically minded critics have reacted in turn against the organicists.

34. Brodtkorb, *Ishmael's White World*, 4.

35. Ralph Waldo Emerson, "The American Scholar," in *Nature, Addresses, and Lectures*, ed. Alfred R. Ferguson and Robert E. Spiller (Cambridge: Harvard University Press, Belknap Press, 1971), 58.

Postscript

These remarks have been published previously: (1) following comments by Hershel Parker, Chair, ALS/MLA Hubbell Committee, in the *Annual Report, 1992*, of the

American Literature Section, MLA (1993), 7–8; and (2) in *Emerson Society Papers* 4 (Fall 1993): 1.

Appendix 4
The Melvilles, the Gansevoorts, and the Cincinnati Badge

1. William Sturgis Thomas, *Members of the Society of the Cincinnati Original, Hereditary and Honorary. With a Brief Account of the Society's History and Aims* (New York: Tobias A. Wright, 1929), 11.

2. Compiled respectively by Francis S. Drake and James M. Bugbee and printed for the Society (Boston, 1873, 1890).

3. The portrait is reproduced in Raymond Weaver, *Herman Melville: Mariner and Mystic* (New York: George H. Doran, 1921), facing p. 40.

4. Thomas erroneously lists the younger Peter Gansevoort as a *grand* son and misprints the date of his admission as 1858; Stanton Garner determined the correct date.

5. The two sketches were first printed, somewhat inaccurately, in *"Billy Budd" and Other Prose Pieces,* ed. Raymond Weaver (London: Constable, 1924); I quoted the relevant passages from manuscripts in the Melville Collection, Houghton Library, Harvard University, in "The Ghost of Major Melvill" (1957) and "Melville's Burgundy Club Sketches" (1958). Both articles were later reprinted in my *Pursuing Melville* (1982), 67–77 and 78–90.

6. See *Pursuing Melville*, 75, 88–89. Melville's *Omoo* (1847) was "cordially inscribed" to Herman Gansevoort "by his nephew, the author."

7. Melville's visit to the front is treated in Stanton Garner, "Melville's Scout toward Aldie" (1982) and more fully in *The Civil War World of Herman Melville*, 298–323. Both Henry Gansevoort and another cousin, naval officer Guert Gansevoort (1812–1868), whom Melville also visited during the war, were potential inheritors of the Cincinnati badge, but their deaths occurred before that of Melville's uncle Peter Gansevoort in 1876.

Books, Articles, and Reviews
by Merton M. Sealts, Jr.

Books

Melville as Lecturer. Cambridge: Harvard University Press, 1957. Reprint, The Folcroft Press, 1970. Reconstructed texts of Melville's lectures reprinted in *"The Piazza Tales" and Other Prose Pieces 1839–1860,* vol. 9 of *The Writings of Herman Melville.* Evanston and Chicago: Northwestern University Press and the Newberry Library, 1987, 398–423.

Billy Budd, Sailor, by Herman Melville. Reading Text and Genetic Text. Edited from the manuscript with Introduction and Notes by Harrison Hayford and Merton M. Sealts, Jr. Chicago: University of Chicago Press, 1962. Reading Text reprinted by the University of Chicago Press as a Phoenix Book, 1962; Genetic Text reprinted as a Midway Reprint, 1978.

The Journals and Miscellaneous Notebooks of Ralph Waldo Emerson, vol. 5 (1835–1838). Ed. Merton M. Sealts, Jr. Cambridge: Harvard University Press, Belknap Press, 1965.

Melville's Reading: A Check-List of Books Owned and Borrowed. Madison: University of Wisconsin Press, 1966.

Emerson's "Nature": Origin, Growth, Meaning. Ed. Merton M. Sealts, Jr., and Alfred R. Ferguson. New York: Dodd, Mead, 1969.

The Journals and Miscellaneous Notebooks of Ralph Waldo Emerson, vol. 10 (1847–1848). Ed. Merton M. Sealts, Jr. Cambridge: Harvard University Press, Belknap Press, 1973.

The Early Lives of Melville: Nineteenth-Century Biographical Sketches and Their Authors. Madison: University of Wisconsin Press, 1974.

Emerson's "Nature": Origin, Growth, Meaning. Ed. Merton M. Sealts, Jr., and Alfred R. Ferguson. 2d ed., enlarged. Carbondale: Southern Illinois University Press, 1979.

Pursuing Melville, 1940–1980: Chapters and Essays. Madison: University of Wisconsin Press, 1982.

Melville's Reading. Revised and Enlarged Edition. Columbia: University of South Carolina Press, 1988.

Emerson on the Scholar. Columbia: University of Missouri Press, 1992.

Articles

"The World of Mind: Melville's Theory of Knowledge" (1940). First printed in Sealts, *Pursuing Melville* (1982), 3–10. Originally written as chapter 3 of an 81-page seminar paper submitted to Professor Stanley T. Williams on 27 February 1940.

"Herman Melville's 'I and My Chimney.'" *American Literature* 13 (May 1941): 142–54. Reprinted in Hershel Parker, ed., *The Recognition of Herman Melville: Selected Criticism since 1846,* 237–51 (Ann Arbor: University of Michigan Press, 1967); in Sealts, *Pursuing Melville* (1982), 11–22, 356–59; and in Louis J. Budd and Edwin H. Cady, eds., *On Melville: The Best from "American Literature,"* 10–22 (Durham, N.C.: Duke University Press, 1988).

"Melville and the Philosophers" (1942). First printed in Sealts, *Pursuing Melville* (1982), 23–30. This essay originally constituted the "Summary and Conclusion" of my doctoral dissertation, "Herman Melville's Reading in Ancient Philosophy" (Yale University, 1942).

"The Publication of Melville's *Piazza Tales.*" *Modern Language Notes* 59 (January 1944): 56–59.

"Melville's Reading: A Check-List of Books Owned and Borrowed." *Harvard Library Bulletin* 2 (Spring 1948): 141–63, (Autumn 1948): 378–92; 3 (Winter 1949): 119–30, (Spring 1949): 268–77, (Autumn 1949): 407–21; 4 (Winter 1950): 98–109. Incorporated in Sealts, *Melville's Reading* (1966, 1988).

"Melville's 'Friend Atahalpa.'" *Notes and Queries* 194 (22 January 1949): 37–38.

"A Note on the Melville Canon." *Melville Society Newsletter* 5 (December 1949): [2].

"Melville and the Shakers." *Studies in Bibliography: Papers of the Bibliographical Society of the University of Virginia* 2 (1949–1950): 105–14.

"Did Melville Write 'October Mountain'?" *American Literature* 22 (May 1950): 178–82.

"Melville's 'Neoplatonical Originals.' " *Modern Language Notes* 67 (February 1952): 80–86.

"Melville's Reading: A Supplementary List of Books Owned and Borrowed." *Harvard Library Bulletin* 6 (Spring 1952): 239–47. Incorporated in Sealts, *Melville's Reading* (1966, 1988).

"The Ghost of Major Melvill." *New England Quarterly* 30 (September 1957): 291–306. Reprinted in Sealts, *Pursuing Melville* (1982), 67–77; error corrected in Sealts, "The Melvilles, the Gansevoorts, and the Cincinnati Badge," *Melville Society Extracts* 70 (September 1987): 1, 4.

"Melville's Burgundy Club Sketches." *Harvard Library Bulletin* 12 (Spring 1958): 253–67. Reprinted in Sealts, *Pursuing Melville* (1982), 78–90; error corrected in Sealts, "The Melvilles, the Gansevoorts, and the Cincinnati Badge," *Melville Society Extracts* 70 (September 1987): 1, 4.

"Approaching Melville through 'Hawthorne and His Mosses.' " *Emerson Society Quarterly* 28, pt. 3 (1962): 12–15.

"Melville's 'Geniality.' " In *Essays in American and English Literature Presented to Bruce Robert McElderry, Jr.,* ed. Max F. Schulz with William D. Templeman and Charles R. Metzger, 3–26. Athens: Ohio University Press, 1967. Reprinted in Sealts, *Pursuing Melville* (1982), 155–70.

"Melville." Chapter 3 in *American Literary Scholarship: An Annual / 1967,* ed. James Woodress, 29–47. Durham, N.C.: Duke University Press, 1969.

"Melville's Chimney, Reexamined." In *Themes and Directions in American Literature: Essays in Honor of Leon Howard,* ed. Ray B. Browne and Donald Pizer, 80–102. Lafayette, Ind.: Purdue University Studies, 1969. Reprinted in Sealts, *Pursuing Melville* (1982), 171–92.

"Herman Melville's Reading in Ancient Philosophy." Ph.D. diss., Yale University, 1942. *Dissertation Abstracts* 30 (1969): 1574A–75A.

"Emerson on the Scholar, 1833–1837." *PMLA* 85 (March 1970): 185–95. Reprinted in *Critical Essays on Ralph Waldo Emerson,* ed. Robert E. Burkholder and Joel Myerson, 368–86 (Boston: G. K. Hall, 1983), and in *The American Classics Revisited: Recent Studies in American Literature,* ed. P. C. Kar and D. Ramakrishna, 127–45 (Hyderabad, India: American Studies Research Centre, 1985). Incorporated in Sealts, *Emerson on the Scholar* (1992).

"Melville." Chapter 3 in *American Literary Scholarship: An Annual / 1968,* ed. J. Albert Robbins, 30–49. Durham, N.C.: Duke University Press, 1970.

"Melville." Chapter 3 in *American Literary Scholarship: An Annual / 1969,* ed. J. Albert Robbins, 33–55. Durham, N.C.: Duke University Press, 1971.

"A Supplementary Note to *Melville's Reading* (1966)." *Harvard Library Bulletin* 19 (July 1971): 280–84.

"Melville and Richard Henry Stoddard." *American Literature* 43 (November 1971): 359–70.

"Melville." Chapter 3 in *American Literary Scholarship: An Annual / 1970,* ed. J. Albert Robbins, 33–54. Durham, N.C.: Duke University Press, 1972.

"Melville." Chapter 3 in *American Literary Scholarship: An Annual / 1971,* ed. J. Albert Robbins, 41–58. Durham, N.C.: Duke University Press, 1973.

"Emerson on the Scholar, 1838: A Study of 'Literary Ethics.' " In *Literature and Ideas in America: Essays in Memory of Harry Hayden Clark,* ed. Robert Falk, 40–57. Athens: Ohio University Press, 1975. Incorporated in Sealts, *Emerson on the Scholar* (1992).

"The American Scholar and Public Issues: The Case of Emerson." *Ariel: A Review of International English Literature* 7 (July 1976): 109–21. Incorporated in Sealts, *Emerson on the Scholar* (1992).

"Mary L. D. Ferris and the Melvilles." *Extracts: An Occasional Newsletter* (The Melville Society) 28 (November 1976): 10–11.

"Additions to *The Early Lives of Melville.*" *Extracts: An Occasional Newsletter* (The Melville Society) 28 (November 1976): 11–13.

"Did Melville Write 'The Fiddler'?" *Harvard Library Bulletin* 26 (January 1978): 77–80.

"Melville's Short Fiction." *ESQ: A Journal of the American Renaissance* 25 (1st Quarter 1979): 43–57. Reprinted as "The Reception of Melville's Short Fiction" in Sealts, *Pursuing Melville* (1982), 232–49.

"The Composition of *Nature*." In Sealts and Ferguson, eds. *Emerson's
"Nature": Origin, Growth, Meaning* (1979), 175–93; and in Sealts,
Emerson on the Scholar (1992).

"A Second Supplementary Note to *Melville's Reading* (1966). *Harvard
Library Bulletin* 27 (July 1979): 330–35. Incorporated in the rev.
and enlarged ed. of *Melville's Reading* (1988).

"Melville and Emerson's Rainbow." *ESQ: A Journal of the American Renais-
sance* 26 (2d Quarter 1980): 53–78. Reprinted in Sealts, *Pursuing
Melville* (1982), 250–77; excerpted in *Critical Essays on Herman
Melville's "Moby-Dick,"* ed. Brian Higgins and Hershel Parker, 349–54
(New York: G. K. Hall & Co., 1992). Trans. into Japanese by Arimichi
Makino of Meiji University, Tokyo, in *University Study Report* (1995):
27–77.

"The Chronology of Melville's Short Fiction, 1853–1856." *Harvard Library
Bulletin* 28 (October 1980): 391–403. Reprinted in Sealts, *Pursuing
Melville* (1982), 221–31; incorporated, with revision, in Sealts, Historical Note to *"The Piazza Tales" and Other Prose Pieces 1839–1860*
(1987).

"Olson, Melville, and the *New Republic*." *Contemporary Literature* 22
(Spring 1981): 167–86. Drawn from Sealts, "A Correspondence with
Charles Olson," then forthcoming in Sealts, *Pursuing Melville* (1982).

"A Correspondence with Charles Olson." Pt. 2 of Sealts, *Pursuing Melville*
(1982), 91–151.

"Melville and the Platonic Tradition." In Sealts, *Pursuing Melville* (1982),
278–336. Excerpted in *Critical Essays on Herman Melville's "Moby-
Dick,"* ed. Higgins and Parker, 355–76.

"A Letter to Henry A. Murray." Pt. 4 of Sealts, *Pursuing Melville* (1982),
337–44.

"Emerson as Teacher." In *Emerson Centenary Essays,* ed. Joel Myerson,
180–90, 210–12 (Carbondale: Southern Illinois University Press,
1982). Reprinted in *Critical Essays on Ralph Waldo Emerson,* ed.
Lawrence Buell, 199–210 (Englewood Cliffs, N.J.: Prentice-Hall,
1992); incorporated, with revision, in Sealts, *Emerson on the Scholar*
(1992).

Resources for Discussing Herman Melville's Tale, "Bartleby, the Scrivener."
Madison: Wisconsin Humanities Committee, 1982.

"Melville and Whitman." *Melville Society Extracts* 50 (May 1982): 10–12.

"Response to Papers by Dunne, Steele, and Rosenthal" (at a Hawthorne-Melville conference in Pittsfield, Mass., June 1992). Abstracted in *Nathaniel Hawthorne Society Newsletter* 8 (Fall 1982): 6; *Melville Society Extracts* 51 (September 1982): 4.

"Innocence and Infamy: Herman Melville's *Billy Budd* and the Critics." In *Innocence and Infamy: Resources for Discussing Herman Melville's "Billy Budd, Sailor."* Madison: Wisconsin Humanities Committee, 1983. Abstracted in *Design, Pattern, Style: Hallmarks of a Developing American Culture,* ed. Don Harkness, papers presented at the biennial conference of the Southeastern American Studies Association (Tampa, Fla.: American Studies Press, 1983), 38–39; incorporated in Sealts, "Innocence and Infamy: [Melville's] *Billy Budd, Sailor*" (1986).

"Mulberry Leaves and Satin: Emerson's Theory of the Creative Process." In *Studies in the American Renaissance (1985),* ed. Joel Myerson, 79–94 (Charlottesville: University Press of Virginia, 1985). Incorporated in Sealts, *Emerson on the Scholar* (1992).

"The Melvill Heritage." *Harvard Library Bulletin* 34 (Fall 1986): 337–61, plus three-page foldout.

"Innocence and Infamy: *Billy Budd, Sailor."* In *A Companion to Melville Studies,* ed. John Bryant, 407–30 (Westport, Conn.: Greenwood Press, 1986).

"Thomas Melvill, Jr., in *The History of Pittsfield."* *Harvard Library Bulletin* 35 (Spring 1987): 201–17.

"A Sheaf of Melville-Melvill Letters." *Harvard Library Bulletin* 35 (Summer 1957): 280–93.

"The Melvilles, the Gansevoorts, and the Cincinnati Badge." *Melville Society Extracts* 70 (September 1987): 1, 4.

"Historical Note." In *"The Piazza Tales" and Other Prose Pieces 1839–1860,* by Herman Melville, ed. Harrison Hayford, Alma A. MacDougall, G. Thomas Tanselle, et al., 457–533 (vol. 9 of *The Writings of Herman Melville* [Evanston and Chicago: Northwestern University Press and the Newberry Library, 1987]). ("Preliminary planning" for this volume "was done by Merton M. Sealts, Jr., during his association with the Northwestern-Newberry Edition, 1965–78. The reading texts of Melville's lectures of 1857–60 and the accompanying notes are his work, based on versions originally prepared for his *Melville as Lecturer* [1957]." —Editorial Appendix, p. 454.)

"An Author's Self-Education: Herman Melville's Reading." *Wisconsin Academy Review* 35 (September 1989): 11–16.

" 'An utter idler and a savage': Melville in the Spring of 1952." *Melville Society Extracts* 79 (November 1989): 1–3. Error corrected in an unsigned note by Sealts in *Melville Society Extracts* 80 (February 1990): 15.

"A Supplementary Note to *Melville's Reading* (1988)." *Melville Society Extracts* 80 (February 1990): 5–10.

" 'Pulse of the Continent': The Railroad in American Literature." *Wisconsin Academy Review* 36 (March 1990): 26–32.

" 'The Flower of Fame': A Centennial Tribute to Herman Melville, 1819–1891." *ESQ: A Journal of the American Renaissance* 38 (2d Quarter 1992): 89–117.

"Emerson Then and Now." *Wisconsin Academy Review* 38 (Summer 1992): 29–32.

"A Second Supplementary Note to *Melville's Reading* (1988)." *Melville Society Extracts* 100 (March 1995): 2–3.

"Melville, Herman." *Biographical Dictionary of Transcendentalism,* ed. Wesley T. Mott. Westport, Conn.: Greenwood Press, 1996.

Reviews

Herman Melville, by Newton Arvin (1950). *American Literature* 22 (January 1951): 518–20.

Die Funktion des Ich-Erzählers in Herman Melvilles Roman "Moby Dick," by Hans Helmcke (1957). *American Quarterly* 10 (Winter 1958): 504–5.

The Letters of Herman Melville. Ed. Merrell R. Davis and William H. Gilman (1960). *American Literature* 32 (January 1961): 473–75.

The Example of Melville, by Warner Berthoff (1962). *American Literature* 35 (May 1963): 247–48.

Moby Dick: The Myth and the Symbol: A Study in Folklore and Literature, by Janez Stanonik (1962). *American Literature* 35 (November 1963): 376–77.

The Wake of the Gods: Melville's Mythology, by H. Bruce Franklin (1963). *American Literature* 36 (March 1964): 86–87.

Pacifism and Rebellion in the Writings of Herman Melville, by John Bernstein (1964). *American Literature* 37 (January 1966): 483–85.

Emerson: Prophecy, Metamorphosis, and Influence. Selected Papers from the English Institute. Ed. David Levin (1975). *English Language Notes* 14 (March 1977): 219–21.

Hawthorne, Melville, and the Novel, by Richard H. Brodhead (1976). *Journal of English and Germanic Philology* 76 (April 1977): 268–70.

The Method of Melville's Short Fiction, by R. Bruce Bickley (1975), *Melville's Short Fiction, 1853–1856,* by William B. Dillingham (1977), and *Going Under: Melville's Short Fiction and the American 1850s,* by Marvin Fisher (1977). "Critical Review: Melville's Short Fiction." *ESQ: A Journal of the American Renaissance* 25 (1st Quarter 1979): 43–57.

Melville, by Edward H. Rosenberry (1979). *American Literature* 52 (March 1980): 138–39.

Stove by a Whale: Owen Chase and the "Essex," by Thomas Farel Heffernan (1981). *Resources for American Literary Study* 11 (Spring 1981): 138–40.

The Unbounded Center: Jungian Studies in American Romanticism, by Martin Bickman (1980). *American Literature* 53 (May 1981): 339–40.

Ralph Waldo Emerson: A Descriptive Bibliography, by Joel Myerson (1982). *PBSA: Publications of the Bibliographical Society of America* 77 (1st Quarter 1983): 87–89.

The House of Emerson, by Leonard Neufeldt (1983). *Journal of English and Germanic Philology* 82 (October 1983): 579–81.

Subversive Genealogy: The Politics and Art of Herman Melville, by Michael Paul Rogin (1983). *South Atlantic Quarterly* 84 (Spring 1985): 225–26.

Hawthorne, Melville, and the American Character, by John P. McWilliams, Jr. (1984). *American Literature* 57 (May 1985): 332–33.

The Province of Piety: Moral History in Hawthorne's Early Tales, by Michael J. Colacurcio (1984). "Hawthorne as Perry Miller." *American Quarterly* 37 (Fall 1985): 614–18.

Pen Friends, by Michael Thorn (1988). *Nathaniel Hawthorne Review* 15 (Fall 1989): 15–16; and *Melville Society Extracts* 82 (September 1990): 12.

White Fire: The Influence of Emerson on Melville, by John B. Williams (1991). *Melville Society Extracts* 91 (November 1992): 17–19; reply to rejoinder by Williams, *Melville Society Extracts* 93 (June 1993): 14.

The American Ideal: Literary Theory as a Worldly Activity, by Peter Carafiol (1991). *Comparative Literature Studies* 31.1 (1994): 96–99.

An Emerson Chronology, by Albert J. von Frank (1994). *Analytical and Enumerative Bibliography,* in press.

Index

Academy, 215
Achilles, 46
ACLS Newsletter, 233
Adam, 46, 48, 228
Adams, Henry, 4, 9, 90; *The Education of Henry Adams,* 90, 92–93, 213
Adams, Richard P., 244
Adams, Samuel, 22
Adler, George J., 23
Adler, Joyce Sparer, 60–61, 221
Aesop, 7
Agrippa, Cornelius Heinrich, 82
Ahab *(Moby-Dick),* 28, 29, 30, 47, 60, 116, 119, 122, 175–88, 228, 230, 231–32, 243
Albany Academy, 68
Albany Argus, 77
Albany Atlas, 240
Albany Classical School, 68
Albany Evening Journal, 77
Albany Evening Tribune, 77
Albany Young Men's Association, 68
Albertus Magnus, 82
Alexander, 46
Allen, Ethan, 59; *A Narrative of Colonel Ethan Allen's Captivity,* 81
Allen, Gay Wilson, 56
American Literature, 189
American Literature Section, Modern Language Association, 189
Ananias, 40
Anderson, Charles R., 45, 56, 126
Appleton's Annual Cyclopaedia, 18
Aranda, Alessandro ("Benito Cereno"), 36
Arms, George ("T. T. E."), 56, 220
Arnold, Matthew, 3–4, 68, 70, 97–98; "Emerson," 211
Arvin, Newton, 45, 56
Astor, John Jacob, 22

Athée (Atheist), 41, 60
Atufal ("Benito Cereno"), 197
Authors Club, 17

Bachelor's Delight ("Benito Cereno"), 28, 37, 195
Balzac, Honore, 70
Barrymore, John, 122, 231
Bartleby ("Bartleby, the Scrivener"), 23, 26–30, 34, 79, 192–93
Bayle, Pierre, *Dictionary,* 82
Baym, Nina, 170, 241
Beaumont, Francis, and John Fletcher, 80
Bellipotent, H.M.S. *(Billy Budd, Sailor),* 40–42, 52, 60, 61, 204, 205, 206
Belzoni, Giovanni Battista, 83
Benson, Earl Maltby, 230
Bentley, Richard, 74, 75, 116–17, 118
Bentley's Miscellany, 74
Benziger, Walter, 246
Berenson, Bernard, 129
Berenson, Mary Smith, 129–30
Berkshire Athenaeum, 70, 72
Berkshire Eagle, 87
Berryman, John, 138, 235
Berthoff, Warner, 183–84, 244
Bezanson, Walter E., 80, 181, 183, 185, 187, 188, 224, 244, 245, 246
Bible, 47, 68, 107, 153
Bickman, Martin, 240
Billson, James, 17
Bishop, Jonathan, 227
Bland *(White-Jacket),* 46–47
Blodgett, Harold W., 234
Bode, Carl, 212
Bodzin, Eugene, 237
Boone, Joseph Allen, 239
Booth, Wayne C., 176, 183, 244
Bradley, Sculley, 234

Brasher, Thomas L., 16, 215
Braswell, William, 243
Breinig, Helmbrecht, 85, 225
Breit, Harvey, 231
Bridge, Horatio, 241
Bridgman, Richard, 235
Briggs, Charles F., 75; *Working a Passage*, 51, 219
Britten, Benjamin, 122
Broderick, John C., 157, 239
Brodtkorb, Paul, Jr., 58, 185, 187, 221, 245, 246
Brook Farm, 163
Brooklyn Daily Eagle, 16, 215
Brooks, Cleanth, 57
Brown, Cecil M., 186–87, 187, 246
Brown, Isaac, 79
Brown, John, 10, 97, 107
Browne, Sir Thomas, 69
Browning, Elizabeth Barrett, 68
Browning, Robert, 68
Bryant, John, 51, 219, 232, 244
Buchanan, Robert, 17, 215; "Imperial Cockneydom," 17; "Socrates in Camden," 17
Buchman, S. R., 231–32
Buckley, Vincent, 243
Budd, William ("Billy"; *Billy Budd, Sailor*), 32, 39–42, 45–47, 48–50, 51, 52, 55–57, 60–61, 199, 201–2, 203–6, 207–8
Buell, Lawrence, 19, 215
Bugbee, James M., 247
Bunyan, John, 92
Burney, James, 80; *History of the Discoveries in the South Seas*, 80
Burton, Robert, *The Anatomy of Melancholy*, 79
Byron, George Gordon, 6th Baron Byron, 68

Cabot, James Elliot, *A Memoir of Ralph Waldo Emerson*, 104
Cambon, Glauco, 185, 186, 188, 245, 246
Campbell, Harry Modean, 56
Carlyle, Thomas, 7, 68, 69, 99; *Sartor Resartus*, 4, 211
Carnegie, Andrew, 99
Carraway, Nick *(The Great Gatsby)*, 94, 184

"Casey Jones," 91
Casper, Leonard, 56, 220
Cellini, Benvenuto, *Autobiography*, 82
Cereno, Benito ("Benito Cereno"), 32, 33, 34–35, 36, 37, 38, 47–48, 195–97
Cervantes Saavedra, Miguel de, *Don Quixote*, 85
Chaplain, the *(Billy Budd, Sailor)*, 205–6
Charles L. Webster & Co., 16
Chase, Jack, 44
Chase, Owen, *Narrative*, 72
Chase, Richard, 56, 57
Chatterton, Thomas, 80
Chillingworth, Roger *(The Scarlet Letter)*, 166–67, 242
China, 149
Cincinnati, Society of the, 209–10, 247
Claggart, John *(Billy Budd, Sailor)*, 32, 39, 40–42, 46–47, 48, 49, 55, 56, 57, 58, 60, 199, 201, 202–3, 203–6
Clapper, Ronald, 236
Claret, Captain *(White-Jacket)*, 59
Clark, C. E. Frazer, Jr., 240
Clark, Harry Hayden, 189
Clemens, Samuel Langhorne (Mark Twain), 7, 15, 16, 24, 37, 65, 67, 92, 105; *Roughing It*, 92
Clift, Rupert C., 230
Coleridge, Samuel Taylor, 68, 69, 103, 176; *Lyrical Ballads*, 176
Collins, William, 80
Colnett, James, 80
Colon, Christopher, 37
Colt, John C., 22
Columbia University, 133
Compson, Quentin *(Absalom, Absalom!)*, 186
Concord, Massachusetts, Lyceum, 147, 148–49, 151
Conrad, Joseph, *Heart of Darkness*, 184
Constable and Company, 121
Conway, Moncure Daniel, 8, 13; *Emerson at Home and Abroad*, 212, 213, 214
Cook, James, 46
Coolidge, Lowell William, 211
Cooper, James Fenimore, 68, 77; *History of the Navy of the United States*, 81; *The Two Admirals*, 51; *Wing-and-Wing*, 51

Cowley, Malcolm, 123–24, 137–38, 232–33, 233, 235, 240
Cowley, William, 80
Cox, James M., 241
Crane, Hart, 90
Crane, Stephen, "The Bride Comes to Yellow Sky," 92
Curtis, Edwin Gansevoort, 210
Curtis, George William, 7, 8, 9, 76, 83, 84, 228; "Emerson Lecturing," 213

Dana, Richard Henry, 77, 230
Dansker, the (Billy Budd, Sailor), 45, 205
Dante Alighieri, 69, 72; The Divine Comedy, 35; The Vision; or Hell, Purgatory, and Paradise, translated by the Rev. Henry Francis Cary, 72
Dartmouth College, 102, 103, 104
Darwin, Charles Robert, 80; Journal of Researches . . . during the Voyage of H.M.S. Beagle . . . , 80
David, 46
Delano, Amasa, 32, 37, 80, 195; A Narrative of Voyages and Travels . . . , 32, 80, 82, 195, 196
Delano, Amasa ("Benito Cereno"), 28, 33, 34–35, 37, 38, 47–48, 195–97
De Quincey, Thomas, 69, 159
Dewey, John, 12
Dick, Bridegroom ("Bridegroom Dick"), 44
Dickens, Charles, 23, 25, 68, 78, 79, 117
Dickinson, Emily, 15, 90–91, 117, 184, 225, 228, 244; "I Love to See It Lap the Miles," 90–91; "Tell All the Truth But Tell It Slant," 184
Dimmesdale, Arthur (The Scarlet Letter), 166–67, 171, 174, 242
Dix and Edwards, 75
Douglas, Ann, 117, 228
Dowden, Edward, 131
Drake, Francis S., 247
Dublin University Magazine, 77
Duyckinck, Evert, 69, 71, 72, 74, 79, 116, 118, 160, 161, 179, 212, 224, 228, 240; "Books Lent," 72
Duyckinck, George, 116, 118, 179
Dwight, Timothy, Travels in New England, 84

Edwards, Jonathan, 193
Edwards, Monroe, 22
Edwards, Mr., 23
Eliot, Thomas Stearns, 57, 67, 232, 233; "Cousin Nancy," 98
Elmore, A. E., 238
Emanuel, James, 227
Emerson, Charles, 241
Emerson, Edward Waldo, 101
Emerson, Ellen, 212, 213
Emerson, Lydia ("Lidian"), 108
Emerson, Ralph Waldo, 3–14, 15, 67, 68, 69, 87–88, 96–101, 102–9, 137, 146, 147, 150, 162–63, 173, 188, 211–14, 226, 226–27, 234; Address on Education, 12; "The American Scholar," 11, 12, 13, 67, 98, 99, 103, 105, 106, 107, 145, 226, 246; "Carlyle," 7; "The Celebration of Intellect," 12; "Circles," 103, 226; Divinity School Address, 10, 12, 99, 106; "Education" (1840), 12; "Find Your Calling," 103; "Intellect," 12; Journals, 96, 101, 103; "Literary Ethics," 12, 102, 104; "The Man of Letters," 105; "Milton," 96; Nature, 98, 241; "Nominalist and Realist," 237; "The Over-Soul," 12; "The Poet," 12, 19, 88, 90; "Power," 100; "The Problem," 85; Representative Men, 105, 109; "The Scholar," 105; "Self-Reliance," 11, 12, 99, 100; sermons, 214; "Spiritual Laws," 12; "The Transcendentalist," 104
Emerson, William, 147
"Enchanted Island," 122
Erkkila, Betsy, 235

Fanny Fern. See Willis, Sara P.
Faulkner, William, 121, 124; Absalom, Absalom!, 186; "The Bear," 95
Feidelson, Charles, Jr., 180, 244
Field, David Dudley, History of the County of Berkshire, 81, 84
Fields, James T., 165, 240, 242
Finn, Huckleberry (Adventures of Huckleberry Finn), 37
Fish, Stanley, 233

Fitzgerald, Francis Scott Key, 94, 184; *The Crack-Up,* 184, 245; *The Great Gatsby,* 94, 184; "Pasting It Together," 245
Fly, Eli James Murdock, 23
Foerster, Norman, 237
Fogle, Richard Harter, 58, 221
Forbes, Waldo Emerson, 101
Forster, Edward Morgan, 122, 239–40
Fox, George, 107
Francesca *(The Divine Comedy),* 35
Francesco ("Benito Cereno"), 197
Frank, Stuart M., 70, 222
Franklin, Benjamin, 7, 81; *The Way to Wealth,* 237
Freeman, F. Barron, 54, 56
Frost, Robert, 225; "A Lone Striker," 93–94; "The Oven Bird," 94; *West-Running Brook,* 93

Gabriel, Ralph H., 244
Gansevoort, Guert, 44, 219, 247
Gansevoort, Henry Sanford, 210, 247
Gansevoort, Herman 78, 210
Gansevoort, Peter (1749–1812), 210
Gansevoort, Peter (1789–1876), 22, 68, 210, 247
Garner, Stanton, 51–52, 53, 55, 59, 209, 220, 221, 223, 247
Geismar, Maxwell, 231
Gentian, Jack (Burgundy Club sketches), 44, 47, 59, 210
Giamatti, A. Bartlett, 100
Ginger Nut ("Bartleby, the Scrivener"), 191
Glendinning, General Pierre *(Pierre),* 59
Glendinning, Pierre *(Pierre),* 30, 31, 56, 67, 184, 212
God, 11, 12, 13, 27, 40, 41, 50, 56, 99, 100, 103, 116, 186
Goethe, Johann Wolfgang von, 68, 69; *The Sorrows of Young Werther,* 105
Gohdes, Clarence, 189
Goldsmith, Oliver, 78
Gollin, Richard and Rita, 51, 219
Grandvin, Marquis de (Burgundy Club sketches), 44
"Great Train Robbery, The," 93
Greek language and literature, 68
Greene, Richard Tobias ("Toby"), 44
Gregg, Edith Emerson Webster, 212, 213

Gribben, Alan, 65, 222
Guttman, Allen, 196, 197

Haden, Francis Seymour, 44
Halverson, John, 243
Harold, Childe *(Childe Harold's Pilgrimage),* 105
Harper and Brothers, 25, 74, 75, 76, 80, 118
Harper's New Monthly Magazine, 25, 26, 74, 75, 76–77, 118
Harriman, Edward Henry, 93
Hart, James D., 229
Harvard College, 3, 5, 7, 114, 147
Harvard Divinity School, 4, 7, 11, 97
Hastings, Jonas, 9
Hautboy ("The Fiddler"), 27, 79
Haverford College, 129
Hawthorne, Julian, 9, 161, 165; *The Memoirs of Julian Hawthorne,* 213
Hawthorne, Nathaniel, 5, 12, 15, 21, 25, 35, 38, 66, 68, 69, 78, 80, 82, 83, 91–92, 113, 114–15, 116, 117, 119, 121, 124, 159–74, 175, 185, 216, 228, 229, 230, 240–42, 246; "The Celestial Rail-road," 92; "The Custom-House," 159, 164, 168, 168–74, 241, 242; "Endicott and the Red Cross," 166; "Ethan Brand," 167; *The House of the Seven Gables,* 91–92; "The Minister's Black Veil," 166, 168; "The Minotaur," 82; *Mosses from an Old Manse,* 85, 113, 159, 160, 169; notebooks, 107, 240, 241, 242; "The Old Manse," 159, 160–64, 166, 168, 170, 172, 174, 212, 241; "Old-Time Legends," 165, 168; *The Scarlet Letter,* 165, 165–68, 169, 171, 184, 233, 242; "Sights from a Steeple," 167; *Tanglewood Tales,* 82; *Twice-Told Tales,* 160
Hawthorne, Sophia, 117, 124, 163, 165
Hawthorne, Una, 160, 165
Haydon, Benjamin Robert, *Life . . . ,* edited and compiled by Tom Taylor, 81
Hayes, Rutherford B., 6, 212
Hayes, Woodrow ("Woody"), 99
Hayford, Harrison, 55, 219, 220, 246;

coeditor, *Billy Budd, Sailor,* by Herman Melville, 51, 54–55, 56, 206, 218, 236; coeditor, *Moby-Dick as Doubloon,* 228, 243

Hays, Peter L., 49–50, 219

Hazel, Robert, 246

Hazlitt, William, 159

Helmstone ("The Happy Fiddler"), 27

Henry, William A., III, 233

Higgins, Bryan, 228, 243

Higginson, Thomas Wentworth, 228

Hirsch, Penny L., 224

Hitler, Adolf, 99

Hoeltje, Hubert H., 240

Holden's Dollar Magazine, 74

Holmes, Oliver Wendell, 8, 9, 11, 83; *Ralph Waldo Emerson,* 213

The Houghton Library, 54, 66, 71

Howard, Leon, 22, 60, 182, 189, 221

Howells, William Dean, 71; *A Hazard of New Fortunes,* 92

Hubbard, Henry F., 82

Hubbard, Sarah, 82

Hubbell, Jay B., 189

Hulbert, Ann, 239–40

Hunilla ("The Encantadas"), 80

Huntington, Collis Potter, 93

Hyman, Stanley Edgar, 156, 239

Iago *(Othello),* 47

Inge, M. Thomas, 23

Irving, Washington, 23, 78, 79, 83, 159, 165; *The Alhambra,* 83; "Legend of the Arabian Astrologer," 83

Isaac, 46

Ishmael *(Moby-Dick),* 15, 29, 66, 72, 114, 116, 119, 175–88, 199, 230, 231, 243

Italian opera, 144

Ives, C. B., 207, 219

Jackson *(Redburn),* 46–47

James, Henry (1811–1882), 2, 8, 211; "Emerson," 213

James, Henry (1843–1916), 15, 104, 166; "Emerson," 226; *Hawthorne,* 240

James, William (d. 1827), *The Naval History of Great Britain,* 51

James, William (1842–1910), 4

Jarrell, Randall, 134, 235

Jekyll, Dr., and Mr. Hyde (Stevenson, "Dr. Jekyll and Mr. Hyde"), 193

Jerrold, Douglas, *Black Ey'd Susan,* 51; *The Mutiny at the Nore,* 51

Jesus Christ, 23, 55, 57, 192

Job, 194

Johnson, Barbara, 58, 221

Johnson, Professor ("The Apple-Tree Table"), 83

Jonah, 115

Jones, Casey, 91, 94

Jones, John Paul, 59

Jonson, Ben, 69

Joseph, 46

Josephson, Matthew, 230

Joyce, James, 24

Jupiter ("The Gold-Bug"), 78

Kennedy, Willam Sloane, 215

Kenosha Democrat, 9, 99

King, Thomas Starr, 6

Kinnamon, Jon M., 221–22

Kipling, Rudyard, 71

Kleinfield, H. R., 97

Lamb, Charles, 23, 78, 79, 159, 169; "Old Benchers of the Inner Temple," 169; "The South-Sea House," 169

Lathers, Richard, 78

Latin language and literature, 68, 152

Lauter, Paul, 227, 230

Lawrence, David Herbert, 10, 183, 214, 244

Lawry, Robert P., 207–8, 219

Lawyer-narrator ("Bartleby, the Scrivener"), 22, 26, 27–31, 37, 79, 191–93, 199

Lease, Benjamin, 241

Lebeaux, Richard, 152, 236, 238

Ledbetter, Jack W., 207, 219

Lee, William, 241

Legrand ("The Gold-Bug"), 78

Levin, Harry, 183, 232, 244

Lewis, R. W. B., 159, 239

Leyda, Jay, 18, 79, 81, 224

Literary World, The, 74, 115–16, 179, 228

Littel's Living Age, 77

Livy (Titus Livius), 49

Lombardo *(Mardi),* 113

London Atlas, 228
London Examiner, 228
Longfellow, Henry Wadsworth, 291
Loving, Jerome, 212
Lowell, James Russell, 6, 7, 8, 9, 87, 97, 100; "Emerson the Lecturer," 212, 213
Lowell, Robert, 196
Lyon, Melvin E., 239

MacDougall, Alma, 217
Machiavelli, Nicolo, *The Florentine Histories,* 82
Maitland, James C., *The Lawyer's Story,* 22, 79
Malthus, Thomas Robert, 237
Mapple, Father *(Moby-Dick),* 185
Mariana ("The Piazza"), 85
Marks, Barry A., 185, 245
Marlowe, Christopher, 69
Marr, John ("John Marr"), 43, 46
Marryat, Frederick (Captain Marryat), *The King's Own,* 51
Mars (god of war), 48
Martin, Robert K., 235
Marx, Leo, 86–87, 225
Mather, Cotton, *Magnalia Christi Americana,* 81, 83
Mathews, Cornelius, 79
Matthew, 193
Matthews, Pamela, 84, 225
Matthiessen, Francis Otto, 72, 153, 174, 180, 190, 212, 218, 222, 238, 242
Maugham, William Somerset, 231
May, Samuel H., 107
McCall, Dan, 23
McElderry, Bruce Robert, Jr., 51, 189, 219
Mead, David, 212, 213
Melvill, Allan (1751–1832), 68, 82
Melvill, Thomas (1751–1832), 82, 209
Melvill, Thomas, Jr. (1776–1845), 43, 68–69, 75, 82–83, 210
Melville, Allan (1823–1872), 22, 53, 69, 77, 79, 81
Melville, Augusta, 76–77
Melville, Elizabeth, 54, 71
Melville, Elizabeth Shaw, 39, 51, 53–54, 71, 78, 83, 229
Melville, Frances, 54

Melville, Gansevoort, 22
Melville, Herman, 5, 6, 12, 15–20, 65–73, 74–85, 91, 110–25, 131, 175–88, 194, 209, 212, 215, 222, 222–25, 227–33, 234; "The American Aloe on Exhibition," 229; "The Apple-Tree Table," 82, 83, 84; "At the Hostelry," 43; "Bartleby, the Scrivener," 21–31, 34, 37, 75, 79, 191–94, 199, 215–16, 223; *Battle-Pieces,* 19, 46, 53, 59, 228; "The Bell-Tower," 22, 84; "Benito Cereno," 28, 32–38, 50, 80, 82, 84, 195–98, 216–17, 223; *Billy Budd, Sailor,* 17, 18, 19, 32, 39–61, 70, 120, 121, 122, 123, 124, 199–208, 217–22, 223; "Billy in the Darbies," 41, 42–45, 206; "Bridegroom Dick," 44; Burgundy Club sketches, 43, 44, 45, 49, 59, 210; *Clarel,* 39, 47, 59, 67–68; "Cock-A-Doodle-Doo!," 26, 27, 75, 79; *The Confidence-Man,* 25, 39, 77, 78, 82, 85, 118–19, 197, 234; "The Encantadas," 75, 80, 82; "The Fiddler," 26, 27, 75, 78; "The 'Gees," 81; "The Happy Failure," 26, 27, 75, 78, 83; "Hawthorne and His Mosses," 35, 37, 78, 85, 227, 231, 244; "I and My Chimney," 82, 83, 84, 85, 223; *The Isle of the Cross,* 25, 75, 80, 118; *Israel Potter,* 22, 25, 50, 53, 59, 75, 80, 81, 118, 223; "Jack Roy," 44; "Jimmy Rose," 82, 224; "John Marr," 43, 44, 45; *John Marr and Other Sailors,* 42–43, 44, 45, 50; "Lecture Engagements," 77; "The Lightning-Rod Man," 81, 84; "Major Gentian and Colonel Bun-kum," 210; "The March into Virginia," 46; *Mardi,* 18, 19, 20, 28, 30, 69, 70, 112, 114, 118, 123, 124, 223; "Misgivings," 228; *Moby-Dick,* 5, 14, 15, 18, 19, 20, 21, 24, 25, 26, 28, 29, 30, 37, 39, 47, 66, 67, 69, 70, 72, 74, 75, 79, 85, 110, 111, 112, 113, 114, 115, 116, 117, 118, 121–22, 123, 124, 175–88, 197, 199, 206, 214, 230, 231, 233, 242–46; "Naples in the Time of Bomba," 43; "Note: The Cincinnati," 210; *Omoo,* 16, 18, 46, 50, 67, 69,

70, 76, 111, 115, 118, 121, 180, 223, 247; "On the Slain Collegians," 46; "The Paradise of Bachelors and the Tartarus of Maids," 28, 37, 79, 84; "The Piazza," 75, 84–85; *The Piazza Tales,* 21, 22, 25, 32, 75, 76, 78, 82, 84, 118, 217; *Pierre,* 18, 19, 20, 21, 22, 24, 25, 26, 28, 30, 31, 32, 59, 67, 70, 74, 75, 76, 79, 83, 117–18, 124, 184, 210; "Poor Man's Pudding and Rich Man's Manure," 79; *Redburn,* 46, 112, 114, 185; "Sketch of Major Thomas Melville, Jr.," 224; "The South Seas," 70, 80; "Supplement to *Battle-Pieces,*" 19; "Thy Aim, Thy Aim?," 110–11; "To the Master of the 'Meteor,'" 44; "Tom Deadlight," 44, 45; "Tortoise-Hunting," 75; "The Town-Ho's Story," 74, 77; "The Two Temples," 75, 79, 84; *Typee,* 16, 18, 21, 32, 46, 50, 67, 69, 70, 76, 80, 110, 111, 112, 114, 115, 118, 119, 121, 122, 123, 124, 180, 223, 230; "A Utilitarian View of the Monitor's Fight," 44; *White-Jacket,* 18, 45, 46, 50, 59, 61, 73, 111, 112, 113, 114, 121, 131, 185

Melville, Malcolm, 49

Melvill(e), Maria Gansevoort, 68, 76–77

Melville, Stanwix, 49

Melville, Thomas (1830–1884), 44

Merrimac, 44

Merrymusk ("Cock-A-Doodle-Doo!"), 27

Metcalf, Eleanor Melville, 54, 70

Meynell, Viola, 121, 124, 230

Miller, Edwin Haviland, 49

Miller, James F., 168–69, 170, 235

Miller, Perry, 5, 189, 212

Milton, John, 4, 24, 47, 68, 69, 72; *Lycidas,* 119–20; *Paradise Lost,* 79, 85

Mitchell, Charles, 57, 221

Moby Dick (*Moby-Dick*), 29, 30, 116, 119, 175–88, 230, 243

Modern Language Association of America, 111

Moldenhauer, Joseph, 151–52, 153, 237, 238, 239

Monitor, 44

Montaigne, Michel Eyquem, 49

Morewood, Helen, 81

Morewood, Margaret, 81

Morewoods, the, 81, 83

Morison, Samuel Eliot, 231

Morley, Christopher, 230

Mott, Wesley T., 238–39

Mumford, Lewis, 26, 56, 236

Murray, Henry A., 183, 244

Murry, John Middleton, 55–56, 220

Myers, Henry Alonzo, 244

Napoleon Bonaparte, 109

Nelson, Horatio, 41, 44, 200, 203, 208

Neufeldt, Leonard, 106, 236, 237

Newark Daily Advertiser, 76

New Criticism, 57, 190

New Historicism, 190

Newman, Lea Bertani Vozar, 216, 217, 223

New York Commercial Advertiser, 228

New York Day Book, 229

New York Herald, 77

New York Press, 227

New York Public Library, 71, 72, 123

New York Society Library, 69, 71, 72

New York Times, 77, 79

New York Tribune, 77, 79, 88, 227, 243

New Yorker, 175

Nicoloff, Philip L., 227

Niebuhr, Reinhold, 233

Nietzsche, Friedrich, 99

Nippers ("Bartleby, the Scrivener"), 191, 192

Norris, Frank, 93; *The Octopus,* 93

Norton, Andrews, "A Discourse on the Latest Form of Infidelity," 97, 211

O'Brien, Fitz-James, 229, 243

Olson, Charles, 56, 57

Osborne, Frances Thomas, 71

Paolo *(The Divine Comedy),* 35

Parker, Hershel, 115, 118, 221, 223, 228, 229, 243; coeditor, *Moby-Dick as Doubloon,* 228, 243

Parrington, Vernon Louis, 237

Partisan Review, 186

Paul, Sherman, 151, 227, 237

Pearce, Roy Harvey, 234

Pearson, Norman Holmes, 241

Peck, Gregory, 122
Peckham, Morse, 180, 244
Peleg, Captain *(Moby-Dick)*, 177, 178
Pequod (Moby-Dick), 86, 179, 181, 183, 184, 188
Perseverance ("Benito Cereno"), 37, 195
Picasso, Pablo, 30
Pip *(Moby-Dick)*, 30, 178, 182, 184
Pittsfield Culturist and Gazette, 77
Pittsfield Eagle, 77
Pittsfield Library Association, 69
Pittsfield Sun, 77
Plato, 5, 47, 68, 69, 103, 157; *Republic,* 100
Plimlimmon, Plotinus *(Pierre),* 31
Plutarch, 49; "On the Cessation of the Oracles," 81
Pochmann, Henry A., 189
Poe, Edgar Allan, 15, 38, 78, 82, 124; "The Gold-Bug," 78
Pommer, Henry F., 227
Porte, Joel, 96
Porter, David, 80; *Journal of a Cruise . . . to the Pacific Ocean,* 80
Potter, Israel, 80
Prescott, Mr., 9
Priestley, Joseph, 193
Proteus, 9
Pry, Paul, 167
Prynne, Hester *(The Scarlet Letter),* 166–68, 171, 174, 292
Prynne, Pearl *(The Scarlet Letter),* 166
Pue, Jonathan, 171, 172
Purser, the *(Billy Budd, Sailor),* 206
Putnam, George Palmer, 75, 76
Putnam's Monthly Magazine, 21, 25, 26, 32, 38, 74, 75, 77, 81–82, 84, 118, 197
Pyncheon, Clifford *(The House of the Seven Gables),* 91
Pyncheon, Hepzibah *(The House of the Seven Gables),* 91
Pyncheon, Judge Jaffrey *(The House of the Seven Gables),* 241

Radney *(Moby-Dick),* 47
Redburn, Wellingborough *(Redburn),* 45–46, 47
Reich, Charles A., 207, 219
Ricardo, David, 237

Rice, Amasa, 82
Richards, Ivor Armstrong, 57
Richardson, Lyon N., 6, 100, 212
Richardson, Robert D., Jr., 238
Richter, Johann Paul Friedrich, 68
Riesman, David, 11
Rights-of-Man (Billy Budd, Sailor), 40, 60
Ripley, Samuel, 7
Robinson, Agatha Hatch, 80
Robinson, Lillian S., 233
Rogin, Michael Paul, 47, 48, 218, 219
Roper, Gordon, 243
Rorschach test, 194
Rosenberry, Edward H., 58
Ross, Harold, 175
Rusk, Ralph L., 213
Rust, Richard Dilworth, 49–50, 219

Sale, Arthur, 56
Salem Register, 241
Sandburg, Carl, 90, 132, 225, 235; "Limited," 91; "Mamie," 90
San Dominick ("Benito Cereno"), 33, 34, 36, 37, 195, 196
Sands, Robert C., *Life and Correspondence of John Paul Jones,* 81
Santayana, George, 4
Santo Domingo, 37, 196
Satan, 55, 57; *(Paradise Lost),* 47
Sattelmeyer, Robert, 66, 153, 222, 238, 239
Schatt, Stanley, 23
Schiffman, Joseph, 56, 220
Schiller, Johann Christoph Friedrich von, 68
Schneider, Herbert, 56
Schopenhauer, Arthur, 68, 71, 120, 125; *The Wisdom of Life,* 229
Schorer, C. E., 213
Scorza, Thomas J., 47, 55
Scott, Eleanor Bryce, 213
"Sea-Beast, The," 122
Sealts, Merton M., Jr., 66, 189–90, 248–56; "The American Scholar and Public Issues," 214; coeditor, *Billy Budd, Sailor,* by Herman Melville, 51, 54–55, 56, 206, 218, 236; *Emerson on the Scholar,* 106–7, 109; "Herman Melville's 'I and My Chimney,' "

224; "Herman Melville's Reading in Ancient Philosophy," 232; "Historical Note" to *The Piazza Tales . . . ,*" 223; "Melville" (1971), 221; "Melville's Chimney, Reexamined," 224; *Melville's Reading,* 66

Sedgwick, Catherine Maria, *The Poor Rich Man and the Rich Poor Man,* 79

Seneca, Marcus (or Lucius) Annaeus, 68

Shakespeare, William, 7, 24, 47, 68, 69, 113, 184; *Cymbeline,* 85; *Hamlet,* 79, 85; *Macbeth,* 85; *Measure for Measure,* 85; *A Midsummer Night's Dream,* 85

Shanley, J. Lyndon, 150, 236, 237, 238

Shaw, Lemuel, 22, 48, 112

Shelley, Mary Wollstonecraft, *Frankenstein . . . ,* 82

Short, Raymond, 56, 220

Simmons, Nancy Craig, 67, 222

Smith, Adam, 237

Smith, Henry Nash, 104–5, 107, 226, 227

Smith, Herbert F., 237

Smith, Joseph Edward Adams, 77; *Taghconic,* 81

Smith, Logan Pearsall, 129–31; *Unforgotten Years,* 131

Smith, Robert Pearsall, 129–30, 234

Smith College, 129

Society of the Cincinnati, 209–10, 247

Socrates, 13

Solomon, 60

Somers mutiny, 44, 45, 50, 56, 219

Southey, Robert, *Life of Nelson,* 51, 218

Spenser, Edmund, 80, 85, 234

Spiller, Robert E., 103, 226

"Spirit-Rapping," 83

Springfield Republican, 77

Staël, Anne Louise Germaine de, 68

Standard ("The Fiddler"), 79

Stanford, Leland, 93

Starbuck *(Moby-Dick),* 128, 182

Stedman, Arthur, 16, 17, 18, 53–54, 119, 122, 124, 215; Introduction to *Typee,* 229; "Marquesan Melville," 229; ed., *Selected Poems of Whitman* and Whitman's *Autobiographia,* 18; ed., Melville's *Typee, Omoo, White-Jacket,* and *Moby-Dick,* 18, 53–54

Stedman, Edmund C., 17, 18, 215; ed.,

Library of American Literature, 16; ed., *The Poets of America,* 18

Stedman, Laura Gould, 18, 215

Steelkilt *(Moby-Dick),* 47

Sten, Christopher, 70–71, 222

Stern, Milton R., 47, 55, 220

Sterne, Laurence, *Tristram Shandy,* 79

Stessel, Edward, 218

Stewart, Randall, 10, 214

Stowe, Harriet Beecher, *Uncle Tom's Cabin,* 117

Stuart, Gilbert, 210

Stubb *(Moby-Dick),* 178

Surgeon, the *(Billy Budd, Sailor),* 204, 206

Swedenborgianism, 83

Symonds, John Addington, 131

Tacitus, Cornelius, 119

Tanselle, G. Thomas, 82, 224, 229, 230

Tappan, Caroline Sturgis, 212

Taylor, J. Golden, 157, 239

Taylor, Mary A., 230

Tennyson, Alfred, 1st Baron Tennyson (Lord Tennyson), 68, 131; "Marianna," 85; "Marianna in the South," 85

Teufelsdröckh, Herr *(Sartor Resartus),* 4, 105

Thackeray, William Makepeace, 25, 117

Thomas, Brook, 48, 55, 218, 221

Thomas, William Sturgis, 210, 247

Thompson, Lawrance, 56, 57

Thoreau, Cynthia, 176

Thoreau, Henry David, 5, 12, 15, 65–66, 68, 111, 117, 121, 124, 146–58, 177, 188, 192; journal, 146, 212; *Walden, or Life in the Woods,* 14, 84, 87, 111, 146–58, 160, 176, 177, 180, 181, 185, 188, 214, 236–40, 243; *A Week on the Concord and Merrimack Rivers,* 66, 147–48, 149–50

Thoreau, John (brother), 146, 147

Thoreau, John (father), 146, 147–48

Thorp, Willard, 189, 229–30

Thurber, James, 175, 243

Ticknor, William D., 216, 229

Ticknor and Fields, 165

Time, 5, 212, 233

Tomlinson, Henry Major, 230

Traubel, Horace, 16; *With Walt Whitman in Camden,* 215
Treeman, Elizabeth, 220
Trollope, Anthony, 174
Trowbridge, James Townsend, "Reminiscences of Walt Whitman," 212; *My Own Story,* 212
Trumbull, Henry, 80; *Life and Remarkable Adventures of Israel Potter,* 81
Tryal, 27, 195, 196
Tucker, Abraham, *The Light of Nature Revealed,* 78
Turkey ("Bartleby, the Scrivener"), 191
Turner, Arlin, 189
Turner, Joseph Mallord William, 44
Turret, Captain ("Bridegroom Dick"), 48
Twain, Mark. *See* Clemens, Samuel Langhorne

Unitarians, 4, 97, 99, 102, 106, 160, 163
Universal Review, 215
Upham, Charles W., 241
Ustinov, Peter, 122

Vere, Edward Fairfax *(Billy Budd, Sailor),* 32, 39, 40–42, 46, 47–50, 51, 52, 56, 57, 58, 59, 60–61, 120, 199, 200–201, 203–5, 206, 207–8, 221, 222
Vincent, Howard P., 23, 182, 244
Vishanoff, Thomas, 238

Wagner, Vern, 42, 56, 218
Wallace, Robert K., 71, 222
Warren, Robert Penn, 49, 57
Watson, E. L. Grant, 55–56, 220
Weaver, Raymond M., 54, 121, 220, 247
Weir, Charles, Jr., 56
Weisberg, Richard H., 51, 55, 207, 219, 220
Werther *(The Sorrows of Young Werther),* 105–6, 227
Whicher, Stephen E., 105–6, 227
Whipple, Edwin Percy, 7, 9; "Some Recollections of Ralph Waldo Emerson," 213
White, Elwyn Brooks, 152, 238
Whitehead, Alfred North, *The Aims of Education,* 13, 123

Whitman, Walt, 5, 6, 12, 15–20, 24, 65, 68, 88–90, 94, 95, 111, 117, 121, 124, 129–45, 185, 188, 215, 233–36; "As I Ebb'd with the Ocean of Life," 145; *Autobiographia: The Story of a Life,* ed. Arthur Stedman, 18; "Calamus," 145, 234, 235; "Crossing Brooklyn Ferry," 139–45; *Democratic Vistas,* 19; *Drum-Taps,* 19, 234; "Emerson's Books, (The Shadows of Them),"
214; "Here the Frailest Leaves of Me," 236; "How Solemn as One by One," 234; *Leaves of Grass,* 5, 14, 18–19, 88, 130, 131, 132, 133, 135, 139, 234, 243; "Out of the Cradle Endlessly Rocking," 145; "Passage to India," 89; "Proto-Leaf," 234; *Selected Poems,* ed. Arthur Stedman, 18; "So Long!", 132, 234; "A Song of Joys," 89; "Song of Myself," 18–19, 20, 111, 135–39, 145, 176, 177, 180, 181, 188, 214, 237; "Song of the Exposition," 88–89, 225; "Song of the Open Road," 129; "Sun-Down Poem," 139; "There Was a Child Went Forth," 133–34, 135, 136, 138, 141–45, 235; "To a Locomotive in Winter," 89–90, 225; "Whoever You Are Holding Me Now in Hand," 131–32, 234; "The Wound-Dresser," 145
Widmer, Kingsley, 57, 221
Wife, the ("The Apple-Tree Table"), 83
Wife, the ("I and My Chimney"), 83
Wiley and Putnam, 160
Williams, Stanley T., 189, 232
Williams, William Carlos, 91
Willis, Sara P. ("Fanny Fern"), *Fern Leaves from Fanny's Portfolio,* 117
Wilson, Edmund, 244
Winters, Yvor, 10, 56, 213, 244
Witherell, Elizabeth Hall, 239
Withim, Phil, 56, 220
Wolfe, Thomas, 94; *Of Time and the River,* 94
Wolpert, Bernard M., 232
Woodson, Thomas, 238
Wooster, The College of, 189
Wordsworth, William, 24, 68, 69, 79, 88, 176; "Essay Supplement to Preface

(1815)," 243; *Lyrical Ballads,* 176;
   The Prelude, 104, 105
Wright, Frank Lloyd, 98
Wright, Nathalia, 232

Yale College, 114
Yale University, 189

Yankee Doodle, 74
Yannella, Donald, 78–79, 216
Yorpy ("The Happy Failure"), 78

Zimmerman, Michael P., 232
Zink, Karl E., 56
Zoroaster, 156, 158